CONTEMPORARY BRITISH HORROR CINEMA

Industry, Genre and Society

Johnny Walker

EDINBURGH
University Press

Edinburgh University Press Ltd
The Tun – Holyrood Road
12 (2f) Jackson's Entry
Edinburgh EH8 8PJ
www.euppublishing.com

First published in hardback by Edinburgh University Press 2016

Typeset in 10/12.5 pt Sabon by
Servis Filmsetting Ltd, Stockport, Cheshire
and printed and bound in Great Britain by
CPI Group (UK) Ltd, Croydon CR0 4YY

A CIP record for this book is available from the British Library

ISBN 978 0 7486 8973 6 (hardback)
ISBN 978 1 4744 2939 9 (paperback)
ISBN 978 0 7486 8974 3 (webready PDF)
ISBN 978 0 7486 8975 0 (epub)

CONTENTS

FIGURES

ACKNOWLEDGEMENTS

This book has been in gestation in my head (and on my shelves) for a few years now. Many amazing people have assisted in its development.

First and foremost, I would like to thank Gillian Leslie at EUP for having faith in this book and for commissioning it in record time, as well as the two (very kind) anonymous peer reviewers. Thanks must also go to the academics that made up the 'British Cinema: International Connections' bursary panel at De Montfort University (DMU) (in Leicester, England), who provided me with the funding that initiated this project. Most of all, my sincere gratitude goes to Steve Chibnall for his friendship, support and reassurance throughout the duration of my research (and for subbing me at the Mirch Masala restaurant on more than one occasion), to Ian Hunter for his constructive criticism, friendly advice and access to his DVD and magazine collection, and to Peter Hutchings, Andrew Spicer and Tim O'Sullivan for their helpful comments on a much earlier draft.

Over the years, several of my lecturers, seminar tutors and my many friends within and beyond the academy have inspired me in numerous ways. In particular, Sarah Leahy, Elayne Chaplin and James Leggott were all hugely supportive and encouraging when I first embarked on writing about contemporary British horror. Conversations and email exchanges with Jonathan Rigby, M. J. Simpson and Robert J. E. Simpson helped to clarify some of my ideas, and helped me to see my project within the bigger picture of British cinema history. (Robert, in particular, was very helpful as I prepared Chapter 6.) Austin Fisher remained a reliable sounding board and therapist in times of crisis and stress, and James Russell was always very accommodating when I turned up at his door unannounced. My new colleagues at Northumbria University (in Newcastle upon Tyne, England) have been especially supportive: Gilbert Cockton, Jacky Collins, Ysanne Holt, Russ Hunter, Mary Irwin, Elizabeth Kramer, Gabriel Moreno, Karen Ross and Jamie Sexton. Neil Jackson provided some helpful feedback on an earlier draft of Chapter 3, and Steve Jones read, and provided feedback on, most of the manuscript. I would also like to extend my gratitude to the following scholars, who have shown their support over the last few years: Wickham Clayton, Kate Egan, John Paul Green, Sarah Harman, Tobias Hochscherf, Beth Johnson, Shaun Kimber, Mark McKenna, Richard Nowell, Alison Peirse, Julian Petley, Clarissa Smith, Iain Robert Smith and Matt Smith.

This book would have suffered greatly if it hadn't been for the cooperation of all of the filmmakers and producers who gave up their time to be interviewed, or who assisted in any capacity. They are: Arvind Ethan David at Slingshot Studios (thanks to Andy Betts at Hassle Records for organising the interview), Jonathan Sothcott at Chata Pictures (formerly Black and Blue Films), Ben and Tom Grass at Pure Grass Films, Richard Holmes at Big Rich, David V. G. Davies, Jon Finn, Jason Impey, Simon Oakes at Hammer, Marc Price, Julian Richards, Matt 'M. J.' Stone and Simon Hunter. I am especially grateful to the writers/producers/directors Adam Mason, Johannes Roberts, Steven Sheil and Jake West for being especially understanding and supportive (and for making some really interesting films). The following production companies/people provided me with films that were otherwise impossible to access: Black Robe Productions, Jinga Films, Cryptkeeper Films, Leigh Dovey, Sean Hogan, Rebekah Smith (The Film Festival Doctor), and J. I. Productions.

Matt Collins, Jonny Rob and Chad Welch were very understanding when I decided to temporarily put punk rock on hold. Hannah Skeldon, Christina Blackadder, Dan Clark, Georgina Corkram, Amy Hegarty and Ben Smart made the insular life of academic research all the more bearable. Alex Rock, Laura Mee and Natalie Hayton offered me an intellectual lifeline many times during this project, and remain some of my closest friends. The PhD students in the Cinema and Television History (CATH) Research Centre at De Montfort also deserve a mention for providing an inspiring and friendly research environment, particularly Eve Bennett, Jilly Boyce Kaye, Paul Gosling and Caitlin Shaw.

In 2005 I started at university and quickly met two of my best friends. I would like to recognise Gary Jenkins, and to thank him for the friendship, support and wisdom that he's shown me over the years. I would also like to thank Tom Watson whose generosity, intellect and words of encouragement have truly helped drive this book forward.

Small sections of Chapters 1, 2 and 5 have appeared in condensed forms in

'A wilderness of horrors? British horror cinema in the new millennium' in the *Journal of British Cinema and Television* 9: 3, pp. 436–56; a shorter version of Chapter 3 has appeared as 'Nasty visions: Violent spectacle in contemporary British horror cinema' in *Horror Studies* 2: 1, pp. 115–30; and bits and pieces from Chapters 2 and 7 have appeared in my contribution to Richard Nowell's collection, *Merchants of Menace: The Business of Horror Cinema* (2014). I am grateful to Edinburgh University Press (EUP), Intellect Books and Bloomsbury Academic (an imprint of Bloomsbury Publishing Inc.), respectively, for allowing me to reprint extracts from these here. Thanks also must go to Hammer Films for granting me the permission to print two of the images that appear in Chapter 6.

Finally, I'd like to thank my family for all of their generous love and support. My parents, Jacqueline and Rob, have always had faith in me, and I truly love them for that. My wonderful partner, Nikki – for some unknown reason – puts up with all this nonsense. She's a total legend and the love of my life. Our dog, Willis, is never likely to read this book. But then again, he's impressed us in so many other ways, I couldn't not include the little guy. As this book was going to print, we lost someone very dear to us. I'd therefore like to dedicate this book to the memory of my dear grandma, Helen Sheriff (1918–2015).

1. LONG TIME DEAD

In 2002, the filmmaker Richard Stanley sounded the death knell of 'the great British horror movie'. His 'obituary', which appeared in Steve Chibnall and Julian Petley's edited volume *British Horror Cinema*, lamented the general absence of any real directorial talent at the turn of the millennium, noting that the horror film directors 'who really knew what they were doing escaped to Hollywood a long time ago' (Stanley 2002: 194). Stanley cited the direct-to-video occult horror *The 13th Sign* (Jonty Acton and Adam Mason, 2000) as offering a glimmer of hope, but concluded that it was 'still a long way below the minimum standard of even the most vilified 1980s product' (2002: 193).

Stanley's pessimism was not unfounded (even if his assessment of *The 13th Sign* was perhaps a bit unfair). Hammer Films – the once-prolific film studio responsible for the first full-colour horror film, *The Curse of Frankenstein* (Terence Fisher), in 1957, and a host of other classic British horrors over the next two decades – buckled under market pressure and ceased making feature films in 1979. The 1980s, therefore, saw the production of only a handful of British horror films, which, at any rate, were mostly thought of as American productions that had peripheral British involvement, such as Stanley Kubrick's blockbuster *The Shining* (1980) and Clive Barker's franchise-initiating *Hellraiser* (1987). Others from the decade were artsy one-offs, such as the Gothic fairy tale *The Company of Wolves* (Neil Jordan, 1984), or (as was most often the case) amateurish flops, such as the cheap and clumsy monster movie *Rawhead Rex* (George Pavlou, 1986). Aside from the *very* occasional hit,[1] most of these were critical and commercial failures (Conrich 1998).

The following decade was similarly dire.[2] With the exception of a smattering of micro-budget releases like Richard Stanley's own *Hardware* (1990), *Funny Man* (Simon Sprackling, 1994), *Razorblade Smile* (Jake West, 1998) and *Darklands* (Julian Richards, 1996), the 1990s did not proffer the most encouraging environment for indigenous horror film production. The 'video nasty'[3] moral panic that had plagued the 1980s was given new life in 1993, when toddler James Bulger was murdered by two children who had allegedly been inspired by the video release of Jack Bender's killer doll film *Child's Play 3* (although no evidence was ever found to support this claim).[4] Moreover, media furores continued to be sparked around the potential corrupting effects that violent films could have on weak-minded audiences (specifically children), following the theatrical releases of controversial titles such as *Natural Born Killers* (Oliver Stone, 1994) and *Crash* (David Cronenberg 1996).[5] As Chibnall and Petley have put it, 'no one in their right mind' would have produced a British video nasty equivalent at this sensitive time, 'and just *imagine* what would [have happened] were a film company to [have suggested] making a film about, say [British serial killers] Fred and Rosemary West . . . or the Bulger murder' (2002: 7–8; emphasis in original).

Despite the premature publication of its obituaries, however, horror became one of the most prolific British film genres in the years following the new millennium, with hundreds of films being produced either in the UK, or elsewhere, with the support of British finance and resources. In fact, the year that saw the publication of Chibnall and Petley's *British Horror Cinema* was also the year that saw the release of one of the highest grossing British horrors of the period, Danny Boyle's post-apocalyptic *28 Days Later* (2002), as well as the release of *Dog Soldiers* (2002), a werewolf movie responsible for launching the career of revered horror darling Neil Marshall. This ironic state of affairs spilled over into the years that followed, with the production and release of a part-British sequel to the film that was said to have influenced Bulger's killers, *Seed of Chucky* (Don Mancini, 2004), as well as the release of *Mum & Dad* (Steven Sheil, 2008): a British film accused by the British press of distastefully turning 'the crimes of Fred and Rosemary West into an exploitation film' (Tookey 2008a). There were also a few international box office smashes such as *Resident Evil* and its sequels (2002–), *The Descent* (Neil Marshall, 2005) and *The Woman in Black* (James Watkins, 2012); widely popular horror-comedies such as *Shaun of the Dead* (Edgar Wright, 2004) and *Attack the Block* (Joe Cornish, 2011); less-popular ones such as *The Cottage* (Paul Andrew Williams, 2008), *Lesbian Vampire Killers* (Phil Claydon, 2009), *Doghouse* (Jake West, 2009), *Zombie Women of Satan* (Steve O'Brien, 2009), *Stitches* (Conor McMahon, 2012) and *Stalled* (Christian James, 2013); regionally set (and sometimes regionally funded) films, such as *Eden Lake* (James Watkins, 2008), *Salvage* (Lawrence Gough, 2009), *Outcast* (Colm McCarthy, 2010),

Citadel (Ciaran Foy, 2012), *The Borderlands* (Elliot Goldner, 2013) and *White Settlers* (Simeon Halligan, 2014); a string of international co-productions such as *The Ferryman* (Chris Graham, 2007, New Zealand/UK), *Wind Chill* (Gregory Jacobs, 2007, US/UK), *Surviving Evil* (Terence Daw, 2009, UK/South Africa), *Strigoi* (Faye Jackson, 2009, UK/Romania), *Black Death* (Christopher Smith, 2010, Germany/UK) and *Let Me In* (Matt Reeves, 2010, US/UK); a huge array of independently produced films for the home video market such as *Dead Creatures* (Andrew Parkinson, 2001), *Sanitarium* (Johannes Roberts and James Eaves, 2001), *The Zombie Diaries* (Michael Bartlett and Kevin Gates, 2006), *Reverb* (Eitan Arrusi, 2008), *The Sick House* (Curtis Radclyffe, 2008), *Bane* (James Eaves, 2008), *Spiderhole* (Daniel Simpson, 2010), *Patrol Men* (David Campion and Ben Simpson, 2010), *Psychosis* (Reg Traviss, 2010), *Devil's Bridge* (Chris Crow, 2010), *Little Deaths* (Andrew Parkinson *et al.*, 2012), *Panic Button* (Chris Crow, 2011), *Truth or Die* (Robert Heath, 2012), *The Reverend* (Neil Jones, 2011), *Deviation* (J. K. Amalou, 2012), *The Captive* (*Armistice*) (Luke Massey, 2013) and *The Clinic* (*The Addicted*) (Sean J. Vincent, 2014); and even some films that deliberately obscured the oft-invoked binary between 'art' and 'horror', such as *The Last Great Wilderness* (David Mackenzie, 2002), *Puffball* (Nicolas Roeg, 2007), *The Devil's Business* (Sean Hogen, 2011), *Kill List* (Ben Wheatley, 2011) and *Under the Skin* (Jonathan Glazer, 2013). Put simply, the 2000s and 2010s marked a dramatic change in tide for the genre, and signalled the first sustained period of British horror production since Hammer's golden era.

Contemporary British Horror Cinema: Industry, Genre and Society charts the rebirth of the British horror film in the twenty-first century, paying close attention to both the cultural and economic factors that contributed to the horror genre's buoyancy amid UK film production. Using primary research – including data from funding institutions and primary interview material with key industry players – and detailed film analysis, this book will show in what ways horror offered a significant contribution to British film production post-2000, and how it evidenced diversity across a broad spectrum of filmmakers, industrial trends, technologies and social issues.

A HERITAGE OF HORROR: THE 'HAMMER HEGEMONY'

Of course, I am not the first person to write of the horror film's 'significance' to British film history and culture. As noted above, one of the most famous horror studios in the world, Hammer Films, is of British origin, and for a period from the late 1950s to the late 1970s it produced a series of films that have since been heralded both for their innovation and parochial inflections. In fact, the popularity of Hammer's numerous loose adaptations of Gothic novels, such as the aforementioned *The Curse of Frankenstein*, *Dracula* (Terence Fisher, 1958) and their many sequels, led critic David Pirie to argue in his landmark work from 1973, *A Heritage of Horror: The English Gothic Cinema 1946–1972*, that Hammer's penchant for the Gothic granted the horror genre a cultural grounding that was *unique* to Britain. As he famously put it:

> [T]he horror genre, as it has been developed in this country by Hammer and its rivals, remains the only staple cinematic myth which Britain can properly claim as its own, and which relates to it in the same way as the western relates to America. (Pirie 1973: 9)

Pirie certainly wasn't wrong to underscore Hammer's significance at this time. The company's period-set films, and others inspired by its successes,[6] would go on to define the Golden Age of British horror film production and would secure Hammer's reputation as a British household name (McKay 2007: 1–5). In Pirie's (1973: 9) view, Hammer's innovation, widespread popularity but, above all, the recurrence of 'various Gothic motifs' in its films evidenced a modality unsusceptible to foreign influence:

> [T]he British cinema (including not just Hammer but other smaller companies: this is a national phenomenon) has effectively and effortlessly dominated the 'horror' market over a period of almost twenty years with a series of films which, whatever their faults, are in no way imitative of American or European models but derive in general from [English] literary sources. (Pirie 1973: 9–10)

Until the publication of Peter Hutchings' academic monograph *Hammer and Beyond: The British Horror Film* in 1993, *A Heritage of Horror* was the only book-length study available on the subject of British horror cinema. Aimed at a more general readership than Hutchings' scholarly tome, Pirie's core argument became a highly influential one in and out of academe. For filmmakers working in the disreputable horror genre, it afforded them a critical reassessment and to an extent 'validated' their work, by situating them amid a rich cultural tapestry, and offering their films some serious analysis. Indeed, while it was common for Hammer's films to have been mocked or shunned by contemporary critics, Pirie conversely heralded one of Hammer's most constant directors, Terence Fisher, an auteur (1973: 50–65). For cultural historians, *Heritage* became the yardstick of British horror film criticism and would occasionally be invoked in later discussions that lamented a perceived lack of nationally oriented contemporary horror productions (Chibnall and Petley 2002). But perhaps the most lasting result of Pirie's tome, however, is what Hutchings has dubbed the 'Hammer hegemony' in British film studies – that is to say, the centrality of Hammer to much of the critical work on British horror that followed Pirie's book, which made difficult the appraisal of films that 'do not sit easily with those critical accounts that have sought to identify British horror as a purely indigenous cultural phenomenon' (Hutchings 2002a: 131). And in spite of the best efforts of a number of scholars to fill gaps in British horror's history (such as Petley 1996 [1986]; Hunt 1998; Chibnall 1998; Rigby 2000, 2002, 2004, 2006), nostalgia for a certain type of Hammer film also retained the upper hand in pop culture throughout the 1980s and 1990s, bolstered by several high-profile conventions and events, a number of Hammer seasons at the National Film Theatre (now known as BFI Southbank), retrospective TV shows such as *The World of Hammer* (Robert Sidaway, 1990), celebratory late-night television screenings of classic Hammer horror films, video re-releases, articles in fanzines such as *Little Shoppe of Horrors*, *Shivers* and *The Dark Side*, and a string of officially studio-licensed merchandise. These factors continued to reaffirm the notion that Pirie initiated: that 'Hammer' would very much remain a catch-all term for 'British horror cinema' in the decades to follow.

As I discuss in Chapter 6 of this book, Hammer actually returned to film production in 2007 to make films aimed at young contemporary audiences. But its name was nowhere near as central to British horror film culture as it had been in previous decades. Indeed, one of the most striking things about British horror cinema after the year 2000 was, on many levels, its variedness. For starters, there was no main horror studio producing films with the visibility or the aesthetic and thematic coherence that Hammer once laid claim to. On the contrary, the British horror revival stretched across many styles, technologies and budgets, and most films were detached from the period style and the 'Gothic tradition' that Pirie deemed so important to British horror. Films like *The Hole* (Nick Hamm, 2001), *The Descent* and *The Devil's Chair* (Adam Mason, 2007) – and hundreds of others – were, as this book argues, influenced by a whole host of cross-cultural factors,[7] so it would be rather limiting to view recent British horror films solely in light of Gothic literary antecedents.

To be clear, in writing this, I am not trying to shut out history in any way and deny the horror genre its legacy in popular culture. After all, tropes that one may dub 'Gothic' can certainly be found across much contemporary horror production. But, to my mind, viewing British horror solely in terms of a literary heritage would be to neglect the many other factors that contributed to the genre's UK revival after 2000. In fact, Pirie himself did attempt to account for the divergences in more contemporary product in a second edition to his original book in 2008 – *A New Heritage of Horror: The English Gothic Cinema*, which features extensive rewrites and, crucially, a lengthy chapter on British horror in the new millennium. However, even in this new edition, in spite of the broader pool of films that Pirie draws on, he maintains his original argument, claiming that although the original Gothic 'novels and poems themselves (with a few exceptions) are now largely forgotten', English Gothic resonates throughout contemporary horror, because the 'idioms and emotions [that the original novels and poems] created have entered our DNA' (Pirie 2008: 221). It is my contention that, for all that Pirie's book is a master class in film history and criticism, we need to move beyond the literary gothic if we are to ever fully understand the real reasons and impetuses that led to the boom in contemporary British horror cinema. Indeed, in a global marketplace, and in a transnational context, a clear understanding of British horror cinema hinges more on an awareness of influencing industrial factors, as well as an understanding of those more direct creative influences that have impacted on contemporary filmmakers (such as cult horror films from Europe and America).

Of course, it should be made clear that Pirie's argument has been debated in academe before, as has the dominance of Hammer Films in academic and nonacademic discussions of the British horror film. For example, Peter Hutchings, in *Hammer and Beyond*, recognised how restricting the analysis of British horror cinema to a literary heritage risks undermining, or avoiding entirely, the 'aesthetic and ideological properties' of certain films, and how such films may draw on, on the one hand, prevalent social concerns, and on the other, broader trends in horror cinema happening elsewhere in the world (1993: 12). Hutchings also made the crucial point that 'the story of British horror involves much more than the activities . . . of Hammer' because 'well over one half' emerged from other companies (1). Indeed, part of the reasoning behind Chibnall and Petley's *British Horror Cinema* was to 'explore more neglected areas' of British horror cinema (2002: 1), while Hutchings' essay in the same volume seeks to further 'challenge . . . the Hammer hegemony' by examining Hammer's main rival, Amicus, in hope of shining some light on the oft-ignored 'heterogeneity of British horror cinema' (Hutchings 2002a: 131). As Hutchings notes, Amicus, which was headed by two Americans, drew mostly on American source material rather than English Gothic novels. Additionally, studies from Leon Hunt (1998) and Steve Chibnall (1998) offered the first lengthy studies on maligned British horror directors such as Pete Walker; Alison Peirse's *After Dracula* (2013) contains a chapter on British horror of the 1930s; while the most rigorous of all studies, Jonathan Rigby's pivotal *English Gothic: A Century of Horror Cinema*, also looked way beyond Hammer to other once-neglected areas. The last editions even included a short section on contemporary films (2002, 2004, 2006), and the forthcoming edition promises to cover even more.[8]

The more recent studies to address British horror – with the exception of Barry Forshaw's tellingly entitled *British Gothic Cinema* (2013) – are even less bound to literary Gothicism, such as: James Leggott's (2008) *Contemporary British Cinema: From Heritage to Horror*, Linnie Blake's (2008) *Wounds of Nations: Horror Cinema, Historical Trauma and National Identity*, James

Rose's (2009) *Beyond Hammer: British Horror since 1970*, I. Q. Hunter's (2013) *British Trash Cinema*, and various articles by Peter Hutchings (2009a) and others (Peirse 2009; Hantke 2010a; Hockenhull 2010; Walker 2011, 2012 and 2014). Yet, while these interventions are helpful starting points for broader considerations of the genre in contemporary British cinema, they are also limited by the small body of films that they cover and the brevity with which they do so. And with the exception of M. J. Simpson's recent *Urban Terrors: New British Horror Cinema, 1998–2008* (2012), which presents the reader with a detailed filmography of contemporary British horror films, elsewhere there remains a general reluctance to consider British horror in any detail at all. A case in point is Andrew Higson's otherwise comprehensive *Film England: Culturally English Filmmaking since the 1990s*, which draws attention to romantic comedies, dramas, thrillers and family films (2011: 30–6) but not to the explosion in British – or for that matter, English – horror film production.

While we are repeatedly reminded in academic literature of the worthiness of horror cinema of yesteryear – such as British horror of the 1950s or American horror of the 1970s – twenty-first century horror films are repeatedly dismissed as being inferior to those that preceded them. Sometimes they are dismissed as derivative; other times they are seen as lacking the radical social critique that critics like Robin Wood (1979) afforded such paradigm-shifting films as *Night of the Living Dead* (George A. Romero, 1968) and *The Texas Chain Saw Massacre* (Tobe Hooper, 1974) (see, for example, Sharret 2009). Other times, contemporary horror cinema is framed, quite simply, as just not being very good. For example, if some journalists and academics were to be believed, the first ten years of the 2000s saw American horror cinema 'at its worst' (Hantke 2010b: vii). The general lack of interest in new British horror cinema at this time, then, may well be attributed to a possible assumption that the films are not dissimilar enough from similarly terrible contemporary American productions to warrant extended analysis on their own terms. (This is certainly an opinion that resonates throughout contemporary film criticism, and will be considered in more detail in Chapter 3 of this book.)

Contemporary British Horror Cinema seeks to address these misgivings, by moving beyond the Gothic tradition and unhelpful accusations of inferiority, to offer the first academic study of British horror cinema in the new millennium. The book charts an era when horror production was arguably at its most global and most varied. Indeed, amid cynical claims in light of a slurry of American remakes that horror is so unoriginal these days that it 'will eat itself' (Newman 2009: 36), horror films in the twenty-first century straddled a broad church of styles and demographics, from big-budget Hollywood efforts such as the *The Twilight Saga* (2008–12) (Clayton and Harman 2014), to low-budget films produced for the DVD market (Wood 2007: 95–6; Bernard 2014), to the corporeal horrors of the torture porn cycle (Jones 2013), and a 'new wave' of European horror in light of the *cinema du corps* ('new French extremism') (Horeck and Kendall 2011; Austin 2012). British horror makers, this book contends, were firmly positioned to respond to the scope and diversity of the genre during this period, and that they did, with gusto.

In light of horror's magnitude and diversity, the genre had a central role in British film production across the board: in relation to what was promoted as being the dawning of a 'new' British film industry following the instating of the UK Film Council (UKFC) quango in 2000 (see Chapter 2), and over the next fourteen years, in relation to smaller, independently/self-funded productions. The British horror films produced after 2000, I argue, testified to the UK film industry's economic and cultural preoccupations of the period, including the successful utilisation of funding initiatives, an increase in the accessibility of filmmaking technologies to up-and-coming directors, the increased economic sustainability of home-viewing platforms, and how such platforms have impacted on what cinema 'means' in the twenty-first century (see Murphy 2002; Petrie 2002; Ryall 2002; Hill 2012; Perkins 2012; Street 2012). Also considered in these pages are several of the major themes and film cycles that became prevalent during the period. I will pay specific attention to the role of the fan filmmaker, as well as to how British horror films have functioned at a socio-political level and have engaged with current national concerns. Ultimately, by considering these factors, this books hopes to offer a sense of coherence to a genre now recognised as a 'considerably more varied and consequently less cohesive phenomenon' (Hutchings 2009b: 149) than it has been thought of in the recent past.

THE NEW FILM HISTORY

It should be made clear from the outset that *Contemporary British Horror Cinema: Industry, Genre and Society* is more a work of film *history* than film *theory*. That is to say, methodologically, it is informed by the philosophies of the 'New Film History', as outlined by James Chapman, Mark Glancy and Sue Harper in their significant edited collection from 2007: *The New Film History: Sources, Methods, Approaches*. Using British horror films released in the 2000s and 2010s, this book will partly 'demonstrate . . . how the principles of historical investigation can be applied in practice in order to illuminate the structures and processes that have determined the nature of the medium of film and its social institutions' (Chapman *et al.* 2007: 1–2). As Chapman persuasively argues, a 'characteristic of the New Film History, as opposed to the old, is that it regards all films, whatever their critical or cultural status, as worthy objects of analysis' (Chapman 2007: 55). This is not, however, to completely discount the many benefits of textual analysis: something that is often solely associated with non-empirical approaches to the study of film. After all, as Jeffrey Richards has argued, neither an empirical approach to film history, nor text-based critical analysis 'has an exclusive monopoly of wisdom' (2000: 21). Rather, it is the case that empiricism should too be recognised as a 'theory', but 'one that is longer established and more thoroughly tried and tested than some of the more fashionable but short-lived theories of recent years' (22). It is certainly true that the study of horror cinema has been particularly limited by voguish cultural theory such as psychoanalysis, where 'history has been conceptualized as nothing more than a discontinuous succession of discrete moments, each characterised by a different basic version of the genre' (Altman 1984 [2004]: 686). Therefore, to avoid such limitations, when critical and theoretical ideas are considered in this book – such as the theories of cult film and gendered practices advanced by Joanne Hollows (2003) and Jacinda Read (2003) in Chapter 4, or Richard Dyer's (2009 [1993]) theories of stereotyping acknowledged in Chapter 5 – these are not used to reify 'the idea that films [possess] a meaning that [is] independent of the prevailing social, cultural, political and economic contexts' (Richards 2000: 22). On the contrary, such approaches are explored in direct relation to historical contexts, or are used to expose and redress the limiting nature of reductive taxonomies, which, in spite of their shortcomings, maintain currency in film studies and society more generally (in relation to, for instance, the 'underclass' in British film and media, as per Chapter 5). As such, it is my contention that empirical research (into industry, production, reception, distribution patterns and social context) can further complement more analytical readings of specific films when their historical and social contexts are explicitly identified.

Categorisations

The pool of films considered in this book was determined, some may say crudely, considering a broad range of factors. First was the understanding that neither 'genre' nor 'horror film' are hermetic concepts but are susceptible to interpretation and categorical overlap. To borrow an expression from Matt Hills, *'the horror genre is not where it is*; it exists, intertextually, rhetorically . . . outside its major and explicitly labelled generic traditions/sites/texts' (2005: 6; emphasis in original). My own research into the horror film is therefore indebted to these kinds of understandings, as well as to Jeffrey Sconce's concept of 'paracinema': 'a most elastic textual category' of 'cult' cinema that covers a wide range of genres,[9] which are typically relegated in cultural hierarchies, and prone to influence and classification by a variety of ways and means (1995: 372). Resultantly, each contemporary British horror film has been incorporated (subjectively, but) sensibly, with consideration given to how the rigid theoretical paradigms imposed on the genre in the past have generated more questions than they have answered – not least in terms of the varied 'philosophical' approaches to the horror film that rarely factor historical context into the equation at all (such as Twitchell 1985; Carroll 1990; Fahy 2010). To this end, I have considered the genre in relation to how it has been approached industrially (by production companies and through marketing), textually (in terms of key tropes and themes, and a historical understanding of horror) and extra-textually (in terms of fan communities and audience demographics). I have therefore relied on my own personal designations as well – 'though the edges may be rather blurred' (Tudor 2003: 6) – and the classificatory system provided by professional industry resources (such as by Screen International and IMDBPro), specific press-releases for films, personal interviews with directors, screenwriters and producers, and the ways that films have been marketed *as horror*, and how they have been discussed within the media, and promoted through their official (and fan-run) websites and discussion forums (such as www.britishhorrorfilms.com). More often than not, I have relied on others' perceptions of what a horror film is (or may be), purely to avoid isolating horror as a genre that is not informed, and infinitely reassessed, by consumers, critics and other culture-makers. In other words, I accept that genre is 'what we collectively believe it to be' (Tudor 2003: 7), but also how 'we' as individuals and communities, within different contexts of production, marketing, textual and extra-textual discussion, contest it, embrace it and interpret it.

Designating films as 'British' here has also relied on a similar looseness. As Andrew Higson has recently discussed, designations such as 'British' or 'English', while still useful in some contexts, are arguably at their most controversial because 'most national cinemas are now a complex amalgam of often competing local, national and international forces' (2011: 5). To this end, I have not subscribed to one cohesive notion of 'Britishness' due to the complex transcultural bases for many British horror films in the 2000s and 2010s (in terms of funding sources, for instance). As discussed above, I also contest the idea that horror is itself an 'English genre' because of its links to English Gothic fiction. That having been said, *Contemporary British Horror Cinema* does foreground what could be understood as 'national' concerns, including the aftermath of the 'video nasties' era, 'New Lad' culture and fears about 'broken Britain': all which have been positioned in media discourse as notably local phenomena despite their similarities with other traits, practices and cultures overseas. But these instances of parochialism on my part are to be perceived as essential in my attempt to locate contemporary British horror and its influences amid more immediate (and, one may argue, more relevant) textual, historical and social trajectories than the English Gothic literature referred to above. In doing so, this book presents a detailed account of British horror cinema, taking note of both national and international factors, and emerges at a time when contemporary British cinema is highly popular all over the world (Perkins

2012), and when the horror genre remains one of the most intriguing, yet overlooked, areas of production.

CHAPTER BREAKDOWN

Chapter 2 contemplates why British horror was revived at the dawning of the new millennium, and also considers some of the reasons why British horror films produced in the 2000s and 2010s can be viewed as constituting a distinctive aspect of contemporary British cinema. I discuss the establishment of the UK Film Council (UKFC) in 2000 and contextualise the contemporary British horror film in the international film marketplace, drawing parallels between British horror and British film production more broadly, British horror and international horror production, and the audience demographics targeted by distributers and film production companies. This involves examining British horror's shift from a theatrical genre to one associated primarily with the home video and online market.

Chapter 3, in light of the broader international concerns outlined in the previous chapter, works towards locating cultural specificities within British horror at a time when it has drifted from its better known 'English' heritage. By considering the social and historical context during which many contemporary filmmakers grew up (namely, the late 1970s and 1980s), I reassess how recent British horror's 'heritage' may be more immediate than we initially presume. To do this, I argue that several films responded to the typically negative British critical response to horror cinema (Petley 2002a), and, through textual analysis, argue that such films are products inspired by nostalgia for the video nasties panic of the 1980s. Through doing so, I consider how cultural specificity can be extracted from films by directors who not only have a passion for the horror film (that is, are self-confessed fans of the genre), but are also aware of how British horror (and horror in Britain) has been figured and derided within British culture.

In Chapter 4, I extend some of the issues surrounding fan filmmakers as discussed in the previous chapter, and deliberate the representation of masculinity and cult film fandom within a series of horror-comedy hybrids. Through acknowledgement of the ways in which cult film fandom has traditionally been gendered as 'male', and often as immature, crude and boyish, I draw parallels between recent horror-comedies that use these stereotypes as ironic self-critiques of the filmmakers' themselves and their desired audience. I ultimately locate these films within discourses surrounding 'New Lad' culture of the 1990s, which has similarly been linked to contemporary cult film fandom (Hollows 2003; Read 2003). Through a discussion of themes, industry statistics and textual analysis, I show how films such as *Shaun of the Dead*, *Doghouse* and *Lesbian Vampire Killers* satirise the social marginality of laddish behaviour by placing fannish 'New Lad' types within a horror film environment, thus literalising many of the stereotypes that have figured within contemporary academic writing on cult film audiences.

The practice of stereotyping is also the focus of Chapter 5, which considers a cycle of films that are designed to elicit fear from media representations of the contemporary working classes. Through analysis of films in the 'hoodie-horror' cycle, which typically presented the youth of the white British under-class as feral and monstrous, I analyse the social context from which these films stemmed and examine how they tapped into current anxieties surround-ing contemporary fears of British youth (an apparent groundswell in gang culture that culminated in the 'August Riots' of 2011).

Chapter 6 returns to industry, and charts the re-emergence of Hammer Films, which, after thirty years, finally went back into film production in the 2000s. Drawing from primary sources such as the industry trade press and interviews, the chapter reflects on Hammer's recent history, considering briefly the tumultuous 1980s and 1990s, before assessing the company's market posi-tioning between its re-launch in 2007 with the web serial *Beyond the Rave* (Matthias Hoene, 2008), through its theatrical success with the blockbuster *The Woman in Black* in 2012, up until the release of its lower-budgeted ghost story, *The Quiet Ones* (John Pogue) in 2014. Ultimately, taking into account Hammer's prominence in much discourse around classic British horror, I use its millennial incarnation to assess its relevance (or not) to the identity of British horror in the twenty-first century.

By considering contemporary British horror in the terms outlined above – from the perspectives of industry, the personal tastes of directors, the ways in which horror audiences have been theorised and how horror cinema can tap into deeper social concerns – I present the contemporary British horror film as curious and varied, but also prolific and distinctive. What will hopefully become clear in this book is how restrictive and unhelpful it is to pigeonhole British horror cinema into one theoretical paradigm or cultural tradition. Conversely, it will be revealed how the genre has been diverse – if, at times, unwieldy – in the twenty-first century and that these factors alone are enough for it to demand our attention.

NOTES

1. *The Shining* and *Hellraiser* fall into this camp.
2. Robert Murphy's collection *British Cinema of the 90s* (1999a) makes no mention of the horror genre at all.
3. 'Video nasty' was a term initially given by the British media and pressure groups to horror/violent films that were released on video in the UK prior to the Video Recordings Act of 1984. It resulted in thirty-nine films being banned by the Director of Public Prosecutions (DPP), and the ruining of hundreds of independent distribu-tors, who could not afford to pay the British Board of Film Classification's (BBFC's)

high classificatory fees. I discuss this era in relation to British horror film production in more detail in Chapter 3. For contextual overviews see Barker (1984), Barlow and Hill (1985), Kerekes and Slater (2000) and Petley (2011).

4. As Kerekes and Slater have noted 'similarities were pointed out between scenes in the film and events of the incident. For instance . . . the killers admitted that Bulger constantly got back on his feet no matter how hard they hit him and the doll in the film shows a similar indestructibility. (The suggestion that Bulger repeatedly rose to his feet after being struck down because of a scene in the film, poses the ridiculous and outrageous notion that Bulger must have seen the film and was mimicking it himself)' (Kerekes and Slater 2000: 325).

5. For an account of the presence of *Child's Play 3* in reportage of the Bulger case see Petley (2011: 87–102). For a detailed account of the '*Crash* controversy' see Barker (*et al.* 2001).

6. Other studios making British horror fare at this time included Amicus, Tigon and Tyburn.

7. Pirie's comparing of British horror with the western – if we are to read the western as representative of cultural purity – is problematic, especially in light of Austin Fisher's recent work on the Italian western, which looks at how a genre deemed so 'American' could communicate 'revolutionary [Italian] political views in the national and international contexts of [Italy in] the late 1960s' (2011: 1).

8. Personal email correspondence with Jonathan Rigby (2013).

9. Sconce does not specifically include horror in this list, but 'splatterpunk, "mondo" films, sword and sandal epics, Elvis flicks, governmental hygiene films, Japanese monster movies, beach party musicals, and just about every other historical manifestation of exploitation cinema from juvenile delinquency documentaries to soft core pornography' (1995: 372). Yet, as Jancovich et al. point out, 'it should be noted that even this list is not even meant to cover all aspects of the cult movie, but only those aspects that Sconce identifies as "paracinema", a small and select subsection of a larger set' (2003: 1). Horror, thus, can also be understood as a cult genre, and is often framed within Sconce's paracinema mantra (see, for example, Hawkins 2003; Hutchings 2003a; Jancovich 2008 [2002]; Willis 2003; Wu 2003).

2. BRITISH FILM PRODUCTION AND THE HORROR GENRE

The first decade of the new millennium saw British horror film production increase exponentially. Whereas only a smattering of horror titles were produced in Britain from 1990 to 2000, by the end of 2010 more than 400 had been released in one format or another,[1] with a further 100 having appeared as of 2014.[2] This 'British horror revival' – as it has subsequently come to be known (Simpson 2012: 11) – ran concurrent with a variety of shifts that were taking place across British film and film culture. These included shifts in the increasingly global prominence of British cinema at the international box office; the changing tastes of domestic audiences; and changing critical attitudes to the horror genre that, for centuries, was subjected to the most vociferous of criticisms by the popular press and society's moralists. Horror film producers in the UK responded to these changes, aided largely by a boom in cheap digital filmmaking technologies, which prompted the production and distribution of micro-budget genre films, as well as some significant shifts in governmental film policy that abetted the development of higher-profile horror movies. While the majority of filmmakers during this period secured funding through private investors (or in many cases self-funded their own films), the introduction of tax relief for British films in 1997 (for films with budgets of less than £15m), and the birth of the UK Film Council (UKFC) in 2000, anticipated financial support for popular genres such as horror – or, to quote the UKFC, 'the development, production and export of films that attract audiences in the UK and all over the world' (UKFC 2000: 3).

This chapter considers the re-introduction of the horror genre to the production slates of British filmmakers after the year 2000, addressing the kinds of films that emerged during this period and what key factors contributed to the horror genre's economic buoyancy amid other production trends in local and international cinema. For neatness, the chapter is split into two sections. The first of these, '(Re)establishing Horror as a popular British genre', considers how the horror film featured amid the 'commercially minded' rhetoric of the UKFC and its supporters from 2000 to 2004 (Leggott 2008: 17). The first section also considers how the genre underwent some critical re-evaluation in this period, and what impact this had on both the visibility and 'respectability' of British horror cinema in critical circles. It is my contention that a positive critical re-evaluation of the horror genre during this period aided in the development of some high-profile British horror releases. The second section, 'Sustaining British Horror: 2005 and beyond', considers how, after a smattering of international successes (but mostly box office flops), filmmakers and producers found means of sustaining their horror output through the 'direct-to-video' market.

(Re)establishing Horror as a popular British genre

In *A New Heritage of Horror*, David Pirie argues that the classic 'English Gothic' films produced by Hammer from the 1950s to 70s were 'in no way imitative of American or European models' (2008: xv). However, in the early 2000s, 'Britishness' was sometimes approached with caution by British film producers who often presumed that indigenous films may run the risk of being too parochial to sell to a global audience. Therefore, the first British horror films that appeared in the twenty-first century were explicitly indebted to 'models' of filmmaking that were proving to be popular in overseas theatrical markets, and, as such, the horror films were cultivated with the broadest possible demographics in mind.

New beginnings

Significantly for British horror's future, international genre successes of the 1990s such as the US-produced *Scream* (Wes Craven, 1996) and *The Blair Witch Project* (Eduardo Sánchez and Daniel Myrick, 1999), and the Japanese *Ringu* (Hideo Nakata, 1998), demonstrated that it was possible to produce cheap genre films that would sell well in foreign territories.[3] However, for one reason or another, it took a while for UK producers to catch on to horror's market potential. The production pages featured in the film industry periodical *Screen International* between the year 2000 and the release of British horror's first major success, *28 Days Later* in 2002, reveal a potential fifty British horror titles that were ultimately never made (including remakes of several

Hammer classics),[4] while those films that did make it through, such as Simon Hunter's slasher film *Lighthouse* (2000), and Neil Marshall's werewolf movie *Dog Soldiers*, had been stuck in development hell since the mid-1990s (see Leake 1999a; Marshall 2003).

It is arguable that prospective horror film producers were exercising caution. After all, the genre had a fraught relationship with British critics that dated back to the publication of the first Gothic novel, Walpole's *The Castle of Otranto*, in 1794. As Julian Petley explains, *Otranto*, and others like it, was subject to the kinds of 'vociferous' criticism that would meet the release of many horror films in Britain in subsequent decades (Petley 2002a: 38; see also Hutchings 1993: 4–7). Moreover, the panic surrounding 'media effects' in the wake of the 'video nasties' scandal in the 1980s remained rife enough in the 1990s to put off most British producers from engaging with horror at all (Chibnall and Petley 2002: 7). What is more, the few British horror films that did manage to slip through the net – such as *Dream Demon* (Harley Cokeliss, 1988) and *I Bought a Vampire Motorcycle* (Dirk Campbell, 1990) – generated very little in the way of box office returns.[5] However, by the 2000s, the global popularity of horror was enough to incentivise British producers to take a gamble on the genre once again, and three films led the way: the UKFC-backed *The Hole* and *Long Time Dead* (Marcus Adams, 2002), and *My Little Eye* (Marc Evans, 2002).

Seen together, these films were aspiring profit-generating combatants against the voluble criticisms that were being launched at the British film industry at the time, for producing films that were not only costly, but also widely unpopular (Petley 2002b: 45). Unlike recent flops such as the comedy *Rancid Aluminium* (Edward Thomas, 2000), which was shot for £6m but only managed to recoup £150k at the UK box office, *The Hole*, *Long Time Dead* and *My Little Eye* were comparatively inexpensive, with budgets all about the £1–2m mark. They were also made up of casts of mostly unknown actors, negating the expenditure of star fees.[6] Keeping the costs down meant that, even if a loss were to befall them, the outcome would unlikely have been as severe as *Rancid Aluminium*'s, nor that of the similarly dire *Honest* (David A. Stewart, 2000): a British crime film that only recouped a miserable £111k of its £3m shooting budget (http://imdb.com/pro).

The makers of *The Hole*, *Long Time Dead* and *My Little Eye* also exercised caution in other ways. With plots surrounding the grisly demise of fresh-faced teenagers, these films were very much riding a wave of highly popular 'teen horror' films from the US, including *The Faculty* (Robert Rodriguez, 1998), *I Know What You Did Last Summer* (Jim Gillespie, 1997), the *Scream* sequels (Wes Craven, 1997, 2000), *Urban Legend* (Jamie Blanks, 1998), *Halloween H20* (Steve Miner, 1998), *Cherry Falls* (Geoffrey Wright, 2000) and *Final Destination* (James Wong, 2000).[7] *My Little Eye* actually paraded as an

'American' production by setting its action in the American wilderness, and casting Canadian actors in American roles,[8] while the marketing campaigns for *The Hole* and *Long Time Dead* resonated loudly with those of their Hollywood counterparts. For example, the British theatrical posters depicted the faces of their cast strategically centred on the respective 'threat' of each film – an abandoned underground bunker ('the hole') in the case of *The Hole*, and a demonic figure in the case of *Long Time Dead* – in turn complying with the marketing style of US money-spinners.

This drive to appeal to an overseas audience proved problematic for some commentators, who argued that British producers were compromising cultural distinctiveness by making films that were simply derivative of (mostly better) American product (Pirie 2008: 218). It was typical in reviews of *Long Time Dead*, for instance, for critics to lambast its employment of the stalk 'n' slash formula, accuse the film of being 'obvious' (Marriott 2002: 8) and having 'ripped off' the director of *Scream*, Wes Craven (Anon. 2002). However, British cultural mores were not wholly absent from the British horror films. In fact, such mores, if not always as prominent as their international allusions, were essential to how the films were made to fit with current trends in British cinema.

Finding an audience: 'Britishness', gender and the mainstream

One way that two of the films hat-tipped British culture – or perhaps, a tourist's eye view of said culture that could be easily marketed to an international audience – was through the employment of settings and locations that would likely have been familiar to international audiences of British cinema. *The Hole*, for example, is set around the campus of a grand, aged British school, not dissimilar in style to the country mansions of highly profitable Jane Austen adaptations, such as *Mansfield Park* (Patricia Rozema, 1999), or the heritage films of Merchant Ivory. Similarly, much of the action in *Long Time Dead* unfolds in the kind of large 'Gothic' house found in thrillers that were enjoying overseas success, such as the British-set *The Others* (Alejandro Amenábar, 2001). It should come as no surprise then that British horror films were engaging with these touristic traits, especially when they were designed to attract international audiences. Perhaps the most important 'British' factor that horror films were engaging with at this time, however, was youth and youth cultures, strategically to appeal to 'the younger, core cinema-going audience' (Street 2009: 135).

Youth cultures have been central to both the narratives and marketing of British horror and exploitation cinema since the 1950s (Hutchings 1993; Hunt 1998). This has mostly been due to the fact that teenagers have been continuously identified as the primary market for horror films, and, also, that horror films themselves have been influenced by other genres popular with young audiences. Often, horror films have 'blended' with other genres popular with a teenage demographic, such as the first American slasher cycle, which fused gory sequences of teenagers being murdered with tropes of contemporaneous 'roller-disco movies' and 'animal comedies' (Nowell 2010: 112–16). The production context of contemporary British horrors such as *The Hole*, *Long Time Dead* and *My Little Eye* was similar.

The specific ways that youth are represented in these three films relates to two primary factors. The first of these is that the films – as mentioned above – were responding directly to the American 'teen horror' films, which typically saw teenagers engage in hedonistic activity, before being killed off in gory ways. The second factor – and that which is most overlooked in discussions of British horror – is that British horror films were also responding to the (continued) popularity of what Karen Lury (2000) has recognised as British 'youth films', such as Danny Boyle's worldwide success *Trainspotting* (1996) and Justin Kerrigan's *Human Traffic* (1999).[9] It could be argued, thus, that the British horror films sought to strike a balance between the universal teenage ambience popularised by the American films – that would potentially appeal to a global audience – and the more overt cultural-specificities of the British youth films – that would appease local cinemagoers and critics. The linking strand in the British horror films, thus, was a focus on sex and drugs. *The Hole*'s plot, for instance, is that a group of rebellious teens spend a long weekend in a secret underground bunker on their school's campus, getting high and having sex. Similarly, *My Little Eye* features a group of carefree young people who are all participants in an online reality game show, and who – as with past contestants on British TV's *Big Brother* (2000–) – get drunk and (among other things) have sex for the camera. While one could argue that these films owe more to the frat house culture explored in the American horror films (and in comedies such as the *American Pie* (1999–) films), *Long Time Dead* more overtly embodies the sex, drugs and dance culture associated with the likes of *Human Traffic* and its 'live-for-the-weekend' mentality, and even features a key scene in which one of the characters is killed off at a dance party by falling through a glass ceiling onto the revellers below. Whereas *Trainspotting* and *Human Traffic* very much celebrate hedonism (Street 2009: 134–5), the British horror films are more conservative in their outlook. As with their self-aware American counterparts they part-function as morality tales that see their young characters 'punished' by death for their waywardness. This was a story trait likely included due to the films' producers' wanting to remain faithful to the many American horror films discussed above, which echoed a highly influential sequence in *Scream* in which horror-geek Randy (Jamie Kennedy) explains the 'rules' of slasher films (you can never have sex, do drugs or say, 'I'll be right back'), and the inevitable fates that await permissive teenagers when such rules are disobeyed

(Harries 2002: 289; see also Hutchings 2004a: 212–13). Nevertheless, it is important to recognise that the British films show an awareness of local trends and (sub)culture(s), even if their 'American' allusions ultimately prevail. At the very least, there is confluence. This is hinted towards in the taglines for both *The Hole* and *Long Time Dead* – 'Desperate to get in . . . dying to get out' and 'Play it to death' – that both chime with the cautionary taglines of films like *I Know What You Did Last Summer* ('If you are going to bury the truth, make sure it stays buried'), but that can also be read as subverting the 'Choose life' sentiments of *Trainspotting*,[10] by offering 'death' as an option (or rather, an inevitability) instead.

The Hole, *Long Time Dead* and *My Little Eye* did relatively well domestically: *The Hole* grossed £2.2m, *Long Time Dead* grossed £1.6m and *My Little Eye* grossed £2.5m (http://imdb.com/pro). Both *Long Time Dead* and *My Little Eye* also enjoyed some success in continental Europe, with the former proving popular in Spain (EURO1.76m) and the latter, in Italy ($750k).[11] All, however, were released directly to video in the US. The video market would become a more sustainable primary outlet for horror film distribution as the decade progressed (discussed below; see also Bernard 2014), but the DTV release of these formative horror movies perhaps testified to the ambivalence felt by American distributors to British horror films, in spite of the British producers' best efforts to prove them otherwise.

In an article published in 2000, Mark Jancovich identified the apparent distinction between masculinised audiences of violent and obscure horror films and feminised audiences of 'mainstream' horror films, and the ways that this perceived binary is negotiated within fan communities. He argued that this split is presented within some fan circles as a divide between fans of 'authentic' horror on the one hand, and fans of 'inauthentic' horror on the other. Using himself as a case study (as both a fan and academic), he argued:

> I have often been accused . . . of not really talking about horror (or at least not 'real' horror), but rather about mainstream commercial horror. To put it another way, [people] claim that what I discuss is not 'real' horror but rather the commercialized, sanitized tripe which is consumed by moronic victims of mass culture. (Jancovich 2000: 25)

He continues, 'many of these horror fans privilege as "real" and "authentic" those films of violent "excess" whose circulation is usually restricted . . . and they do so specifically to define their own opposition to, or distinction from, what they define as inauthentic commercial products of mainstream culture' (ibid.). The films of violent excess that Jancovich is referring to are the 1960s films of cult B-movie director Herschell Gordon Lewis, although one could easily read more recent, micro-budget, British splatter films such as Alex

Chandon's *Cradle of Fear* (2001) in their place.[12] And the mainstream horror films identified in Jancovich's article are the *Scream* films because of their mass-market visibility and teen-focus; yet he could easily have been referring to *The Hole* or *Long Time Dead*. British film producers were aware of this binary, and were straying from optioning material that was likely to only appeal to a niche, straight-to-video horror crowd. Instead, they were looking beyond the 'B-movie' type, to a kind of horror that would reinstate the genre beyond the male fannish associations that the genre has so-often characterised (Cherry 2002; Chapter 4 of this book), as something that was far more commercially ambitious.

Another way of targeting a young audience was through studio-backed 'labels' that would attempt to recapture the kind of British horror branding that Hammer had once had. One failed attempt at launching a horror label came from Hammer itself, which, prior to being acquired by the consortium Cyrte Investments in 2008, mooted a series of UK/Australian co-productions (see Chapter 6). Another attempt came from Random Harvest, which established the 'Four Horsemen' label with the intention of producing twelve horror films over three years in association with Buena Vista (Minns 2002). In the end, only two films were produced. The first was a teen vampire film from the director of *Long Time Dead*, Marcus Adams. Entitled *Octane* (2003), it was scripted by UK Gothic stalwart Stephen Volk and was clearly devised to capitalise on the huge successes of 'leather-clad vampire' epics such as *Blade* (Stephen Norrington, 1998) and *Underworld* (Len Wiseman, 2003). The second film from Four Horsemen was yet another in the 'teen horror' mould, *Lethal Dose: 50 (LD50)* (Simon De Selva, 2003), which borrowed themes of infection from the zombie film *28 Days Later* (discussed in more detail below) and starred former pop star Melanie 'Scary Spice' Brown. The Four Horsemen venture, while an ambitious project (twelve films were planned!), misjudged the faltering demand for teen-oriented horror at this time, as popular horror became more visceral and remake-centred. Accordingly, *Octane* flopped at the box office and *Lethal Dose: 50* went straight to video. Four Horsemen ceased as a production company shortly after.

Another attempt to create a British horror brand came from Lizzie Francke, chief executive of Little Bird Films (and former Edinburgh International Film Festival (EIFF) director), whose subsidiary 'The Ministry of Fear' was established in 2001 solely to produce horror films for a mainstream audience (Bacal 2004: 16). Francke was among the first to anticipate the market potential of new British horror, and, through trying to appeal to two traditionally disparate audiences – the young female audience of the romantic drama and the young male audience of the horror film – sought to produce 'crossover' horror films that were, to her mind, 'more intelligent' and psychologically grounded than the visceral slashers that had come to be associated with the male horror crowd

(Macnab 2004a: 6). However, the first and only release from Ministry of Fear, *Trauma* (Marc Evans, 2004), demonstrated the difficulties of this approach.

On paper, the film had many bases covered to be a success. Described by one reviewer as 'a haunting mediation on grief and self-delusion' (Brown 2004: 34), *Trauma*'s themes of mental illness, the death of loved ones and ghosts, chimed with several popular psychological Hollywood horror films of the day, including *What Lies Beneath* (Robert Zemeckis, 2000) and *The Sixth Sense* (M. Night Shyamalan, 1999). It also starred two widely recognisable British actors, Colin Firth and Naomie Harris, both of whom were probably cast to appeal, in one respect, to prospective female audience members and, in another, assumedly male horror fans. Firth had become somewhat of a national heartthrob following his portrayal of Mr Darcy in the 1995 TV production of *Pride and Prejudice*, and also had several box office hits to his name; including *Bridget Jones's Diary* (Sharon Maguire, 2001) in which he played another Darcy. Meanwhile Harris, though at this point not as famous as Firth,[13] had recently appeared as Selena, the strong-willed heroine of *28 Days Later*, and, as such, may have invited empathy from both the female audience members and the core horror crowd. *Trauma*'s makers also strategically cast a cool and sexy American teen idol, Mena Suvari of the *American Pie* series, and gave the role of director to Marc Evans, whose *My Little Eye* had recently enjoyed success at the domestic box office and at international horror film festivals.

In spite of these promising commercial aspects, *Trauma* never did see its August 2004 cinema release, but ended up going straight to video the following year. A possible reason for this was Francke's misjudging of the key audience for horror, who, at the time of the film's production, was already flocking to see pastiche-heavy films such as *The Texas Chainsaw Massacre* (Marcus Nispel, 2003), *Saw* (James Wan, 2004) and *Shaun of the Dead*. These were films that were far more grounded in horror fan culture and viscera than the psychological horrors upon which Francke has based her venture. By casting Firth, by holding back on the gore, and by repeatedly using the somewhat condescending phrase 'girly horror' to sum-up horror's growing popularity among women (Macnab 2004a: 6), Francke ran the risk of, to use Jancovich's terminology, 'sanitizing' her film, by at once excluding the male core of the genre audience and patronising women by assuming that the presence of Colin Firth would somehow guarantee their attendance.

Audience crossover worked better for *28 Days Later* in 2002 and *Shaun of the Dead* in 2004, which were two of the highest grossing British horror films released from 2000 to 2004. Their success with wide audiences can be put down to two main factors: both had large advertising budgets, and both featured elements that were deemed in some way relatable to female audiences (that is, not the usual horror crowd). Indeed, *28 Days Later* had one of the biggest marketing budgets yet seen for a British horror film, which included a

£600k television campaign, a £170k prints campaign, a sophisticated online marketing campaign, as well as the projection of the film's poster on to the Irish parliament building[14] – while *Shaun of the Dead* had a combined prints and advertising (P&A) budget of £1.7m ($3m).[15] The films were also engineered to attract men and women and to cover a variety of age groups in a way that did not alienate potential audience members, or – to use fan terminology – 'disrespect' the genre texts that they pastiched or parodied. For instance, Selena in *28 Days Later* offered a strong, complex, moral centre to an otherwise run-of-the-mill zombie narrative (an infection turns the majority of England's inhabitants into blood-hungry subhumans). The character also was different to the white, teenage and suburban 'final girls' that had preceded her in horror history, the character owing more to resourceful action heroines of the period such as Ripley in *Alien: Resurrection* (Jean-Pierre Jeunet, 1997). Meanwhile, *Shaun of the Dead*, as a horror-comedy, focused more on character types associated with British romantic comedies of the period that were widely popular with female cinema-goers: Shaun (Simon Pegg) is a bafoonish man in the Hugh Grant mould who is actively trying to rekindle his failed relationship with his ex-girlfriend (see Chapter 4). The film's 'romantic comedy' aspect thus offered a potent thematic diversion that was thought to have sat well with female audiences to the otherwise trivia-based, fannish references that the film made to (what is often thought of as being) male-oriented American splatter cinema of the 1970s. To this end, while both *28 Days Later* and *Shaun of the Dead* both retained the intertextual aspect likely to appeal to horror fans, it was clear at their time of release that their production companies desired to appeal to an audience far broader than this.

Changing attitudes

In *Hammer and Beyond*, Peter Hutchings notes how horror has generally been judged negatively or with embarrassment by the British critics (1993: 4–11). Such reactions, he argues, have in a sense 'validated' the films, and affirmed their transgressive potential. He concludes the book by arguing, that, to render 'these films worthy and respectable would be doing them a disservice', as it is 'a fundamental condition of British horror's existence that no one "really" takes it seriously' (187). However, the period from 2000 to 2004 indicated a wide shift in British critical attitudes towards the genre that, in turn, impacted indigenous genre production in various ways.

For example, the retirement of James Ferman as Secretary of the British Board of Film Classification (BBFC) saw the immediate theatrical and video re-release of several once-banned and/or controversial films, including *The Exorcist* (William Friedkin, 1973), *The Texas Chain Saw Massacre* and *The Last House on the Left* (Wes Craven, 1972). This suggested that the 'video nasty era' was (finally) well and truly over, and that opinions on the genre in Britain were certainly softening. Furthermore, the slasher film *Lighthouse* was placed on a multiplex double-bill with the one of the most notorious of all 'video nasties', *The Evil Dead* (Sam Raimi, 1981) in 2002. And while it was a modest release – it only played in a smattering of Odeon cinemas – the double bill at least looked towards the shift of British horror and horror cinema more generally from the margins, to the critical mainstream.

During October and November 2002 both *My Little Eye* and *28 Days Later* were released. Both were heralded as 'good' horror films, both made a substantial profit and both were deemed technologically innovative, having been shot on Mini Digital Video (MiniDV) – a domestic, home-recording medium – as opposed to the more commonplace 35mm film. The choice to shoot on DV set them apart from the arguable Hollywood gloss of *The Hole* and *Long Time Dead* and other mainstream films, without impeding their box office successes. As was recognised by the trade press at the time, the similar styles of *My Little Eye* and *28 Days Later* resonated not only with other low-budget and highly profitable horror films such as *The Blair Witch Project*, but also the transgressive Dogme 95 movement in Denmark.[16] Not insignificantly, in 2001, Zentropa Films (Dogme 95's production company) had in fact produced *The Last Great Wilderness*, a film shot on DV that, on the one hand displayed thematic allegiance to *The Wicker Man* (Robin Hardy, 1973) and *Straw Dogs* (Sam Peckinpah, 1971), but, on the other, chimed stylistically with contemporary art house trends. It had little mainstream recognition beyond the trade press, but nevertheless hinted towards a new – and, as far as the critics were concerned, more 'respectable' – type of British horror.[17]

Indeed, *My Little Eye* and *28 Days Later* were distributed more-widely,[18] and, as such, afforded the British horror film some much-needed credibility: specifically Boyle's film, which was one of the first films developed by the Conservative government's (but subsequently adopted by the Labour party in 1997) much-criticised Film Consortium to make a substantial amount of money (£6m in the UK, $45m in the US) (Minns 2001: 13). More than this, it had the added credibility of being shot by an award-winning British filmmaker, Danny Boyle, and for being photographed by Anthony Dod Mantle, who had also been cinematographer on the critically regarded Dogme 95 film, *Festen* (Thomas Vinterberg, 1998).[19]

My Little Eye was released almost exactly one month prior to *28 Days Later* in the UK. The earlier release date (4 October) eliminated the risk of it being overshadowed by Boyle's film, which was subsequently released the day after Halloween (1 November). Moreover, the critical reaction to *My Little Eye* afforded Evans the opportunity to appear, alongside British cinema stalwart Mike Leigh, and up-and-comer Lynne Ramsay, above the headline 'The Confident New Face of British Cinema' on the cover of October 2002's *Sight and Sound*. Significantly, *Sight and Sound* was the very same magazine that published Derek Hill's infamous 'The Face of Horror' article in 1958, which argued that the genre was a social problem – not something to be nationally embraced.[20] Indeed, the cover of the October 2002 edition implied that it was possible not only for traits of popular genres to fuse with those of the art house, but also that horror films could be read critically and in relation to revered and respectable areas of British cinema that had, for a long time, been considered segregated from it. For the first time in British cinema history, horror was readily accepted as a welcome part of the filmic patchwork and as indicative of 'the diversity and daring of indigenous film-makers' (Hunter 2002: 1), rather than as a canker on the national cinema.[21]

The lengths that British horror producers stretched to produce commercially viable horror productions in the first five years of the new millennium were varied, yet were also linked by the solitary desire to attract as broad an audience as possible. As we have seen, this involved capitalising on popular international genre successes, filtering through subtle British resonances, as well as producing 'crossover' films with a broad market remit. These are all aspects of British horror that spilled over into the second half of the decade. However, what became clearer after 2005 was that, if the first five years of the decade represented the genre 'finding its feet' in the UK, the latter years clarified British horror's 'place' within a crowded market of increased horror production.

Sustaining British Horror: 2005 and beyond

Two things are implied by the fact that *28 Days Later* and *Shaun of the Dead* were the only major global successes for British horror from 2000 to 2004. First, it suggests that most film producers were unsure as to which avenues to take with the genre, seeing as there had been no singular trend-setting text, as there had been with Hammer's *The Curse of Frankenstein* in 1957.[22] Second, it also implies that the genre need not have been restricted to just one outlook or style, but rather that it was, as UK horror director Steven Sheil acknowledged, a 'broad church' and capable of straddling many (Sheil 2010a). In the years after 2005, British horror production increased threefold, and most films were being made beyond the purview of major film studios and funding bodies. Thanks to the rise in new technologies, producers were taking advantage of a lucrative home-viewing market, and, in the majority of cases, were bypassing theatrical releasing altogether.

This is not to say that horror was not, on the whole, popular at the UK box office, or that theatrical success for British horror films had been fully surpassed. Christian Grass of Fox Atomic – the company behind the successful Hollywood remakes *The Grudge* (Takashi Shimizu, 2004) and *The Amityville*

Horror (Andrew Douglas, 2005) and also *28 Days Later* – noted that, in 2005, the UK was one of the highest grossing territories for horror cinema, and that it was also one of the most consistent in terms of performance (cited in Mitchell 2005a: 24). Moreover, *The Woman in Black*, when released in 2012 to record-breaking box office returns, was christened 'the highest grossing British horror film of all time' by the British media (see Chapter 6).

Yet, in the early to-mid 2000s, the most popular horror films to be screened in the UK were the American remakes *The Texas Chainsaw Massacre* and *The Amityville Horror*.[23] Unlike British studio one-offs like *Trauma* and *Long Time Dead*, these films had major cultural weight due to their status as remakes of well-known and controversial films, as well as substantial marketing budgets that helped promote them all over the world.[24] The success of Working Title Films's *Shaun of the Dead* in the US in 2005 could also be partially attributed to the nostalgia for a bygone era of American exploitation cinema. The film's nostalgic undertones were anticipated by the cinematic re-release of *The Exorcist* to large box office in the UK in 1998 (£7.1m), and sustained by grindhouse-influenced torture porn films such as *Saw II* (Darren Lynn Bousman, 2005) and *Hostel* (Eli Roth, 2005). And although *Shaun of the Dead* cloaked its intertexuality within an affectionate parodic framework,[25] strove for comedy more than horror and contained many of the indigenous inflections that was typical of other films produced by Working Title Films (Street 2002: 206), it also proved that a 'British take' on cult American material could prove highly successful in the global marketplace.[26] As Sarah Street (2002: 206) has argued, one of the defining features of Working Title Films in the mid-1990s and beyond was its 'undoubted ability to produce films that demonstrate[d] both indigenous and export appeal' – and *Shaun of the Dead* very much continued this trend.

The Descent and new markets

The release of Neil Marshall's *The Descent* in 2005 was well-timed. *The Descent* embodied the penchant for paying homage to American horror of the seventies that had contributed to the commercial and critical success of *Shaun of the Dead*. Indeed, its plot – a group of outdoorswomen come face to face with flesh-eating humanoids in the cave systems of the Appalachian Mountains – has subsequently invited comparisons to staple rural horror films such as *The Texas Chain Saw Massacre* and *Deliverance* (John Boorman, 1972), in which city dwellers leave the safety of the metropolis only to encounter horrors in the countryside (Clover 1992: 124–37; Rose 2009: 137–9; Bernard 2014: 168). In fact, Marshall has himself described the film as '*Deliverance* goes underground' (cited in Macnab 2005a : 17).

Released in UK cinemas in July 2005, *The Descent* significantly became the first horror film to attract about as many women to British theatres as men (UKFC 2005: 54). While it grossed a commendable £2.6m in the UK,[27] the real surprise came when it was released in America the following year, generating $26m (http://imdb.com/pro). Setting the action in America gave the film more market scope than otherwise provincial horror films of the period – a case in point being Marshall's own *Dog Soldiers*, in which a group of British squaddies are attacked by werewolves in Scotland. As David Martin-Jones has noted, the film's foregrounding of Scottish customs and traditions limited its prospects for international distribution (2011: 115–23).[28] Moreover, the gory nature of *The Descent* helped with its global success; its instances of bodily mutilation and cannibalism chimed with the visceral nature of *Saw* and *Hostel*, while also tapping into the DVD market for trends in 'Extreme' cinema from Europe, in films like *Haute Tension (Switchblade Romance)* (Alexandre Aja, 2003), and Asia, in films like *Ichi the Killer* (Takashi Miike, 2001).[29]

However, *The Descent*'s success cannot be isolated to the cinema-goers' so-called 'contemporary taste for extreme violence' (Wood 2007: 96), nor its cult allusions nor its US setting. Its take on gender is also significant. The all-female cast of well-rounded and plausible characters – all active/outdoor types in their mid- to late thirties – subverted the masculine dominance of its generic forbears and out-stepped the 'boys-only' aura of other British horror films of the period, such as *Dog Soldiers*, and 'military horror' films such as Rob Green's *The Bunker* (2001) and Michael J. Bassett's *Deathwatch* (2002).[30] As with *28 Days Later*, *The Descent* was a film at odds with Lizzie Francke's clean-cut idea of 'girly horror' in that it was as much a psychologically oriented tale as a visceral genre piece. Of course, it also shared the maternal and psychological concerns of the films that Francke name-checked, namely *The Others* and *What Lies Beneath*: the main protagonist, Sarah, loses her daughter in the film's opening moments. However, as with Selena in *28 Days Later*, Sarah is also a strong-willed action heroine, made in the mould of Sigourney Weaver's Ripley, and was also poles apart from the suburban 'final *girl*' of the American slasher.[31] Of the two different cuts of the film that were released – the UK theatrical cut, in which Sarah remains trapped in the caves at the end of the film, and the US version, in which she escapes – it was the latter, in which Sarah prevails, that proved a hit with audiences at the time, and has contributed to its enduring global popularity. The film's distributor acknowledged that, by not underestimating the fluid taste capacities of a horror film audience, and by acknowledging that '[m]ovie-goers are much more complex' than gender binaries, age and taste distinctions can predict (Ortenberg cited in Kay 2006a: 20),[32] horror could attract an adult audience of both sexes.

Upon its initial release *The Descent* appeared to hint towards a bright future for British horror production. As with *28 Days Later* and *Shaun of the Dead*, it had achieved the seemingly impossible and broke America. However, in spite of its noted similarity to other horrors of the period, it was still an anomaly as far as British production was concerned. Therefore, its global achievements at the international box office were unlikely to be emulated by other British horror films; not least because US distributors were already beginning to corner the market with gory horror films for an adult audience (such as with the *Saw* series). It soon became apparent that, unless a film was a sequel to a popular British hit from earlier in the decade – such as *28 Weeks Later* (Juan Carlos Fresnadillo, 2007) and *The Descent: Part 2* (Jon Harris, 2009) – or a follow-up – such as Edgar Wright's successor to *Shaun of the Dead*, *Hot Fuzz* (2007) – a profile at the international box office was not guaranteed for British genre production. To capitalise on *The Descent*'s local and international profile, producers therefore turned to the home video market, where distribution rights are cheaper, where distributors can easily acquire lower-budgeted films and where some profits are almost always guaranteed for distributors.

Video markets

Under these circumstances, over the next ten years the market was flooded with an array of low- (and in most cases micro-) budget horror films. These kinds of films would often be screened at specialist festivals in the UK, such as Fright Fest (London), Mayhem (Nottingham), Grimm Up North (Manchester), Dead By Dawn (Edinburgh), Raindance (London) and Abertoir (Aberystwyth), or abroad such as Midnight Madness (Canada), Lund International Fantastic Film Festival (Sweden), Fantasporto (Portugal), International Festival de Catalunya – Sitges (Spain) and Fantafestival (Italy), before going direct to home video platforms (DVD, Blu-ray, Video on Demand (VoD)). Others would bypass the festival circuit altogether and go straight to video, or would receive a very limited theatrical release in an effort to generate additional exposure. Examples include gory rural horrors like *Broken* (Adam Mason and Simon Boyes, 2006), *Wilderness* (Michael J. Bassett, 2006), *Eden Lake*, *The Fallow Field* (Leigh Dovey, 2013) and *White Settlers* (Simeon Halligan, 2014); chillers about mental instability, such as *Venus Drowning* (Andrew Parkinson, 2006), *Shrooms* (Paddy Breathnach, 2007), *The Daisy Chain* (Aisling Walsh, 2008) and *Psychosis* (Reg Traviss, 2010); vampire films, such as *Night Junkies* (Lawrence Pearce, 2007), *Vampire Diary* (Mark James and Phil O'Shea, 2006) and *Strigoi*; supernatural/spiritual horror films, such as *The Dark* (John Fawcett, 2005), *Dead Wood* (David Bryant, Sebastian Smith and Richard Stiles, 2007), *Credo* (Toni Harman, 2008), *Red Mist* (*Freakdog*) (Paddy Breathnach, 2008), *The Torment* (*The Possession of David O'Reilly*) (Andrew Cull and Steve Isles, 2010), *Hollow* (Michael Axelgaard, 2011) and *Soulmate* (Axelle Carolyn, 2013); creature features, such as *Cold and Dark* (Andrew Goth, 2005), *Forest of the Damned* (Johannes Roberts, 2005), *Isolation* (Billy O'Brien, 2005),

Wild Country (Craig Strachan, 2005), *Salvage, Splintered* (Simeon Halligan, 2010) and *Outcast*; 'family horror' films, including *Mum & Dad, Gnaw* (Gregory Mandry, 2008) and *Community* (Jason Ford, 2012); gory horror comedies, such as *Boy Eats Girl* (Stephen Bradley, 2005), *Botched* (Kit Ryan, 2007), *Graveyard Shift: A Zomedy of Terrors* (Sapphira Sen-Gupta and Denise Channing, 2010), *Kill Keith* (Andy Thompson, 2011), *Stitches* and *Stalled*; films shot in the 'torture porn' model,[33] such as *w Delta z* (Tom Shankland, 2007) and *Spiderhole*; sci-fi horror crossovers, such as *Infestation* (Ed Evers-Swindell, 2005), *Bane, Beacon 77 (The 7th Dimension)* (Brad Watson, 2009) and *Storage 24* (Johannes Roberts, 2012); and zombie films, including *The Zombie Diaries, The Dead Outside* (Kerry Anne Mullaney, 2008), *The Vanguard* (Matthew Hope, 2008), *Zombies of the Night* (Stuart Brennan, 2008) and *Night of the Living Dead: Resurrections* (James Plumb, 2012).[34] The earlier films were often compared unfavourably to *The Descent*, in both critical and commercial terms,[35] while those films that opened theatrically usually only did so for about two weeks and, in some instances, a few days, before appearing on DVD and VoD. These included *Salvage, Surviving Evil, Tony (Tony: London Serial Killer)* (Gerard Johnson, 2009) and *Zombie Undead* (Rhys Davies, 2010). An exception was Steven Sheil's *Mum & Dad*, which on 26 December 2008 was made available simultaneously across multiple platforms: theatres, the pay-per-view service Sky Box Office, other VoD platforms and DVD. In bypassing the standard sixteen-week gap that usually separates a film's theatrical from its home video release (see Henderson 2009: 475–6), this strategy represented a tacit acknowledgement that the audience for British horror was too small to offset the substantial costs of theatrical distribution. As the CEO of *Mum & Dad*'s UK distributer, Revolver Films, has noted, this cross-platform release simply 'made business sense' (Marciano cited in Anon. 2008a: 38).[36]

Several hybrid genre pictures were also made with a view to securing a DVD and VoD release and were typically funded by first-time private investors who were trying their luck in the movie business. Many of the films were either furnished with slapstick comedy, as was the case with *Evil Aliens* (Jake West, 2005) and *Kill Keith* – both of which had short theatrical runs – or with gangster and hooligan types of contemporary British crime movies such as Nick Love's *The Football Factory* (2005) and *The Business* (2005). As Jonathan Sothcott, the CEO of low-budget exploitation producer Black and Blue Films, has explained, the presence of British crime film star Danny Dyer on a DVD cover could almost guarantee the sale of 60,000 to 100,000 units: more than double that of the company's other releases (Sothcott 2011).[37] This form of British exploitation cinema was again often closely modelled on commercially successful cultural products. For example, Black and Blue's *Devil's Playground* (Mark McQueen, 2010) imbeds into the crime film format a tale of zombies spawned by a virus caused by corporate malpractice, which its makers drew from the highly popular *Resident Evil* series and *28 Weeks Later*. Similarly, the filmmakers behind the gangster/vampire picture *Dead Cert* (Steve Lawson, 2010) borrowed from HBO's hit television drama series *The Sopranos* (1999–2007) and *True Blood* (2008–). While genre-mixing permitted the makers and distributor of these films to maximise their profits by evoking a range of previously lucrative properties, it was their availability on DVD and VoD that truly facilitated the measure of success they enjoyed. Had the films incurred substantial losses from a wide theatrical run, the profits they made on home video would have plummeted or have been erased entirely. The same was also true of the first film to be released by the newly re-launched Hammer, *Beyond the Rave*, which was designed specifically for the social networking site Myspace.com, where it also premiered. The fact that Britain's most iconic producer of horror films chose to use a web-based platform to launch a hotly anticipated comeback provides perhaps the clearest indication that British horror would continue to be sustained not by theatrical exhibition but by home viewing (see Chapter 6).

A number of British filmmakers saw this period as an opportunity to make films without subsidy from private investors and without the small studio-like infrastructure of Black and Blue and its contemporaries. As I have discussed in more detail elsewhere (Walker 2014), a true 'DIY' approach was adopted by several amateur filmmakers, including Robbie Moffat, Ian Weeks, Neil Jones and Matt 'M. J.' Stone, who self-released their self-funded films *Cycle* (Moffat, 2005), *Red Canopy* (Weeks, 2006), *The Lost* (Jones, 2006) and *Ouija Board* (Stone, 2009) respectively, via re-recordable DVD-Rs.[38] Similarly, Northampton-born amateur director Jason Impey cast his family, friends and local actors in a series of violent and sexually explicit films for overseas release on DVD and online, such as *Cut & Paste* (2009), *Deranged* (2009) and *Tortured AKA Sex Slave* (2011), while Marc Price shot his self-funded zombie film, *Colin* (2009), on a standard definition digital video (DV) camera for (an alleged) £45 (Manzoor 2009).

These examples have shown how the days of British horror competing for a major theatre release were over for the foreseeable future (at least until the release of *The Woman in Black*). Bigger investors and the likes of the UKFC directed their attention to international bankable projects such as *The Dark Knight* (Christopher Nolan, 2008), *Mamma Mia!* (Phyllida Lloyd, 2008) and the *Harry Potter* films. Horror, meanwhile, was mostly self-contained within the peripheral festival, rental and sell-through markets inhabited by the genre's small, although 'very defined', audience (Kuhn cited in Macnab 2005b: 12).

More 'national' than 'international'

Unlike in the 1950s and 1960s, when Hammer's Gothic films were made with the support of Hollywood majors (Meikle 2009), the American film industry mostly steered clear of British horror in the 2000s and 2010s. This was a curious state of affairs, particularly as Hollywood producers had bolstered their enthusiasm for British film in other areas, such as romantic comedy, action and the family film (Jones 2007: 12; Lyons 2007: 13; Quinn 2007: 12; Mitchell 2008). Indeed, the highest grossing British films of the period – including 'Britbusters' such as *Harry Potter and the Philosopher's Stone* (Chris Columbus, 2001), *Bridget Jones's Diary*, *Casino Royale* (Martin Campbell, 2006), and *Mamma Mia!* – had all received significant financial input from the US (BFI 2012: 25).

Of course, the *Resident Evil* zombie series, the *Underworld* vampire films, *The Wolfman* and *The Woman in Black* all had US involvement.[39] But their lavish sets, high production values and state-of-the-art special effects chimed more with blockbuster culture than horror film trends. Indeed, whenever Hollywood majors proclaimed that 'Americans are interested in the British film industry', they were often only referring to the likes of *Trainspotting*, the Bond movies and actors such as Daniel Craig and Keira Knightley, who 'everybody seems to know' (Jones 2007: 12). This was something that most British horror, by way of its modest nature, could neither compete with, nor realistically aspire to be.[40]

To this end, tax relief abroad made it increasingly attractive for British producers to shoot their lower-budgeted horror films. Examples include *My Little Eye*, which, according to the producer Jon Finn, was shot in Canada partly because 'Canadian tax relief ... reduced Universal's outlay' (Finn 2014). Most popular with UK horror producers, however, was Europe: specifically countries such as Luxembourg, Romania and Germany. *Dog Soldiers*, which was originally planned to be shot in Scotland, was eventually shot in Luxembourg, and reportedly had its budget increased by a third as a result (Jones 2001: 17). Similarly, *Deathwatch* – a ghost story set in trenches during World War I – saved a remarkable $2.5m by shooting in the Czech Republic (Macmillan 2002: 14). Over the coming years, British horror films such as *Creep* (Christopher Smith, 2004), *Dead Even (Method)* (Duncan Roy, 2004), *Spirit Trap* (David Smith, 2005), *Snuff Movie* (Bernard Rose, 2005), *Severance* (Christopher Smith, 2006), *Hush* (Mark Tonderai, 2008), *Black Death* and *Deranged* (Neil Jones, 2012) would also financially benefit from utilising European locations, including Germany, Switzerland, Spain and Romania.

When coupled with the UK's tax incentives,[41] shooting films in Europe could help films 'qualify as British via international co-productions', where the UK was typically utilised for its post-production facilities and high-end studios, and the other countries were used for their scenic locations, inexpensive extras and low construction costs (Dams 2003: 25). Moreover, shooting in Europe and casting European actors offered commercial potential to British films in foreign territories. This was true of *Creep*, which is mostly set in the iconic London underground, but was shot mostly on sets in Germany. It also stars the popular German actress Franka Potente, familiar to German audiences and horror fans for her performance in the cult hit *Anatomie* (*Anatomy*) (Stefan Ruzowitzky, 2000), and to the rest of the world as the star of Tom Tykwer's highly popular *Lola rennt* (*Run Lola Run*) (1998). As Sarah Street and Charlotte Brunsdon have argued of Danny Boyle's depiction of London in *28 Days Later, Creep* was evidently shaped to appeal to both local and international audiences, by fusing elements of cultural specificity with more general, and touristic, iconography (Street 2009: 136–7; Brunsdon 2007: 49–51; see also Hutchings 2009a: 195–9). Indeed, there are several scenes in the film in which Potente's character, Kate, runs through the labyrinthine London subway, passing a number of identifiable signifiers such as 'UndergrounD' and 'Charing Cross' roundels.

In 2007, a points-based 'Cultural Test' was introduced for British cinema that was designed to determine 'the "Britishness" of a film production and therefore its eligibility for public funding and/or tax relief' (Higson 2011: 56).[42] There were also notable changes in Section 42 of the Finance (No. 2) Act's (1992) tax relief guidelines. Whereas the guidelines once had offered relief on 100 per cent of a film's budget, it now stated that relief would only apply to money spent in the UK. As one European filmmaker commented in 2008, the new rules meant that in many cases it was simply easier for producers to 'make a national project than an international one' (Macnab 2008a: 6), and for lower-budgeted British films to shoot solely in the UK.[43] This led to the production of British horror films with a more parochial agenda that displayed little regard for mainstream or transnational appeal.[44]

The UKFC distributed Lottery money through its New Cinema Fund, initially designed to 'support unique and innovative filmmakers' (that is, those with a marginal or non-existent market presence), to assist in the production of lower-budget, digitally shot films,[45] including the horror films *Exhibit A* (Dom Rotheroe, 2007) (awarded £9,999) and *Tony* (*Tony: London Serial Killer*) (awarded £150,000). As with the other non-horror movies that benefited from the fund, both examples given here were modest productions, were shot on location and embraced an inexpesive realist aesthetic. Other films that benefited from the fund include the higher-profile, but no-less parochial, films, *Cherry Tree Lane* (Paul Andrew Williams, 2010) (awarded £155,000), *Chatroom* (Hideo Nakata, 2010) (awarded £700,000) and *Donkey Punch* (Oliver Blackburn, 2008) (awarded £445,000). As with *Exhibit A* and *Tony*, these films accordingly dealt with decidedly British concerns. However, as means of targeting a wider audience demographic, the more expensive films tended to focus on youth culture: *Donkey Punch* offers a commentary on British 'clubbing' holidays, in which a young woman – during an orgy – is accidentally murdered; *Chatroom* explores 'cyber bullying', and sees a group of teens with mental health issues try to overcome the taunts and murderous threats of another; and *Cherry Tree Lane* explores the potent fears of 'Broken Britain', by pitching a group of working-class teens against well-to-do middle-class adults (see Chapter 5). Such films were also supported by the UKFC's Distribution and Exhibition Fund (to assist in the distribution of films in the UK), from which *Colin, Exam* (Stuart Hazeldine, 2009), *Mum & Dad* and *Cherry Tree Lane* each received £5,000, *Heartless* (Philip Ridley, 2009) £30,000 and *Chatroom* £200,000.[46]

The parochial-positioning of much British horror proved enticing to several local governments interested in investing in British cinema, and, in the process, help fund genre films that were regionally themed and that were both set and shot locally. With the aid of the UKFC, organisations such as Screen West Midlands helped fund *Tormented* (Jon Wright, 2009) and *The Children* (Tom Shankland, 2008); East Midlands Media assisted with *Donkey Punch*, *Hush* and *Mum & Dad*; Northwest Vision + Media helped to fund *Salvage* through a scheme backed by Liverpool City Council, 'Digital Departures'; and Screen Yorkshire assisted in the development of *Inbred* (Alex Chandon, 2011).[47] Meanwhile, the Irish Film Board co-funded/funded horror films such as *Freeze Frame* (John Simpson, 2004), *Isolation*, *Wake Wood* (David Keating, 2009), *Citadel* and *Byzantium* (Neil Jordan, 2012); while Scottish Screen distributed funds to the likes of *The Last Great Wilderness*, *Clive Barker's Book of Blood* (John Harrison, 2009) and *Outcast*. The funding of these films by national bodies attested to their assumed national – or even their *regional* – appeal. This was specifically the case with *Salvage*, which gained additional exposure from having been shot on the abandoned set of the once-popular, Liverpool-set, British soap opera *Brookside* (1982–2003), as well as *Outcast*, a monster film shot in and around desolate council blocks likely to resonate with those familiar with the films of Lynne Ramsay and Andrea Arnold (both of whom had also received funds from Scottish Screen for various projects). Moreover, *Wilderness*, which sees a group of young offenders sent to an island for behavioural rehabilitation, was shot with support from the Northern Irish Television Commission, and draws exclusively upon quintessential British pre-texts, from William Golding's novel *Lord of the Flies* (1997 [1954]) to Alan Clarke's seminal prison dramas, *Scum* (1977/9) and *Made in Britain* (1982).[48]

The localised focus of these horror films, while clearly a factor that reduced their chances for international theatrical distribution, did not mean that they remained 'unseen' abroad, however. Once DVD had a firm grip of the market, specialist labels such as Dimension Extreme in the US (owned and operated by The Weinstein Company) and Optimum and Tartan Terror in the UK, were then able to funnel out niche international horror films to cult sell-through and rental audiences: audiences that are typically 'more tolerant of the foibles of cheap production' (Williams 2005: 290).[49] As *Screen International* reported, in North America specifically, the emergence of a 'straight-to-DVD' market in 2005 opened the floodgates for low-budget horror (George *et al.* 2005: 15). As a result, British films as disparate as *Broken*, *Gnaw*, *Eden Lake*, *w Delta z*, *The Cottage* and *The Zombie Diaries* were grouped with other American/international titles in DVD series, offering obscure British films an opportunity to flower in markets where they might otherwise never have been seen.[50]

CONCLUSION

This chapter has shown how, since the year 2000, horror film producers navigated a tumultuous genre terrain to try to produce widely successful horror films that appealed to audiences both at home and abroad. The genre, I have argued, straddled not simply a variety of styles, themes and approaches, but also a variety of budgets, distribution outlets and, crucially, audiences. The films, it has been revealed, testified to a diverse film culture (or film *cultures*) simultaneously representative of commercial potential and niche appeal. Indeed, this chapter has examined how, in spite of the international success of *28 Days Later*, *Shaun of the Dead*, *The Descent* and *The Woman in Black*, the main market for British horror films has been in the UK itself. I have shown how filmmakers and funding bodies had a freer rein to explore local and national cultures, and that the release of these films on DVD in foreign territories has meant that 'regional' British horror films have been able to reach an international audience without theatrical exposure. For a short time, the success of *The Woman in Black* (considered in more detail in Chapter 6) hinted towards a possible 'Gothic revival' à la David Pirie's *A Heritage of Horror*. At about the same time, a few other dark, period-set films, emerged, including the ghost story *The Awakening* (Nick Murphy, 2011), Andrea Arnold's realism-inflected *Wuthering Heights* (2012) and Ben Wheatley's art film *A Field in England* (2013). But none had any major impact on the production trends of the British horror film, which continued to remain most visible in the DVD, and increasingly the VoD, sector.

Having established the industrial context of contemporary British horror cinema in this chapter, the next chapter looks at cultural issues in response to some of the claims that recent British horror's allegiances to contemporary trends in international horror cinema have impeded its potential to be nationally resonant. I make my argument in relation to two of the most visible developments in contemporary horror cinema, the 'torture porn' and 'found footage' cycles, and examine how certain British filmmakers have contributed to these trends through a series of horror films that are nostalgic for the 'video nasty' era.

NOTES

1. This figure is based on primary data acquired by the author. The raw data can be found in Appendix I of Walker (2013).
2. See M. J. Simpson's comprehensive blog, http://british-horror-revival.blogspot.com, as well as his recent book *Urban Terrors: New British Horror Cinema, 1998–2008* (2012).
3. *Scream* was shot for approximately $14m (approx. £8.9m) and generated $172m (approx. £110m) worldwide and *The Blair Witch Project* was shot for approximately $60k/£35k and generated $248.6m/£150m (http://boxofficemojo.com) (see also Telotte 2008 [2001]). Unfortunately, statistics for *Ringu* are not readily available, although the eventual blockbusting American remake of the film (2002) at least testifies, to some extent, to its initial popularity.
4. This information is taken from the issues published from 2000 to 2002. However, it does not factor in the British horror films that were made during this time but had minor straight-to-video releases, such as Richard Driscoll's *Kannibal* (2001) that would be released by straight-to-video-specialist Film 2000 in the UK, and Manos Kalaitzakis's *Sentinels of Darkness* (2002), which, to this day, remains only available on DVD in Greece.
5. As Ian Conrich (1998) notes, *Dream Demon* 'failed commercially and critically' (28) and generated only £28,404 in its first week, and *I Bought a Vampire Motorcycle* grossed a mere £19,193 (31).
6. Thora Birch, who plays the lead in *The Hole*, was the exception here, as she had starred in *American Beauty* in 1999. *The Hole* also featured Keira Knightley, but she had yet to command any star power.
7. That had recently peaked at the box-office with the international release of *Scream 3* (generating £5.6m in the UK and $89m in the US (http://imdb.com/pro)).
8. As was common in reviews of *My Little Eye*, a critic for the *Observer* stated that 'it is hard to tell that *My Little Eye* is a British movie' (Maher 2002).
9. See also Street (2002: 206–10) and Street (2009: 134–8).
10. 'Choose life' was the film's tagline.
11. For information of *Long Time Dead*'s performance in Spain, see Anon. (2005a: 8–9). For more information on *My Little Eye*'s performance in Italy see *Screen International* Box Office Data, no. 1406, 2003: 20.
12. The film, unlike most mainstream horror releases at that time, was laden with prosthetic effects reminiscent of 1980s 'body horror' films such as *The Thing* (John Carpenter, 1982) and *The Fly* (David Cronenberg, 1986) (for a discussion of body horror, see Brophy (2000 [1985]). The film starred Dani Filth, the lead singer of the metal group Cradle of Filth. It also had a running time of 120 minutes at a time when most horror films lasted for about ninety minutes. This suggested a more direct fan address (and an assumption that most audiences wouldn't last that long, nor know/care who Dani Filth was). The director, Alex Chandon, was known among horror fans for his lo-fi feature film in the 1990s, *Pervirella* (1997). Not insignificantly, Chandon first came to the attention of the horror community when he won the short film competition ran by *The Dark Side* magazine for his film *Bad Karma* in 1991 (for a discussion of which, see Reed (2012)).
13. Harris has gone on to play significant blockbusting roles in recent years, including Moneypenny in *Skyfall* (Sam Mendes, 2012), and Winnie Madikizela-Mandela in *Mandela: Long Walk to Freedom* (Justin Chadwick, 2013).
14. *28 Days Later*'s official website, which included short animations based on the film's opening London sequences, acted as a 'prologue to the film', establishing a mythology before the film went on general release (Mitchell 2002: 6; see also

Cherry 2010: 79). Later films would follow suit, including *The Descent*, which was the first film to advertise on the London Underground's 'digital projector panels', and *Creep* (a film set in the London Underground) that had its Underground-themed ad campaign banned from the Tube, resulting in the distributer '[strapping] ads to railings outside stations instead' (Seguin 2005: 26).

15. As Peter Buckingham, then exhibition chief at the UKFC, argued of the film: 'It is a small British film that became a hit with the benefit of a big spend to get it out there' as well as being indicative of films that 'if they make big splash in their home market, they have got the chance of a better wider release overseas' (Buckingham cited in Minns 2004a: 8). *Shaun of the Dead*, which originally stemmed from a zombie sequence in the cult British TV series *Spaced*, was marketed in such a way in the UK, with the intention of attracting US distributers (especially since the film's cast was not made up of notable stars) (Minns 2004b: 7).

16. Dogme 95 was a Danish avant-garde film collective established by Lars von Trier, Thomas Vinterberg, Søren Kragh-Jacobesen and Kristian Levring in 1995, and was underpinned by a manifesto and so-called 'Vow of Chastity' (Hjort and MacKenzie 2003: 2): 'motivated by idealism, but it is also a deeply pragmatic undertaking' (2). One of its central traits was its preference for digital technologies and, in particular, DV (see Hjort 2003).

17. Of course, the production schedule of *My Little Eye* benefited from this too. 'The advantage of MiniDV . . . was that its inherently small cameras could be set up quickly' (Bankston 2003: 83).

18. *My Little Eye* was released in the UK at 255 sites and *28 Days Later* at 316 (as well as 1,407 in the US) (http://imdb.com/pro). Figures for *The Last Great Wilderness* are unavailable, but it is fair to estimate that the release was very limited, and was mostly restricted to film festivals such as Edinburgh, where it debuted (N. Hunt 2002: 14). Despite its obscurity, the film has featured in one notable discussion of Scottish identity onscreen (see Martin-Jones 2005), while Jonathan Murray has argued in a more recent article that, due to its status as a co-production, 'a non-nationally specific reading seems both more obvious and plausible' (2012: 407).

19. On the Film Consortium – and early criticisms – see Murphy (2002) and Hill (2012: 335–6).

20. Hill's article would, in many ways, pre-empt the video nasty debate of the 1980s. He argued that (young) audiences were becoming desensitised to cinematic violence, and that this was inextricably bound to their inner-perversions. Moreover, he implied that the 'new horror gimmick is repulsive physical detail: so the next horror film, if it is to compete with the last, must always be that much bloodier, that much closer in its concentration on nauseating matter' (Hill 1958: 10).

21. It was at this time that several up-and-coming directors, Lynne Ramsay and Jonathan Glazer, were enlisted to shoot the high-profile genre films *The Lovely Bones* and *Under the Skin*, following the success of the magic-realist *Ratcatcher* (Ramsay, 1999) and the gangster film *Sexy Beast* (Glazer, 2000), respectively, as a means of capitalising on the success of ghost stories such as *The Sixth Sense* and *The Others* (the latter was a based on British source material, but was a Spanish/US co-production). *The Lovely Bones* would eventually be directed by Peter Jackson on the back of his success with the *Lord of the Rings* franchise, and was released in 2009. *Under the Skin*, however, would not be shot until much later, and was finally released in 2014.

22. It could be argued that *28 Days Later* initiated a resurgence in the zombie subgenre, which included *Shaun of the Dead* and Zack Snyder's 2004 remake of *Dawn of the Dead* (George A. Romero, 1978), although this trend was largely isolated to DVD releases.

23. *The Texas Chainsaw Massacre* grossed £3.8m, and *The Amityville Horror* £5.3m (http://imdb.com/pro).
24. The earlier attempts from Hammer to remake films such as *The Quatermass Xperiment* (Val Guest, 1955) testify to the fact that, at this time, classic British horror was not perceived to be worthy of a big investment.
25. Edgar Wright is a self-confessed fan of American horror cinema (Wright 2005).
26. In fact, so popular was this film that Simon Pegg and Edgar Wright were subsequently cast as bit-part zombies in Romero's *Land of the Dead* (2005). There is also a sequence in Wes Craven's *Scream 4* (2011), in which a group of teens gather to watch *Shaun of the Dead* on DVD.
27. It was thought that it would have done a lot better had it not been released the week of the '7/7' bombings in London. As Marshall has commented: '*The Descent* did a fraction of the business it was expected to do that weekend' (cited in Carolyn 2009: 112).
28. As a result, *Dog Soldiers* was released direct-to-video in most foreign territories.
29. On Europe, see Horeck and Kendall (2011); on Asia, see Shin (2008).
30. The British 'military horror' trend would continue with *Outpost* (Steve Barker, 2008). See Hantke (2010a).
31. James Rose considers Sarah's problematic status as a 'final girl' in more detail in *Beyond Hammer: British Horror Cinema since 1970*. He argues, 'Sarah almost fulfils Clover's criteria for Final Girl status as she is both resourceful . . . and capable of defensive actions . . . but her role as a mother isolates her from the totality of this role' (Rose 2009: 146).
32. Indeed, Tom Ortenberg of Lionsgate had a better understanding of the horror film's audience than Lizzie Francke had at this point, having released films such as *Cabin Fever* (Eli Roth, 2002) and *Hostel* to huge box office revenues all over the world.
33. The 'torture porn' label is discussed in more detail in the next chapter.
34. This list is offered as a guide. There are inevitable sub-generic crossovers.
35. Most, however, did not get mainstream coverage at all, but were reliant on genre websites such as *DreadCentral.com*, *BloodyDisgusting.com* and *Twitchfilm.com* for exposure.
36. Ben Wheatley's 'psychedelic historical film' *A Field in England* would follow suit (Andrews 2014: 190), appearing across seventeen cinema screens, on VoD, DVD and Blu-ray, and on free-to-air television on 15 July 2013 (see Andrews 2014: 190–2). Although this film was cited as owing a debt to horror film traditions, it was marketed as more of an art movie than a genre film, and can thus be easily be set apart from the core demographic of a film like *Mum & Dad*.
37. For more on the popularity of Danny Dyer with DVD audiences see Godfrey and Walker (2015).
38. These films were released through an initiative launched by Amazon.com, CreateSpace: 'a self-distribution platform with no physical inventory – all its films are digital files that can be streamed or purchased as download-to-own' or bought via the company on made-to-order DVD-Rs (Cunningham and Silver 2012: 56). Such a strategy meant that films could have an international release while avoiding the costs commanded by the BBFC and self-releasing through other means: 'The deal . . . enables producers to retain copyright through a non-exclusive license and incorporates a fixed revenue-sharing split that begins from the first sale' (ibid.).
39. The film's budget came in at $150m (http://imdb.com/pro).
40. Of course, Keira Knightley had appeared in a British horror film: *The Hole*. However, this was before she was a 'star' (she had played a small role in *Innocent Lies* (Patrick Dewolf, 1995) and a peripheral role as Natalie Portman's double in *Star Wars Episode I: The Phantom Menace* (George Lucas, 1999).

41. As Tim Dams of *Screen International* explains, Section 42 of the Finance (No. 2) Act 1992 offered 'a 100% tax write-off over three years – about 10% of a film's budget. To access the tax relief, a film must first qualify as a UK production: it must spend at least 70% of its budget in the UK, set up a UK company and employ UK, European or Commonwealth nationals comprising at least 70-75% of the payroll' (2003: 25).

42. The cultural test awarded points (up to thirty) based on, for instance, whether or not the film was set in the UK, whether or not it was shot in the UK, or if the script was based on British source material (Milmo and Gibson 2005).

43. Hans De Weers, a European film producer, noted that 'in the UK, they've gone from a system where there was too much abuse, to another system that is too local' (cited in Macnab 2008a: 6).

44. As Sarah Street has argued of *28 Days Later*, the film's 'basic topographies could also be identified with other cities and landscapes, evoking a kind of shorthand familiarity that opens up these films to international audiences' (2009: 136–7).

45. The open support from the Film Council given to shooting films digitally was welcomed. As Marc Evans once argued at the turn of the century, 'I would much rather be shooting a feature for $1.5m (£1m) on digital than waiting around in development hell for three years struggling to secure a larger budget' (cited in Hunter 2002 : 2).

46. All UKFC data obtained from the online UKFC (now BFI) Awards Database, http://industry.bfi.org.uk/awards.

47. For further information on the Digital Departures Scheme, see http://industry.bfi.org.uk/10328 (accessed 19 July 2012). Hannah Andrews (2014: 126–7) also considers the Digital Departures scheme in detail in her book *Television and British Cinema: Convergence and Divergence since 1990*.

48. For example, Dave (Jon Travers) slits his writs following repeated bullying by the other lads, in a bleak scene highly evocative of *Scum*, in which Davis (Julian Firth) commits suicide after being gang raped. Moreover, one of the central characters in *Wilderness* – a skinhead – Steve (Stephen Wight), bears an uncanny (and deliberate) resemblance to Trevor (Tim Roth), the lead character in *Made in Britain*.

49. For a discussion of 'speciality DVD markets' see Seguin (2007: 14–15). In direct relation to the horror film, see Shin (2008).

50. For a more thorough discussion about the American horror DVD market in the new millennium see Bernard (2014).

3. NASTY RESURRECTIONS

In the previous chapter I acknowledged the various industrial factors that led to, and helped sustain, British horror film production after the year 2000. In this chapter, I want to consider the more immediate cultural antecedents that have influenced the content of recent British horror films before considering a selection of case studies in close detail. What follows is inspired by an early idea of Andrew Higson. In 1989, Higson argued that a 'national cinema' is indebted not only to the films made within or by a specific country but also the kinds of films that are especially popular with local audiences. The main example he offered with respect to Britain was Hollywood cinema (Higson 1989: 39; see also Higson 2011: 1). In the 2000s and 2010s, many British horror filmmakers were inspired by non-British films that developed a unique *national* significance. I am referring, of course, to the films involved in the 'video nasty' panic of the 1980s, when it was thought that children may watch violent horror films on video and then re-enact the mostly grisly scenes in the 'real world'. Fears surrounding this possibility led to the eventual banning of thirty-nine horror/exploitation videos by the Director of Public Prosecutions (DPP) under the Obscene Publications Act 1959 (OPA) and the passing of a new piece of legislation, the Video Recordings Act (VRA), in 1984.[1] The VRA detailed that all films to be released on video had to undergo the same procedure as those films being theatrically distributed, and be certified by the British Board of Film Censors (BBFC). Those films likely to 'deprave and corrupt' its audience, as per the OPA, needed to be banned outright, or heavily censored. As Kate Egan (2007) and others have acknowledged, although other countries have experienced similarly turbulent reactions to controversial films,[2] nothing has been quite so centred on home video technology. As such, the films that made the infamous video nasty 'list' (in its various incarnations)[3] – despite representing an array of transnational films with their own indigenous preoccupations – constitute a body of films that, in Britain, have been historically and culturally homogenised (Kerekes and Slater 2000; Egan 2007: 128–53). In other words, just as Hollywood has been positioned as central to discourses around British national cinema, the nasties have been collectively 'naturalised' as 'part of the national culture' – if for reasons of controversy rather than widespread popularity (Higson 1989: 39). In light of this notion, this chapter examines the ways that the video nasty era and specific video nasties impacted on the creative directions of British horror filmmakers after the year 2000.

The (British) cultural moment of video violence

Contrary to David Pirie's notion that British horror production in the new millennium remained connected to the English Gothic tradition, it was more often the case that horror filmmakers pastiched the modern American and European horror films that flooded the British video market in the late 1970s and early 1980s. Steven Sheil's *Mum & Dad*, for example, adopted the 'cannibal family' theme that was popularised by a particularly controversial video release, *The Texas Chain Saw Massacre*, and was also initially pitched to its potential funders as *The Heathrow Chainsaw Massacre*.[4] Critics and journalists were also quick to identify similar parallels across British horror. For example, traces of the 'backwoods horror' tradition, which was pioneered by the video nasty *The Last House on the Left*, were identified by reviewers of *Eden Lake* (Dennis 2008; Tilly 2008).

The filmmakers themselves were enthusiastically open about their fan allegiances to the era in question. Neil Marshall, for example, claimed that the video nasty, *The Evil Dead*, was a major influence on *Dog Soldiers* (Marshall cited in Carolyn 2009: 53), and Simon Pegg noted that the zombie films of George A. Romero – that were first brought to Pegg's attention when he was at school during the video nasties era – heavily influenced *Shaun of the Dead* (2011: 199). Moreover, amateur filmmakers such as Jonathon Ash and Bryn Hammond sought to promote their fandom for video nasties by giving their movies titles like *Zombie Ferox* (Ash, 2002) and *The Summer of the Massacre* (Hammond, 2006) in response to Italian splatter films (*Cannibal Ferox* (Umberto Lenzi, 1981) and *Zombie Flesh-Eaters* (Lucio Fulci, 1979)), and American horror films (*The Texas Chain Saw Massacre* and *California Axe Massacre* (*Axe*) (Fredrick R. Friedel, 1974)) that would later be caught up in the video nasties panic. Even when filmmakers were not so overt about their inspirations, call-backs to video nasties were still to be found in, for instance,

Philip Ridley's *Heartless* and Johannes Roberts' *F*. The former employed garish light filters in a way that recalled Dario Argento's *Suspiria* (1977) and the banned *Inferno* (1980),[5] while the score of *F* was peppered with haunting, child-like voices as though in homage to the ethereal soundtracks of the electronica group Goblin, which was best known for having scored some of Argento's films that were banned in the UK, as well as the video nasty *Zombie Creeping Flesh* (Bruno Mattei, 1980).[6]

Although some critics responded avidly to these instances of pastiche and textual allusion, others were inclined to dismiss many of the films as evidence of the British merely pandering to recent trends in contemporary exploitation cinema, marked by retroactive films such as *Hostel* and *The Devil's Rejects* (Rob Zombie, 2005), the remake of *The Hills Have Eyes* (Alexandre Aja, 2006) and later *The Last House on the Left* (Dan Iliadis, 2009) and *I Spit on Your Grave* (Steven R. Monroe, 2010). Such films, which were condemned by the media for being part of the recent 'torture porn' trend (due to their prolonged sequences of gore and physical torture),[7] led Kaleem Aftab (2009) of *The Independent* to deduce that they supplemented 'arguably the worst movement in cinema history'. 'The greatest shame', he continued, 'is that modern British [horror] films such as *Eden Lake, Donkey Punch* and *Severance* [have taken] their leads from torture porn rather than British classics such as Michael Powell's *Peeping Tom*' (Aftab 2009).

Two significant things are implied by this assessment, and both problematise our understanding of the cultural make-up of contemporary British horror cinema. First, Aftab implied that new British horror films were lacking cultural specificity, at least aesthetically speaking, due to them having less in common with 'classic' British horror and more in common with recent developments in the 'extreme' cinema from the United States, Australia and Europe. For films to pay homage was fine, it seems, but for British films to reference contemporary (inferior) foreign product was considered detrimental to the films' overall quality, their originality and, perhaps most explicitly, their preservation of a generic heritage. As such, contemporary British horror was characterised as derivative of tasteless torture porn, as though this trend, and the negative responses it provoked, was resultant of a frankly *un-British* approach to filmmaking.[8]

Second, Aftab (2008) argued that the key traits of torture porn consist of a 'placed emphasis on visuals' and a disregard of plot. However, I would argue that 'visuals' – that, in this instance, refers to the depiction of graphic/ prolonged violence on-screen – were utilised in certain films in such a way that, even if the films were lacking in plot or overt cultural referents, the employment of gory violence ascertained a cultural significance all of its own. This relates specifically to the national context of the British films that Aftab cited, where the BBFC and the news media have had a notoriously tenuous relationship with the horror genre's gory spectacle.

It is apparent, thus, that the nostalgia felt for international exploitation cinema by British filmmakers, and the subsequent content of their films, rests upon a cultural legacy of censorship, social speculation and moralising. This is an allegation given credence in a review of the aforementioned *Mum & Dad* by British journalist Chris Tookey (who, significantly, writes for one of the frontrunners in the original nasty press campaign, the *Daily Mail*):

> Inexperienced writer-director Steven Sheil attempts to play for black comedy as well as thrills, but ends up celebrating sleaze, gloating in gore, and revelling in the repulsive.
>
> As if that wasn't bad enough, you helped pay for this pointlessly unpleasant torture porn through the UK Film Council, the European Regional Development Fund and your BBC licence fee. I make no further comment. (Tookey 2008a)

Although this kind of reaction has characterised much British horror film criticism, it is specifically evocative of the video nasty era (Egan 2007: 25–41). This era has become so well woven into the cultural tapestry of Britain to the extent that some have argued that the spectre of the video nasties still haunts the UK today (Kendrick 2004). To this end, we can consider a number of contemporary British horror films as being not *merely* imitative of international product, but, rather, as decidedly 'British' in their makers' self-reflexive and nostalgic interpretations of such material.

Recently, Brigid Cherry reiterated the academic consensus that horror films are socially reflective and 'tap into very specific elements of the zeitgeist or cultural moment' (2009: 169). However, in light of contemporary British horror's penchant for the visceral, and the distinctive legacy of critical opinion that precedes it, discerning one 'cultural moment' for these films is problematic. The films that were cited earlier were all inspired by, or can be stylistically/thematically likened to, certain horror films that were all, in some form or another, caught up in the video nasties panic in the 1980s.[9] In light of this, one could suggest that those especially violent and exploitative contemporary British horror films were not simply referents of particular texts or filmic trends. They also recalled a stigmatic era that is specifically bound to British cultural memory. As such, the significance of these films' influences is not just hermetically intertextual, but also culturally and *historically* resonant, because the films refer not just to a list of controversial videos, but an era of reception that helped define them as part of British culture. As Kate Egan states,

> Not only has the video nasties term been used to refer, over time and in different contexts, to a set of film titles, a specific set of video versions, a set of historical events and a personal consumption experience, but

clearly, and in line with [Robert] Altman's arguments, the way in which the term and category has been defined and approached has depended 'heavily on the identity and purpose of those [British critics] using and evaluating' it. (Egan 2007: 5)

The remainder of this chapter builds on the idea that recent British horror films have stylistically and thematically recalled the video nasties, and that they have self-reflexively acknowledged the kinds of concerns that have historically characterised the moral panic. I have chosen to single out four films for close analysis: *Creep*, *The Devil's Chair*, *The Last Horror Movie* (Julian Richards, 2003) and *Resurrecting the Street Walker* (Özgür Uyanık, 2009). These films have been chosen because, to my mind, they represent a fair cross-section of twenty-first century British horror production: *Creep* had some theatrical success in the UK and Europe; *The Last Horror Movie* was a cult hit across international horror film festivals and sparked a minor moral panic of its own; *Resurrecting the Street Walker* was similarly successful on the festival circuit and was also a production of Scala Films, a later incarnation of Palace Pictures (the company that originally released *The Evil Dead* on VHS in the UK); while *The Devil's Chair* is an example of micro-budget production, having been shot for £150,000, and ghettoised with other low-budget straight-to-video horror movies. All of these films explore the same kinds of binary opposites that epitomised many of the arguments being made during the infancy of video consumption in Britain: good taste/bad taste, acceptability/unacceptability, reality/fantasy and text/spectator. My first case studies, *Creep* and *The Devil's Chair*, consider these factors in relation to discourses of class and taste: in particular, how the upper classes are presented as indistinguishable from, or as more corrupt, than the lower classes, and also, how these dynamics are interspersed with allegorical nods to horror cinema's violent content, and its perceived effect on those who enjoy it.

MATTERS OF CLASS AND TASTE: *CREEP* AND *THE DEVIL'S CHAIR*

In *Creep*, after attending a cocktail party, our lead protagonist, Kate (Franka Potente), falls asleep in Charing Cross tube station and misses the last train of the evening. As a consequence, she is trapped until dawn. The film sees her relentlessly pursued by a deformed subterranean 'creep' by the name of Craig (Sean Harris) who has managed to survive in the tunnels since childhood.[10] *The Devil's Chair*, comparatively, concerns Nick West (Andrew Howard), a man committed to an asylum after being accused of murdering a girl who he claims was the victim of an electric chair that opens a door to a parallel universe. Nick, who also narrates the film, is temporarily released to assist a Cambridge University study into his ordeal and psychotic visions. Nick and the researchers return to the site of the murder, where they discover, and individually fall victim to, the electric chair.

Although Kate in *Creep* and Nick in *The Devil's Chair* are presented as being of different social strata to each other, there is considerable overlap between how they are respectively characterised. Kate, for instance, is projected as upper class: 'a coke-snorting, dope-smoking rich kid directly descended from the yuppie Thatcherites of the 1980s' (Blake 2008: 178). The people who she associates with are conveyed as 'colleagues' as opposed to 'friends', and are similarly preoccupied with drinking, consuming drugs and remaining separate from the 'invisible' underclass that live on the streets and in the stations of the London Underground. In an early scene, for example, Kate's colleague, Guy (Jeremy Sheffield), offers her cocaine on the condition that she panders to his misogynist bravado, while later in the film Kate dismisses a homeless man's plea for change, being instead preoccupied with finding the club where George Clooney is rumoured to be in residence, so that she can track him down for a one night stand. In *The Devil's Chair*, Nick's existence similarly owes allegiance to the transient pleasures of drugs and sex. 'We are gonna get off our fuckin' nut!' he will say to his girlfriend in the opening scene. However, his attire of hooded sweatshirt and jeans codes him – in relation to contemporary British fashion trends at least – as of a lower social class, and contrasts distinctively with Kate's bright, floral dress.[11] Nick, like Kate, is also shown as having no true friends to speak of, only his girlfriend, who is also given limited characterisation, portrayed solely as someone who Nick wishes to have sex with while stoned on acid. And, in contrast to Kate's loathing of the homeless, Nick loathes the university students, shown when he remarks that they constitute 'educated nothingness . . . houses in France and stuff that could never mean anything to me. Vacuous little cunts!'

These class representations are roughly sketched, and they function most practically in relation to the ways in which each film self-reflexively addresses contemporary perceptions of taste. James Kendrick has discussed how 'the political rhetoric surrounding the [video nasties] social panic was geared specifically toward the protection of children and child-like adults, which essentially meant the working class' (2004: 155). It was argued that being subjected to violent videos would inspire the working-class spectator (specifically their children) to re-enact the on-screen horrors of films like *I Spit on Your Grave* (Meir Zarchi, 1978) in their day-to-day lives. Kendrick continues, stating how the news media 'divided the public into two separate communities: those "reasonable" people who are grossly offended by [the video nasties]' – the middle to upper classes – 'and those who are not' – the lower/working classes (2004: 165). Director Christopher Smith seems to knowingly build on these binaries in *Creep*, during a sequence in which an Underground security guard has his throat slit, by Craig, in close-up:

> I very much wanted to make it as graphic as possible, because when I was a kid and growing up . . . I used to see all those video nasties . . . [and] would always prefer the one that never cut away from the violence . . . So I felt [sic] to myself: if I get the chance to make a horror movie, I'm going to cut back to some more neck cutting. (Smith 2005)

Evidently, Smith desires to ruffle the feathers of the film's detractors while also delivering the goods to the audience with whom he empathises. This technique is provocative, in that it is deliberately designed to combat the kinds of excesses that were deemed reprehensible during the video nasties era, but it is also a wink to the fans who understand the genre and its history. Smith is similarly mischievous in his placing of an 'upper-class' character within the heart of the London Underground – here to be read as the cult 'underground' of horror cinema and video nasty fans – and being disorientated, scared and unable to successfully navigate the terrain. Kate, is not, contra Kendrick, characterised by how 'reasonable' she is, but conversely by how superciliousness. She is not 'respectable', nor 'likeable'. Nor is she designed to generate the empathy that other 'final girls' of horror cinema – who are 'intelligent, watchful and level-headed' – do (Clover 1992: 44). Comparatively, Kate represents a 'spoilt', privileged culture, and her arrogance, selfishness and screaming render her comparable to the shrieking tirade of moralists during the early video era, who strove to promote an 'us' versus 'them' social outlook (Egan 2007: 33).

With that said, I would be reluctant to go as far as Linnie Blake, who describes Kate as being conveyed as a 'prick-teasing bitch who, in fighting off the sexual attentions of the attempted rapist Guy, has brought her troubles on herself' (2008: 179). On the contrary, and as Blake herself implies, every character in this film is 'vacuous' to some degree, mostly driven only by artificial, fabricated (and socially condemned) pleasures: heroin (the homeless), cocaine and rape (Guy), sex (Kate) and violence (Craig). But rather than perceive these character traits as 'so disengaged from historical materiality', as Blake does (2008: 179), I would propose instead that *Creep* relies on this prevalent emptiness as a position from which to propel its socially resonant and thus 'historically material' elements of violent spectacle that, in turn, connects it to the legacy of the video nasty. For, in *Creep*, negative social habits stem not solely from the working class/'uneducated', but also from the middle/upper class, who are traditionally coded as society's moral centre. If these class binaries are vacuous, in that they serve no separatist social function in the labyrinthine Underground, violence functions as the most validated aspect of the diegesis: as a counterpoint to the mundanity of Kate's associates, drugs and money. This is seen most clearly when, later in the film, Kate rediscovers Guy, bloodied and close to death on the train track. She calls the security guard for help using the platform intercom service. After correcting Kate's insolent request for a security 'guard' – 'I am the security *supervisor!*' he exclaims – and refusing to believe her wild circumstance, he requests that she drag the body into view of the CCTV cameras. It is only then, when the guard has visual confirmation of Guy's death, that he attempts to act, only to be attacked by Craig from behind. This offers an ironic opposite to the imperious moralists that had rarely seen any of the video nasties before launching their campaign (see Petley 2000). In presenting the scene in this way, Smith confirms what so many wanted to believe during the video nasties furore: that on-screen visuals could kill, that (simulated) on-screen violence was considered as dangerous as (or more dangerous than) real-life violence itself. In doing so, *Creep* can be read as a metaphorical response to the video nasties campaign, in which Smith can playfully mock and circumvent the era's inconsistencies and class-based contradictions in his own nasty homage.

Director Adam Mason (2010) has commented that the violent content of *The Devil's Chair* functions primarily at a level of 'shock value', as though in echo of his own memories of 'growing up in the UK [during the video nasties era]'.[12] This is successfully conveyed when Nick refers to certain horror films during his narration, citing the audience's pre-knowledge of films that were made in the late 1980s, such as *Hellraiser* and *Pumpkinhead* (Stan Winston, 1988), as reasoning for why we have decided to watch this particular film. He not only addresses 'the audience' here, but, like the films he mentions, an audience of a *certain kind*: a community of aesthetes whose tastes rest upon scenes of violent, special-effects-heavy body-horror. In other words, Nick is not addressing the cultural elite, those who do not have any investment in 'the onscreen action in terms of a heritage of genre knowledge, which absolutely precludes the possibility of sadistic titillation' (Kermode cited in Kendrick 2004: 154). Instead, he offers his own trajectory – in this case, the death of his girlfriend and his subsequent committal to an asylum – as a means of entertainment for horror fans ('If you stick with me I promise you it will be worth your while!' he later exclaims), thereby conflating the 'reality' of death with the 'artificial' entertainment factor of horror cinema. This is a distinction that is as deliberately confused in this film as it has so often been within discourses of British horror film criticism (and the films themselves).

The Devil's Chair mischievously replicates the anxieties of those that presumed that such films were, to quote the infamous hyperbole of a 1983 edition of the *Daily Mail*, responsible for the 'Rape of our children's minds' (Hebdige 1983: 6). This is shown most clearly in the final ten minutes of the film, in which Nick and Rachel (Elize du Toit) – one of the students assisting in the Cambridge study – having passed through the Chair's vortex, must battle an evil demon that inhabits the parallel world. Having defeated the demon, Nick and Rachel embrace. As they kiss, there is a cut to a graphic match that reveals that they are no longer embracing, but rather that Nick is holding Rachel down on the bloodied floors of the asylum, raping her. Surrounding them is the rest of the research group, and the professor, writhing in blood. Nick has fooled us. The trust we placed in him as our narrator diminishes, and his allusions to cinema have given credence to the notion that he has been educated/ influenced by an array of violent films. The parallel universe is conflated with reality: Nick massacres the students and rapes Rachel, as his movie-influenced fantasy has 'raped' his mind.

Nick's entire trajectory is governed by the artifice of cinema, and the willingness of the audience to succumb to the 'promises' and 'truths' of narrative before having the carpet ripped from under them in the film's final moments.[13] But, as we come to learn in the film, illogicality is, frankly, all part of the experience. As though to recall the infamous tag line from the video nasty *The Last House on the Left*, 'Just keep repeating: it's only a movie . . . only a movie', Nick repeatedly underscores the narrative and illogical contradictions of *The Devil's Chair*. He mocks and condemns the plot, as when he is released from the asylum: 'It really was this ridiculous,' he explains to us, 'like a bad *Scooby Doo*.' And in a sequence that sees the university professor shout mythic, nonsensical jargon at the demon near the end of the film, Nick exclaims, 'Enough of this melodrama!' before making the cut back to 'reality' in the film's final scene. This stresses the capabilities of audience manipulation, as we have fallen victim to the narrative and Nick's assertions, a paradigm upon which we initially predicated the 'truth'. But, when Nick directly addresses the audience as 'torture porn gore whores' near the end of the film, the validity of his story becomes increasingly questionable, and increasingly ridiculous, as he both recognises the competency of a contemporary horror film audience (surely no one would be corrupted or influenced by anything this ludicrous!) and recalls the video nasty panic in doing so. 'B-Movie banality', to quote Nick, is ultimately all that *The Devil's Chair* – or any horror film, for that matter – is. It *really is* only a movie.

Linnie Blake's reading of one of *Creep*'s most notorious scenes complicates this:

> In a breathtaking hateful scene the homeless woman Mandy, flat on her back and with her legs strapped in stirrups, is 'operated upon' by the Creep who . . . takes an 18-inch curved serrated knife and thrusts it, repeatedly and with great force, into her vagina. Beyond even the wider shores of Dario Argento's imagination, it is difficult to imagine such a horrific violation being committed to celluloid for mainstream consumption. It serves no narrative or thematic purpose. (Blake 2008: 179; my emphasis)

As Steve Jones has noted, Blake's response to *Creep* is flawed, because '[h]er argument hinges on the same supposition that pervades popular journalistic responses torture porn: that such violence requires justification' (2013: 197). In other words, Blake's conceit is that violence needs to be in some way narratively contextualised (and must conform to an explicit left-wing agenda) in order for it to be morally sound and therefore passable. Indeed, Jones is correct to compare Blake's response to that of journalists who condemn horror cinema, as Kaleem Aftab's article cited here, as well as the critical discourses that surrounded the negative reception of the video nasties (Egan 2007: 78–101). This is hinted at in Blake's nod to Argento (often targeted as a 'reactionary' filmmaker) and the evident offence caused by the nature of the violence on screen, and also by her dismissal of *Creep* as being 'entirely typical of the under-conceived and flashly [sic] executed pastiche of earlier films better done' (2008: 180). All of these factors chime with the typical responses of video nasty critics, who often sought to distance the video nasties as a 'new threat' from the older, and therefore 'safer', films of, say, Hammer and Universal.[14] As any discerning film scholar knows, the horror films of the past were as much loathed upon their initial release as many contemporary films are now, and often for reasons relating to graphic violence (Hill 1958; Pirie 2008: 37–45). Films such as *Creep* and *The Devil's Chair*, therefore, deliberately sought to push the boundaries of the horror genre. Their directors' refusal to conform to common notions of good taste functions to draw a line in the sand between the anachronistic moralising that characterised the video nasty era and the future of horror film production.

RESURRECTING HORROR VIDEO AESTHETICS

If there is one thing that truly binds *The Devil's Chair* and *Creep* together, it is that, although bloody violence is at the core of their aesthetic, they function primarily as metatexts with plots that are not in and of themselves predicated on believability. Fantasy is at their forefront. However, when video nasties were first subjected to any critical judgement by the British press, it was usually at the expense of comparing the films to notions of reality and realism, and thus stripping them of their primary, fantasy-based function. As Egan has argued, 'they [were] not considered in relation to the idea that they [were] commercial ventures with plots based around spectacle and fantasy' (2007: 26). Yet the line between fantasy and reality was often indistinguishable for many commentators, to the extent that some people believed that the videos featured real-life footage of people being murdered in the name of entertainment. As Julian Petley has explained:

> Of all the myths generated by controversies about horror films, and especially about 'video nasties' in the UK, that of the 'snuff' movie is the most persistent and hardest to dispel . . . These, allegedly, were hardcore sex

films featuring prostitutes who were actually murdered on screen as the climax to the 'entertainment'. (Petley 2000: 205)

As Petley notes (210), 'snuff' films have never been found to exist.[15] Yet, the most notorious suspects – the video nasties *Cannibal Holocaust, Faces of Death* (John Alan Schwartz, 1978) and *Snuff* – did not help matters, as they all attempted to claim authenticity by adapting a documentary style, capitalising on the snuff myth and parading as the real thing.[16] This style, and the mythology that surrounds the snuff movie in Britain, was since echoed in British horror films in the 2000s and 2010s, in which issues of filmed death, and historical linkages with video technology, came to the fore.

However, before I move on to interrogate some of the films, it is important to make clear that our understanding of 'video' in this context should not be restricted to simply an aesthetic style that corresponds with realist discourses.[17] It also needs to be understood as evocative of the specific cultural moment and experience of viewing a video nasty. One of the main reasons why so many obscure and low-brow titles found their way on to video in the 1980s was due to the major American film studios being sceptical of video (see McDonald 2007: 89–92, 107–42). This spurred an influx of hundreds of savvy independent video labels to acquire the rights (or not) for low-brow exploitation films, cheaply, to bulk-out their catalogues.[18] Thus, video was immediately positioned as working in competition with mainstream cinema culture and, as a result, has been characterised in much writing as cinema-going's inferior 'other'. As Joan Hawkins argues in her book *Cutting Edge: Art-Horror and the Horrific Avant-Garde*, the horror film is especially suited to the video medium, because 'video itself has made possible a certain desacrilization of cultural forms . . . that theatres by their very nature simply cannot achieve' (2000: 34).

The 'otherness' of video technology is realised in Julian Richard's *The Last Horror Movie* and Özgür Uyanık's *Resurrecting the Street Walker*. The films deal directly with several prominent issues that have continued to surround British horror film criticism since the dawn of VHS: the spectatorial 'consumption' of film violence, cinema's alleged vicarious power to corrupt an audience, as well as the ways in which video technology itself has been able to trigger nostalgic responses in specific viewers.[19] As such, both of these films trace the psychological descent of male protagonists who are obsessed with horror films, are compelled to kill and who film their murders in compliance with established codes and conventions of horror cinema.

THE LAST HORROR MOVIE

Julian Richards's *The Last Horror Movie* belongs to the recent trend of 'POV' or 'found footage' horror films (Heller-Nicholas 2014). Shot in 2003, it followed hot on the heels of *My Little Eye*, which, as detailed in Chapter 2, had brought the found footage mode to the UK with great success. However, Richards's film was not released until 2005, when, following a smattering of festival appearances and cinema showings, it was released to VHS and DVD.

The film begins in the mould of late-90s slasher movies, but, following a tokenistic death scene at an American diner by a masked killer, is soon revealed as a London-based serial killer's video diary. The film's conceit is that we, the audience, have hired a video from a video shop (a slasher movie, 'The Last Horror Movie'), and the serial killer – Max, played by Kevin Howarth – has dubbed over it with recordings of his grisly murders. Throughout the film Max repeatedly confronts the audience with probing questions about the ethics of horror film spectatorship, asking why 'we' as 'decent people' would want to continually subject ourselves to such unsavoury material in the name of entertainment. In other words, the film is a commentary on the 'media effects' debate and, as a result of this, has its interests firmly within the critical and cultural legacy of the video nasty (Barker and Petley 2001).

Julian Richards (2005) has mentioned in several interviews how the opening scene of the film was designed to satirise mainstream teen horror cinema: something that he saw as lacking the intellect and conviction of the horror films of the 1970s and 1980s that have influenced him. *The Last Horror Movie* was therefore conceived out of Richards's own nostalgia for the horror films of yesteryear and, perhaps most significantly, the medium of videotape with which they have associations. As such, the opening scene of the film is played out with melodramatic fervour, and, like many of the slasher films that followed *Scream* in the 1990s, contains stilted acting, clichéd dialogue ('Who's there?') and a paint-by-numbers plot structure. Over the soundtrack to the scene a radio broadcaster warns us that a serial killer has recently escaped from a 'correctional facility' and is on the loose. We then cut to an establishing shot of an American diner, in which a teenage girl is closing up for the night. Suddenly her mobile phone rings; it is a young boy, presumably her younger brother, who, despite his sister's warnings – and in keeping with the film's nods to the video nasty era – has scared himself watching horror films at home. 'You shouldn't be watching that by yourself!' she exclaims. 'I told you it was scary!' The line goes dead, and a strange noise is heard off-screen. The girl foolishly investigates and, as a victim of her own curiosity, she is murdered by a killer (played by British horror regular Chris Adamson). The sequence serves to offer overt stylisation, against which the subsequent naturalism of the remaining narrative is to be juxtaposed. It is not supposed to be convincing. As the girl is stabbed, analogue static fills the screen, and the face of the smug-looking Max greets us. He goes on to explain how he has hijacked our evening's entertainment: 'I realise that this isn't what you were expecting. Let me explain . . .'

Through its adoption of video technology, a first-person narrative and documentary-style camera work, *The Last Horror Movie* qualifies as 'realist horror' as defined by Cynthia A. Freeland (1995). This fact is integral to our understanding of the film as a homage and critique of the video nasty era. Freeland argues that, whereas Noël Carroll's concept of 'art horror' (1990: 12–42) is theorised as being 'a distanced emotional response to representation', whereby monsters of horror cinema frighten us but are never thought to be tangible beings (Freeland 1995: 127), in realist horror 'the monster is . . . true-to-life rather than supernatural' (130). In keeping with the belief that much video nasty rhetoric was based on the possibility of audiences watching horror videos and mimicking what they saw in such films, it may be argued that the technological switch that occurs between the 35mm slasher film and VHS in *The Last Horror Movie* marks this said transition from 'impossibility' to 'possibility'. James Rose, for instance, has suggested that 'the impact of [the] film depends upon the audience's acceptance of realism: the viewer has hired out the film . . ., that Max's intervention into that film is real and that the subsequent events Max chooses to show the audience are also real' (2009: 116). However, this is a problematic and misleading assessment for it implies passivity on behalf of the audience, as though we are somehow 'duped' into believing that what they are watching is in fact real. In contrast to this position, I believe that film is driven by its audience's recognition of the film's ironic self-awareness – we all know we are watching a horror film – as well as by a repeated acknowledgement of well-established horror film conventions, and the history that underpins them.

As several authors have noted (Kermode 2005; Jolin 2005; Rose 2009), the film adapts both concept and structure from other films and, because of this, 'every element . . . smacks of hackneyed imitation' (Kermode 2005: 57). Indeed, by the director's own admission, the video-diary style and themes of *The Last Horror Movie* were lifted from controversial fan favourites such as *Man Bites Dog* (Rémy Belvaux, André Bonzel and Benoît Poelvoorde, 1992) and *Henry: Portrait of a Serial Killer* (John McNaughton, 1986) – the latter of which had numerous run-ins with the BBFC in the UK (Kimber 2011: 31-50) – while the pseudo-documentary element is grounded within the aesthetics of video nasties such as *Cannibal Holocaust* and *Faces of Death*. Indeed, similar to these kinds of films, when we witness Max murder his victims, there are rarely cutaways. More often than not we also see the impact of the various weapons he uses, and on one occasion we view a montage of four different impacts – a blow to the head by a frying pan, a baseball bat to the neck of a woman who is tied to a chair, a man being repeatedly hit in the face with a brick – occurring (presumably, as narrative formalisms dictate) in chronological sequence. Rose (2009: 116) has noted that the lack of cutaways during the scenes of violence emphasises the film's realist tenor (even *Snuff* granted the audience cutaways!). However, these sequences in *The Last Horror Movie* adopt a cinematic quality through montage and temporal rhythm, countering the amateurish associations of wobbly camera movements and a lack of professional lighting, as the audience also bears witness to otherwise professional editorial techniques and slick post-production values. It is also the case that, on a number of occasions, we are shown Max's victims renting, and then watching, 'The Last Horror Movie'. Like us, they willingly follow Max's video diary as though they are used to such gimmicks, and have no reason to question it (at least until Max knocks on their door, that is).

Max himself is an ironic testament to the obtuse confusion that surrounded horror film spectatorship in Britain in the 1980s. He is a well-spoken middle-class gentleman *and* a 'depraved and corrupt' serial killer. Indeed, his killings are not simply a knee-jerk reaction to horror movie spectatorship, nor are they mindless. In fact, they are experiments governed by questions tantamount to academic enquiry. Perversely, thus, Max can be read as a literal realisation of Julian Richards himself: someone who is a fan, who understands the genre and, according to fan lore, is thus 'qualified' to comment on it. It is not that Max, as Freeland has argued of Norman from *Psycho* and Mark from *Peeping Tom* (Michael Powell, 1960), is a man 'unable to connect with the reality around' him (1995: 127). On the contrary, Max and the questions he asks do connect with a reality: one in which horror films have figured as the scapegoats for society's utmost perversions. Max, in many ways, is a video nasty realised.

The Last Horror Movie, in this regard, should not simply be read as an interrogation into the pleasures of the horror genre *de facto*, but, above anything else, as a horror film that operates within the parameters of specific conventions and amid a historical legacy of horror film spectatorship in Britain. The film does not openly acknowledge that it was shot during an era of home-viewing technological advancement and that the majority of audiences would be seeing this film on either DVD or at the cinema, and not re-recordable VHS.[20] But it is not so much about blurring the line between fantasy and reality that is interesting here, but rather accepting that the contemporary horror genre is predicated on the audience's awareness that it is a fiction. Rather than seeing the use of videotape as one of the film's failings, as others have done, I contend that it is precisely the video medium that is presented as the real source of horror here, and our understanding of these fears is founded upon an awareness of the outmodedness of the technology. What is perhaps most ironic in this context is that the film endured its own media controversy, when it was accused of influencing twenty-year old Tom Palmer to kill two of his friends (Pyatt 2007). The distributor, Tartan, withdrew the film after these claims – arguably making *The Last Horror Movie* the closest thing to a video nasty in the new millennium.

RESURRECTING THE STREET WALKER

The allusions to the video nasty in *Resurrecting the Street Walker* are less subtle than those posited by *The Last Horror Movie*. First, *Resurrecting the Street Walker* is not presented as 'found footage' on a hijacked videotape but, rather, as a mockumentary. That is to say, the film plays out as a professional documentary, which cuts in 'video diary' footage of the main protagonist, James (James Powell). However, in a similar way to *The Last Horror Movie*, *Resurrecting the Street Walker* explores the influence of horror cinema on the spectator, by presenting James, like Max, as someone fascinated by horror films and as someone who wants to question and test the limits of the genre.

In the film, James works for an independent British film company as a runner. As he catalogues reels of film in the company's basement, he stumbles across cans of celluloid for 'The Street Walker', a British horror film (we are told) about a serial killer, that was abandoned during the video nasties furore after a cast member was murdered on set. The mockumentary chronicles James's quest to raise finance to finish the film by casting new actors, in the vain hope of making his first break into the movie industry. Posing as a retrospective look at James's time as a runner, the mockumentary shows interviews with his friends, colleagues and family, who comment on his psychological descent, as he adopts the persona of the Street Walker (the serial killer of the lost film) and, in the final scene, films himself murdering one of his colleagues. Allusions to snuff, and the mythology's prominence within the video nasty debate, resonate throughout the film.

The first allusion comes at the very beginning of the film, when a title card displays a quote from the notorious cult leader Charles Manson, followed by a dictionary definition of 'video nasty'. The Manson quote reads as follows: 'If you are going to do something, do it well and leave behind a mark to say that you were there.' The significance of this cannot be understated. Throughout the 1960s, Manson led a cult in America (commonly referred to as 'The Family' in media discourse) that, in 1969, was blamed for the murder of Roman Polanski's wife, Sharon Tate, and then accused of filming other bloody crimes for distribution throughout North America (Kerekes and Slater 1993: 3–4). The term 'snuff film' was first used in reference to these accusations in Ed Sanders' study of Manson's gang in 1971. The deployment of a Manson quote in *Resurrecting the Street Walker* thus invokes the legacy of snuff in a general sense but, more specifically, the legacy that underpins Manson as the godfather of the snuff movie in horror film circles – the 'mark' in question, perhaps. The dictionary definition of 'video nasty' that follows in the film underscores this legacy, by figuratively resituating the snuff movie – and Manson's place within its history – in a British context:

video nasty n

A video film of (allegedly) sensational nature, usually including scenes of explicit sex, violence, and horror.

Although the narrator frames the video nasty as a historical event (and the nasties themselves as a 'menace to society'), the Manson quote, and the subsequent narration that charts the nasties panic and the place of 'The Street Walker' within this, anticipates that 'the resurrection' of the film and the legacy of the video nasties will be essential not only to the psychological descent of James but also to the film's overall critique of the condemnation that the video nasties faced by reactionary moralists. For instance, at the beginning of the film, James' cameraman and best friend Marcus (Tom Shaw), exclaims to the interviewer – in recollection of the kinds of rhetoric employed by video nasty campaigners – that James was 'obsessed with film' from a young age, and that, in a world where most budding filmmakers come to terms with the actuality that their chance of making a living in the business is very slight, '[James] wasn't going to let reality *snuff out* his dreams.' This instance is significant for two reasons in relation to the legacy of the video nasties. First, it immediately aligns James and his ambitions of being a filmmaker with Charles Manson and his desire to 'leave a mark'. Filmmaking, thus, is to be read as being interchangeable with, or indistinguishable from, murder. Second, it also recalls – and problematises – the said distinction, between, on the one hand, the faux-snuff footage that was perceived to be real by those who spoke out against the video nasties in the 1980s, and on the other, the logic, knowingness and common sense of those spectators who were not taken in by the snuff myth, but were able to recognise it as a marketing gimmick. Thus, by having the narrator claim that 'James wasn't going to let reality snuff out his dreams', 'reality' is presented as a threat to 'snuff', as it is *through* snuff that James attempts to realise his dreams, by 'snuffing out' out his colleague, thereby 'leaving a mark'.

The Manson quote anticipates James's downfall, as he reiterates similar rhetoric in his quest to complete 'The Street Walker', as when, after an actress dies on set, he channels any sympathy initially felt for her back to his own obsession with recognition and fame: 'That's what life is: it's short and it ends so fucking quickly; and if you don't make your mark ... fuck!' However, it is important to note that the Manson quote used in the film is fabricated. In the actual reported quote, which was said during an interview between Manson and Diane Sawyer in 1991, Manson does not actually say 'leave a mark to say that you were there', but rather says the more ambiguous 'leave something *witchy*'. While one may be able to claim that such misquoting adds another layer of ambiguity to *Resurrecting the Street Walker* that further brings into question notions of truth and authenticity within the narrative, the term 'witchy' has a certain resonance with the video nasties era. It suggests, among other things, a cult (cult cinema, Manson's cult), but most significantly perhaps, enchantment and the allusions to 'witch craft' that Martin Barker has identified as being employed by the news media around the time of the Video Recordings Act's initial inception,[21] and the destructive effect that *The Street Walker*, as an alleged film from the nasties era, has on James himself.

Yet James's downward trajectory is not simply bound to the corrupting effects of films themselves, but also the cult legacy that films such as *Snuff* have subsequently acquired through various fan communities. For instance, his, in his words, 'stumbling across' reels of film in the company basement, echoes the famous anecdote about the original *Snuff*, 'that for four years prior to its release [in North America] . . . sat gathering dust in a New York distributer's office' before being picked up by exploitation producers, 'completed' with a faux-snuff ending and eventually distributed as 'the real thing' (Kerekes and Slater 1993: 8). In a similar regard, this element of *Resurrecting the Street Walker* also recalls the television campaign replicated in the 1985 television debate *Suitable for Viewing in the Home?*, which depicted two naive children wandering into a video store and 'uncovering' an obscure horror film, which they take home and sadistically enjoy. But more than this, the fact that James wants to complete and repackage a film from the video nasty era for a contemporary audience, attests to the cult(ural) longevity of the nasty as realised by video distributors such as VIPCO (Video Instant Picture Company) and Shameless in the UK, which have attested to the era's 'historical significance' by boasting specific films' statuses as 'original' nasties within their marketing materials for video nasty DVD re-issues (Egan 2007: 193–4). This desire to culturally and nostalgically re-appropriate is suggested in a later sequence of *Resurrecting the Street Walker* when James is typing up a script report, in which he states that the film he is reporting on is 'reminiscent in style of the evil dead [*sic*] movies'. Not only does this statement refer directly to *The Evil Dead* – as we have seen, one of the more controversial video nasties[22] – it also resonates with the idea that the video nasties were, in the words of several video nasty campaigners, 'evil'[23] and void of any cultural worth (that is to say, 'dead'). It is therefore up to James and other filmmakers to 'resurrect' the video nasties and reinstate their significance.

Resurrecting the Street Walker sees the movie business finish off James once and for all. Like Max in *The Last Horror Movie*, he makes his own video nasty and thus physically embroils himself within its mythology. By doing this, both Julian Richards and Özgür Uyanık recognise the contemporariness of the video nasties debate and its potency within the cultural memory of horror film audiences. Their films also identify the excessive nature of the films and the illogicality of those who connected social and moral corruption with horror videos.

In doing so, *The Last Horror Movie* and *Resurrecting the Street Walker* not only recall, but seek to expose, pastiche and parody the panics at the heart of the video nasties era, and the creative impact had upon contemporary horror filmmakers in Britain who have sophisticatedly deconstructed and critiqued the mythology that sparked their interest in horror films in the first place.

CONCLUSION: THE CONTINUED IMPACT OF THE VIDEO NASTY

In this chapter, I have shown not only how the video nasty era has had prominence in British cultural memory, but also how it has been recalled and critiqued by British directors who wished to explore violent spectacle in their horror films.

Of course, the examples that I have chosen for close analysis are only part of a broader spectrum of violent films such as *Shaun of the Dead* and *Eden Lake* (of which I offer closer analyses elsewhere in this book). Moreover, additional British horrors have continued to promote the snuff mythology, such as Bernard Rose's *Snuff Movie*, which tells the story of a director who, after it has been revealed that one of his films influenced a Manson-style gang to film a murder, retires from filmmaking. Other examples include *Donkey Punch*, in which a group of teenagers make a sex video, and accidentally murder a woman in the process; *Dread* (Anthony DiBlasi, 2009), which sees a man entrap a woman in a room, and videotape the process of starving her to death; and *Exhibit A*, a film framed as evidence in a 'real-life' murder trial, presented as a 'real' family video, that charts the mental deterioration of a father who kills his family.[24]

DVD advertising in the UK has also taken to recalling the video nasty era. This is not only true of international films such as the *Saw* and *Hostel* franchises, both of which are available on UK DVD proclaiming to be 'Uncut', 'Extreme' or 'Unseen' editions, but it is also true of British films such as *Cradle of Fear* – that boasts an 'uncut, two-hour version' of the film – and *A Day Of Violence* (Darren Ward, 2010), which presents itself as being 'complete' and 'uncut', as though to emphasise its forbidden-ness and to suggest it has bypassed the notorious British censor.[25] Even Adam Mason, who, after *The Devil's Chair*, began making films in Hollywood, has retained the video nasty angle with his Internet film *PIG* (2010): the downloadable DVD art is a direct replica of the video covers used by VTC, a British video distributor that went bust during the nasties panic (see Figure 3.1).

The kind of material explored in the case studies examined in this chapter may continue to resonate as unpleasant, disgusting, tasteless and/or sadistic, all over the world. Yet, at a time in Britain when censorship was less restrictive than it was in the past, horror directors have been permitted to be playful with the excessiveness of era-defining British moral panics. And although films

Figure 3.1   DVD artwork, video nasty style: Adam Mason's *PIG*.
© Omar Hauksson.

such as *Creep*, *The Devil's Chair*, *The Last Horror Movie* and *Resurrecting the Street Walker* may continue to be internationally overshadowed by contemporary American cinema, or lost amid developments in Euro horror and beyond, when they are considered in light of their own cultural history, they have a nasty taste all of their own.

Notes

1. This era marked the first time in British history that the OPA was used to prosecute films that were not pornography. See Petley (2011: 23–32).
2. Many of the video nasties discussed below were similarly banned in foreign territories, such as *Snuff* (Michael and Roberta Findlay, 1976), *Cannibal Holocaust* (Ruggero Deodato, 1980) and *Cannibal Ferox* (Umberto Lenzi, 1981).
3. The DPP drafted up several different lists before settling on a final thirty-nine. See Petley (2011).
4. This was always intended to be a working title, as a ploy to gain interest from funders (Sheil 2010b).
5. For a discussion about colour in Italian horror cinema, see Carter (2013: 127).
6. *F* was scored by Neil Stemp, who was given – among other things – Goblin's soundtrack to *Suspiria* by Roberts, for inspiration (Roberts 2010a).
7. Film critic David Edelstein first coined the phrase 'torture porn' in an article for *The New York Times* in 2006, and it has subsequently been debated within recent scholarship on the horror film. See Jones (2013) and Kerner (2015).

8. For a discussion of the 'value-judgements' made against torture porn by the press see Jones (2013: 28–30).
9. Although *The Texas Chain Saw Massacre* was never a 'true' video nasty because it did not make the official DPP list, it was caught up in the video controversy, along with two other notorious movies that did not make the list, *A Clockwork Orange* (Stanley Kubrick, 1971) and *The Exorcist*, but have often been presumed to be video nasties. However, as David Kerekes and David Slater argued in 2000 (just before these films were re-released on video in the United Kingdom), 'Indeed, the [alleged] ban imposed on these three particular films has been so long and so often debated in the media that their unavailability has been absorbed as *part of British culture*' (2000: 354; my emphasis).
10. Incidentally – and contra the aforementioned article by Kaleem Aftab (2009) – this is the first of several allusions to Powell's *Peeping Tom* (1960), which also depicts a father experimenting on, and thus corrupting, his son. It has also been common in some reviews and in academic criticism of the film to note *Creep*'s similarities to the British horror film *Death Line* (Gary Sherman) from 1973 (Blake 2008; Hutchings 2009a). While these comparisons are valid, Christopher Smith (2005) denies having ever seen *Death Line*, preferring instead to credit the video nasties as having provided most in the way of inspiration. On *Death Line* see Perks (2002).
11. I investigate the class associations of the hooded sweatshirt in Chapter 5. Smith deliberately bought Kate's dress from an expensive store on London's Oxford Street to signify her class status (Smith 2005).
12. Coincidentally, *The Devil's Chair* was distributed by a company called Soho Square Films; 'Soho Square' was also a nickname given to the BBFC due to the location of the board's offices (in Soho Square) in London (Johnson 1997: 11).
13. The 'truths' of narrative are alluded to in Seymour Chatman's pioneering essay 'The structure of narrative transmission' from 1972. Although largely dealing with literature, he argued that, in relation to the narrator – something that, for our purposes, can be linked to the cinematic voiceover, or what Chatman refers to as 'a disembodied narrative voice' (98) – 'It is clear that the author [or director/ screenwriter] must make special efforts to preserve the illusion that the events [of a story, or in our case, a film] are literally happening before the reader's [or spectator's] eyes' (Chatman 2004 [1972]: 98).
14. An example of this in practice can be seen in a televised discussion about the video nasties in the early 1980s, when broadcaster and novelist Claire Rayner, after being asked to define a 'video nasty', states: 'films that we used to call "horror" . . . are mild when compared with some of these [video nasties]' (the origins of this clip are unknown, although it is featured in the documentary *Ban the Sadist Videos* from 2005).
15. The snuff mythology has recently been ignited beyond the horror film by Canadian porn star Luke Rocco Magnotta, who was blamed for sending body parts of a man he murdered through the mail, and for 'allegedly filmed himself hacking his victim's body up with an ice-pick and then posting the sickening video online' (Anon. 2012).
16. *Snuff*'s publicity materials bellowed: 'The actors and actresses who dedicate their lives to making this film were never seen or heard from again'.
17. Linda Badley (2010) discusses the aesthetic potential of video as pertaining to realism.
18. The securing of rights was a grey area and often involved various companies releasing different versions of the same film within months of one another. To select a couple of examples at random, the Italian rape revenge drama *Night Train Murders* (Aldo Lado, 1975) was released twice in the UK: first by the company Video

Warehouse as *Don't Ride on Late Night Trains* and second by Cinehollywood as *Night Train Murder*. Another example is the Nazi-exploitation film *Love Camp 7* (R. L. Frost, 1968), which was released by Abbey Video and also by Market Video in the UK.

19. Not unlike the experiences of video nasty collectors. See Egan (2007: 154–81) for a detailed discussion of this culturally specific fan practice.

20. By 2005 – the year *The Last Horror Movie* was released on DVD in the UK – 9.9m DVD players had been purchased, compared to 3m VCRs (UKFC 2006: 64).

21. Barker discusses this at some length in Jake West's documentary *Video Nasties: Moral Panic, Censorship & Videotape* (2011).

22. That the film is produced by Scala Films, an offshoot of the company Palace Pictures, that originally distributed *The Evil Dead* in the UK, further nuances this. As Richard Stanley notes, Palace 'outraged the rest of the British film industry which, at that time, was still terrified that video was about to finish off the movie business once and for all' (2002: 183–4).

23. In Jake West's video nasties documentary, the Tory MP Graham Bright, who was behind the Video Recordings Act 1984, refers to the video nasties as 'evil'. Martin Barker talks at length about how it was not uncommon for religious imagery to be invoked in press about the scandal (something that was partly to do with the fact that Mary Whitehouse, the leader of the campaign against video nasties, was a Christian).

24. Alexandra Heller-Nicholas considers *Exhibit A* in some detail in her study of found footage horror films (2014: 170–3).

25. As an added touch, *A Day Of Violence* also stars famous Italian actor Giovanni Lombardo Radice (often credited as John Morghen), who is recognised all over the world for featuring in some of the most famous nasties: *Cannibal Ferox* and *Cannibal Apocalypse* (Antonio Margheriti, 1980).

4. IN THE DOGHOUSE

Andrew Spicer begins the final chapter of his important study *Typical Men: The Representation of Masculinity in Popular British Cinema*, with the following statement:

> One of the most striking features of masculinity in contemporary British cinema is its heterogeneity and hybridity: the range of male types is much wider than before, and the types themselves more complex. (Spicer 2001: 184)

He continues, partly explaining this shift as being due to the 'the present state of British filmmaking which has become decentred and eclectic, lacking the studio infrastructure or dominant producers of the earlier period' (ibid.). Recent British horror film production has testified to this industrial decentralisation, due, among other things, to the independent work carried out by specific filmmakers, independent production companies and the dedicated cult audience for horror films on DVD. Furthermore, Spicer's recognition of onscreen 'hybrid' male types in British cinema at the dawning of the new millennium extends across many of the films that fall within the remit of this book. This has already been noted to some extent in the recent scholarship of Linnie Blake, who explains the hybridity of male identities in British horror as being reflective of 'the erosion of the British man's traditional role as head of the family' in the face of Tony Blair's New Labour government and, specifically, his hybrid 'third way . . . that had been engendered by the destruction of the nation's industrial base and the ongoing realisation of women's longstand-ing calls for economic, political and cultural equality' (2008: 162). As such, in what Blake rightly identifies as 'self-reflexive films' such as *Shaun of the Dead*, *Dog Soldiers* and *Reign of Fire* (Rob Bowman, 2002), there was 'an extraor-dinary proliferation of what Noël Carroll would term "fusion monsters" [that is, humans who mutate into monsters such as werewolves or zombies]: which our questing heroes must invariably overcome in order to forge themselves a mode of masculinity fitted to their time and place' (Blake 2008: 158). As a result, Blake identifies 'a new kind of "fusion hero"' in British horror, 'one who undertakes a hybridisation of earlier models of British masculinity in his mission to conquer the monster and become a man' (ibid.).

In this chapter, I explore the problems involved when attempting to totalise contemporary masculinity as it appears in British horror cinema, and the sur-rounding 'cult' discourses that feed the self-reflexivity that Blake discusses. However, while I concur with Blake that some British horror films have been seen to '[reject] gender essentialism' (2008: 159), many films also examine the significance that gender essentialism has had to cult film arenas (fan communi-ties, fanzines and a love for the horror genre) where the source materials that they pastiche and parody have acquired specific (gendered) meaning. Through this examination, I propose that such 'fusion heroes' are perhaps not as reli-able as Blake implies – after all, has masculinity truly ever been a homogenous entity? – and, in moving away from the hierarchal male hero-type, examine how nerdy and 'fan-boy' types are parodied and critiqued in the recent male-centred subgenre of slapstick horror-comedies.

Central to my analysis is an awareness of the kinds of ways that masculin-ity and masculine personae have been approached within, first, contemporary British cinema – whether onscreen in relation to the cast, or beyond the diege-sis in terms of the writer, director and the actors' other works – and second, the ways in which masculinity has been *stereotyped* within the fan discourses surrounding cult cinema and the horror film and within British culture more generally.

Cult males, male cults and the 'New Lad'

Xavier Mendik and Ernest Mathijs recognise that nostalgia is 'a core feature of many cult films' (2008: 3). As discussed in the previous chapter, in the early 2000s it was often the case that the films that had most cult impact on contem-porary British horror filmmakers were horror and exploitation titles that were first experienced on home video during the early 1980s. Therefore, a partial reasoning for the care-free, violent and morally ambiguous tone of films such as *Creep* and *Mum & Dad* was due to a fannish drive to homage the weird, wonderful and illicit exploitation/horror films of the filmmakers' youth. Put differently, the filmmakers were 'yearning for an idealized past' by producing works that were comparable to their favourite cult films (Mendik and Mathijs 2008: 3).

Of course, as was also discussed in Chapter 3, such violent imagery has not been without its critics, especially if the violence is carried out towards women. Blake, for instance, has suggested that *Creep* is so hateful a film, and its violence towards women is so prominent, that the film and its director testify to an alleged male insecurity that stems from a decrease in patriarchy's social control, and man's reluctance to come to terms with the 'very existence of non-submissive women' (Blake 2008: 177). Blake's opinion is not a new one of course. Indeed, within film studies, since the publication of Laura Mulvey's influential article 'Visual pleasure and narrative cinema' (1975), films have often been read as representative of male's voyeuristic objectivity, with horror cinema – and other 'gross-out' cult genres – being an easy target for readings identifying a 'perverse' and insecure masculinist gaze (Williams 1984; Clover 1992; Creed 1993). Moreover, even recent British horror films with strong female leads, such as *28 Days Later* and *The Descent*, have been accused of reducing these women to monstrous or, at best androgynous, stereotypes.[1] Such readings are not eased by the fact that it is often accepted that it is mostly men who consume (and produce) 'cult' genres such as horror,[2] and the fact that the 'fans' of these genres are often coded as 'male' within surrounding academic discourse (irrespective of their gender), or at the very least, are thought to operate within communities that 'privilege masculine competencies and dispositions' (Hollows 2003: 39; see also Hunt 2003). Viewed in this way, cult genres have been said to inhabit a gendered space bound to patriarchal hegemony, where practices and associated ephemera such as fanzines are accused of replicating philosophies and objects typically associated with a nostalgia for politically incorrect (heterosexual) male pleasures (such as, photographs of scantily clad women and a prose-style drenched in provocative sexism). These factors, so the argument goes, work to exclude female fans (Hollows 2003: 41; see also Cherry 2002).

Within the UK, this fanzine/fan culture can be likened to the kinds of men's magazines that materialised in the 1990s, such as *Loaded*, which followed a 'backlash against feminism' postulated by the 'New Lad': a new social type dismissed as juvenile, vulgar and regressive due to his opinions of women and his pursuit of casual sex, football and booze (see Whelehan 2000: 58; Gauntlett 2008: 170; Genz and Brabon 2009: 141–2).[3] Certainly, contemporary fans of cult film, and 'the masculinity of cult' they have been said to reinforce, genders what is niche and obscure *as* 'male' in opposition to the so-called 'feminized mainstream' (Hollows 2003: 41), as though men, now the increasingly marginalised sex, must recreate their crumbling patriarchal kingdom on the verges of society, by refuting responsibility and having a good time doing things where increasingly powerful and forward-thinking women cannot tell them otherwise. As Jacinda Read (2003) has it, there remains a coalescing between the masculine communities surrounding cult cinema – that she sees as transferring beyond typical fan circles into the academy – and what she discusses as the 'nationally specific "cult of masculinity"' of the New Lad (Read 2003: 55). In her view, the 'cult of masculinity' within British fan and scholar-fan communities represents 'an opportunity to reassert a masculine (sub)culture and politics in the perceived institutionalization of feminism and its subsequent colonization and feminization on the margins' (Read 2003: 61).

Read's theory has rightfully been challenged for being essentialist and for failing to consider the legions of female fans who would refute her assertions (Mathijs and Sexton 2011: 110; Duffett 2013: 194). Nevertheless, British horror cinema repeatedly addressed ideas central to the cult of masculinity paradigm in the 2000s and 2010s. As discussed in Chapter 3, and similar to how Imelda Whelehan has defined the lads' mags of the 1990s, certain films bolstered a nostalgic 'celebration of the boyish', with 'endless references to "trivia" from the seventies and eighties' (2000: 64). Indeed, the jovially juvenile nature of the New Lad stereotype, who revelled in excess, told politically incorrect jokes (often about women) and who dismissed anyone who failed to 'get the joke' as a spoil-sport,[4] is essential to the tone of many of the British horror films discussed so far. Furthermore, the professional community that surrounded contemporary British horror in this period, generated by the reappearances of the same actors, the employment of the same writers and directors,[5] as well as the ghettoisation of the films at specialist festivals such as Fright Fest and Midnight Madness, similarly echoes the ways in which the 'subculture' of cult film has been theorised, because the films constituted a marginal, cultural and industrial presence that is not usually thought of as fitting within the aforementioned 'feminised' mainstream of production and distribution.[6] After all, with a cluster of exceptions, it was unquestionably this parallel existence to the theatrically prioritised British film industry of the early twenty-first century – and, arguably, society as a whole – that the British horror film mostly inhabited.

In what follows, I consider the oft-overlooked area of horror-comedy as fallow ground for parody and self-deprecation of British horror's low-cultural status, the filmmakers, and the fan communities that surround the genre.[7] While it is true that self-reflexivity is evident in 'straight' horror films as well,[8] and that the presence of the New Lad is also strongly felt in films such as *Dog Soldiers* (see Peirse 2009 and Martin-Jones 2011), it is also true that the slapstick horror-comedies produced in the wake of 2004's *Shaun of the Dead* addressed horror and surrounding discourses from a 'sillier' perspective, and can therefore more obviously be accredited with a laddish streak. Indeed, in films as popular as *Shaun of the Dead*, to the more marginal *Doghouse* and critically reviled *Lesbian Vampire Killers*, there is a certain emphasis placed on a type of humour that one would typically associate with the laddish stereotype – including, but not limited to, fart gags and lesbian fantasies and the refuting of anything 'serious'[9] – as well as differing strains of alleged laddish insecurities, from geekishness and sexual-inability to overcompensating hypermasculinity.

Among all of this, intertextual references to horror films and the fan cultures that surround them, abound. In essence, the laddism explored in British horror-comedies is presented *as a cult* in itself – as a 'cult of masculinity' reinforcing the 'masculinity of cult' – but not in a way that would necessarily connote with what Hollows has recognised as a power-aspiring '"hardness" of cult' (2003: 43). Rather, the films can be read as mocking their own cult niche and the rejection of the feminine that film cults have been said to evidence, by drawing parallels to the cult audience of fans along the way, and the stereotypes that have often been read in their place.

BOYHOOD DREAMS COME TRUE: *SHAUN OF THE DEAD* AND THE CONTEXT OF CONTEMPORARY HORROR-COMEDY

Although there was, as David Pirie states, a definite increase in female audience members for horror films at the turn of the millennium (2008: 217),[10] the UK cinema audience for horror (or horror-related)[11] films comprised mostly young males aged from fourteen to thirty-four (UKFC 2004: 41; UKFC 2005: 51; UKFC 2007: 99; UKFC 2008: 108; UKFC 2009: 116; UKFC 2010: 112). Upon a closer look at 2004, one of the benchmark years for horror and the year that the highly popular horror-comedy *Shaun of the Dead* was released, it was revealed that men, as well as having preferred traditionally male-coded 'action-led' genres such as thrillers and science fiction, [12] also had a preference for 'certain types of comedy', of which *Shaun of the Dead* is listed as a chief example (UKFC 2005: 51). If we consider how other comedies that were released that year had a greater female audience share – notably romantic comedies such as Beeban Kidron's *Bridget Jones: The Edge of Reason* (2004) – and identify that the *types* of comedy men were going to see were largely of a slapstick and scatological nature,[13] the phrase 'certain types of comedy' can be comfortably appropriated to mean something that is different/oppositional to the more conventional, mainstream or 'feminised' rom-com.[14] Indeed, the ambiguous nature of the phrase 'certain type' can be read as connoting something decidedly peculiar, specific, niche and – in regards to the gory, juvenile humour of *Shaun of the Dead* (that includes slapstick decapitations and recurring childish jokes) – a 'type' with a laddish appeal and sensibility. Indeed, Edgar Wright's open reverence to the cult films of horror auteurs George A. Romero, Lucio Fulci, John Carpenter, John Landis and Sam Raimi,[15] supports his admission on *Shaun*'s DVD commentary that making the film was 'a boyhood dream come true'. Moreover, the film's plot about two adult men who reject adulthood (by, for instance, playing video games) and end up fighting in a zombie apocalypse, echoes the aforementioned 'trivia of the 70s and 80s' obsessions of the New Lad and supports Wright's description of the film as being 'very indulgent on [his and, writer/star, Simon Pegg's] behalf' (Wright 2005). Indeed, many of the laughs in the film arise from its clear 'celebration of the boyish'. A prime example is the moment when Shaun and Ed attempt to kill zombies by hurling unanimously terrible vinyl albums from Shaun's collection at them, or when Ed repeatedly dispels any moments of seriousness in the film by expulsing potent farts (an insincere 'I'm sorry' is always the punchline to the gag).

Shaun of the Dead, therefore, partially operates in relation to the nostalgic recollection of fannish trivia framed explicitly as being associated with an immature boyish past, from the obvious pun in its title, to its multitudinous geekish intertextuality and body humour. From a marketing perspective, it could be argued with no hesitation that its zombie element was paramount to its appeal: not least because the film stemmed from an episode of the British hit TV series *Spaced* (1999–2001), in which Tim (Simon Pegg) and Daisy (Jessica Stevenson) fend off a group of zombies in the style of the popular videogame *Resident Evil*. Moreover, the *Resident Evil* movie franchise was going from box-office strength to strength in the early to-mid-2000s, and the demand for horror parody at the cinema was at an all-time high, as shown the year previously when the third instalment of the highly popular goofball spoof series, *Scary Movie 3* (David Zucker, 2003), had taken almost $200m worldwide (http://imdb.com/pro).

That said, as argued elsewhere in this book, the makers of *Shaun of the Dead* had their eye on more than *male* cult film fans (or, for that matter, the cult audience of *Spaced*). Resultantly, the film offered more pleasures than those typically sanctioned as male. In fact, one can logically surmise its mainstream popularity with both genders as having something to do with its prominent love story arc rather than its gross-out comedy elements. Indeed, its tagline, 'A romantic comedy. With zombies', emphasised its user-friendly mainstream capabilities, as though speaking out to women, who, statistically, would have been less likely to attend if it was simply 'a horror film'. This may appear to problematise reading the film as 'laddish', when laddism, by its nature, is said to *exclude* women. However, even the emphasising of its rom-com elements in the marketing was done so in a cheeky 'naughty-lad' kind of way (Whelehan 2000: 72). 'With zombies' was tagged on as though a guilty admission of the 'boyish', 'niche' and 'geeky' pleasures the film showcased *in addition to* its romance arc. The tagline clarified the 'type of comedy' later alluded to by the UKFC when describing the film, encasing the boyish humour within the conventional framework of mainstream cinema – including Shaun doing a 'Hugh

Grant running back moment' to get his girlfriend back (Wright 2005) – that widened its appeal, and also suppressed/'excused' its jokey boyish overtones.

Through doing so, rather than simply affirming the New Lad stereotype, the film has been said to offer a critique of what can be read as 'laddish' traits. As Linnie Blake argues, writing about Shaun and Ed specifically:

> Theirs is a mode of masculinity endlessly trapped in its own fast-receding adolescence, where a great deal of time is spent avoiding meaningful contact with one's biological family and no effort is made to establish an adult home and family of one's own; the preferred alternative being a life of computer games and corner-shop lager, fart gags, dead-end jobs and small-scale dope deals. (Blake 2008: 167)

After all, the reason that Shaun's girlfriend, Liz (Kate Ashfield), leaves him in the first place – and what spurs on his quest to battle through zombified London to save her – is due to the fact he prioritises his 'alternative' life with Ed over spending 'quality' and meaningful time with her. Therefore, come the end of the film, once Shaun has proven himself to be a competent decision maker after having saved the day, the objects of his laddism are literally banished to the garden shed: a zombified Ed waits for Shaun in front of a TV, games controller in hand. Back in the house, Shaun can rekindle his faltering relationship with Liz (who has moved in in Ed's place) by 'growing up' and assuming the role of a mature husband-figure. The rest of society, meanwhile, indulges in zombie mania (including charity festivals such as *Zomb-Aid*): a horror that is now coded as mainstream and 'safe', not unlike zombie cinema itself in the wake of blockbusters such as *Resident Evil* and Snyder's *Dawn of the Dead*. In turn, *Shaun of the Dead* echoes its own status as a 'mainstream' film – it was produced by Working Title and distributed by Universal – and by having Shaun go to the shed to play games with zombie Ed literalises the cult of masculinity, presenting it as something that can only be enjoyed on the margins, in private, away from the familial household and as decidedly different to the mainstream zombies that the rest of society consume. The film therefore casually (and affectionately) satirises any male's nostalgic, regressive boyish desires to return to the cults of his youth. In doing so, however, it also distinguishes such pleasures as immature, as typical of the 'fan-boy'. In other words, it positions them as not fully concurrent with 'mainstream' thought and responsibility, which, it appears, has a female stronghold, with Liz calling the shots.

The light-hearted critique of laddish behaviour that lies at the heart of *Shaun of the Dead* is, perhaps unsurprisingly, less evident in those films that sought to emulate it. The films that followed in the wake of *Shaun*'s success, including *Lesbian Vampire Killers*, *Doghouse*, *The Cottage*, *Stag Night of the Dead*

(Neil 'Napoleon' Jones, 2009) and *Zombie Women of Satan* were unquestionably cruder in their sensibilities, and, by extension, were narrower in terms of their audience appeal. As with several British films of the 1990s such as *Nil By Mouth* (Gary Oldman, 1997) and *The Full Monty* (Peter Cattaneo, 1997), which, in Claire Monk's (2000a) view, allegorise a post-Thatcherite society where women are succeeding in industry and men are becoming increasingly disempowered, several post-*Shaun* horror-comedies presented their vision of laddish masculinity as peripheral to the workings of mainstream society. Resultantly, these films maintained a social presence not unlike newer lads' weeklies such as *Nuts* and *Zoo*, which materialised in the early 2000s and were considered to have further regressed in tone the lads' mags of the 1990s, by having a vulgar tone and a considerably smaller readership. To this end, the general unpopularity of these laddish British horror-comedies chimed, first, with the scatological tone of New Lads' weeklies, and, second, with the marginal market presence of a male cult film audience and fan base.

On-screen fanzines?

Much in the same way that lads' mags were, and continue to be, criticised for their regressive politics and low humour, horror fan cultures and their associated magazines have frequently been derided as juvenile, of encompassing 'the sophomoric ramblings of overgrown adolescents' (Sanjek 1990: 151) and perpetuating 'near pornographic' images and 'negative female stereotypes' (Cherry 2002: 50). Indeed, David Sanjek once acknowledged that some (albeit, American) horror fanzines produced in the latter part of the 1980s tended to revel in a sarcastic, arrogant vernacular that was 'often laced with self-conscious misogyny, racism and sexism' (Sanjek 1990: 154). Such a 'jocular tone' and a 'smart-alec' yet 'self-conscious' masculine persona (ibid.), certainly resonates with the accusations directed towards New Lad publications (and the 'it's only a joke!' defences of those editors under fire). It is appropriate – particularly in a British context – that some parallels should be drawn between the attitudes of this British stereotype, horror film fandom, and, by extension, contemporary British horror-comedies that satirise such caricatures.

It could be argued that British horror films post-2000 represented a cinematic extension of the horror fanzine. Similar to British fanzines such as *Samhain*, *Scream* and *Shock Horror*,[16] such films were often modest productions that were worked on by a small dedicated team. This ethos was certainly apparent in the development of horror-comedies such as *Doghouse* and *Lesbian Vampire Killers*, which were shot for about £1m each and had small production teams. The films not only navigated the genre terrain with astute knowingness (some may even say in a 'smart-alec' kind of way) by alluding to notable horror films and other cult obscurities, they also looked towards a particular style of vulgar humour, or what has commonly been referred to within the study of British comedy cinema as 'low-comedy', which has been aligned with 'laddism' on several occasions (see Hunt 1998: 120; Hunter 2012).[17] Certainly, the occasionally sexist tone and the persistence of innuendo within British fanzines such as *The Dark Side*, its racier sister publication *Video World* (that, since the 1990s had scantily clad cover girls not unlike pornographic publications), and *Gorezone* (that would later change its name to *GZ* in echo of men's magazine *GQ*, and feature a monthly cover girl),[18] reveals a vernacular similar to that of new 'low-brow' lad publications.[19] By extension, this tone was also to be found in the likes of *Lesbian Vampire Killers*, which was protested against by radical feminists, The Angry Lesbians, even before shooting began,[20] and the particularly laddish-sounding *Stag Night of the Dead*. The lo-fi 'cultness' that surrounded the majority of the horror-comedies paralleled that of the horror fanzine, as well as what Feona Attwood (2005: 86) sees as a 'downmarket drift in men's print media' in publications such as *Nuts* and *Zoo*, or what Horvath *et al.* recognise as their 'lower production values and . . . content about less globally famous female celebrities' (2012: 2). Certainly, contemporary fanzines such as *Gorezone*, which in recent years had a 'Goremates of the GZ mansion' special (#63, January 2011), and *The Dark Side*, which has ran a number of 'Scream Queen' specials in the past, echoes the marginality that adjectives such as 'low-brow' and 'cheap' have come to signify of cult film and paracinema. In other words, they are obscure, counter-cultural and politically incorrect (Sconce 1995). Moreover, the coverage of 'less globally famous female celebrities' in such magazines mirrors the kinds of cult film actresses who have featured in contemporary horror fanzines and in contemporary British horror-comedies, and who are little-known beyond the parameters of the cult community, such as the model, TV presenter and 'scream queen' Emily Booth (who also features in *Doghouse*), the actress MyAnna Buring (of *The Descent*, *Lesbian Vampire Killers* and *Kill List*), and ex-Bond girl Honor Blackman (of *Cockneys versus Zombies* (Matthias Hoene, 2012)).[21]

The similarity is continued with the levels of obscurity and the fannish niche that the films have characteristically maintained. That the imitators of *Shaun of the Dead* were made with less concern of amassing the same success would suggest that a reason for this was that *Shaun* was *too* 'mainstream' for the niche DVD audience of most contemporary British horror films. After all, it was a hit *across* genders and age groups, which was very unusual for horror. In other words – its subject matter notwithstanding – it was a commercial risk, and, considering the limited success of British horror up to this point, too big of a risk for most production companies to take – specifically when the small (male) audience for horror had shown itself to be the most reliable market in the years after 2005. Indeed, as discussed in Chapter 2 of this book, mainstream theatrical horror hits like this were, by and large, one-offs (*28 Days Later*), with most British horror films not necessarily anticipated to do *that* well in cinemas. (Most of the films that sought to bank on the success of *28 Days Later* – with the exception of the remake of *Dawn of the Dead* – descended rapidly into DVD obscurity.) With some anticipation, thus, subsequent horror-comedies had limited box-office presences, or went directly to DVD, or used their limited theatrical run as an additional platform to raise awareness of their forthcoming (and almost immediate) DVD release among cult film fans who were assumed to be male.[22]

The limited commercial appeal of *Shaun*-style films, such as *Doghouse*, *Lesbian Vampires Killers*, *Severance* and *The Cottage*, and those direct-to-DVD titles such as *Zombie Women of Satan*, was evidenced by their more pronounced masculine-oriented storylines, which took more from the continuing ripples of laddish crime/hooligan films that were enjoying success on video beyond the 1990s[23] by placing less of an emphasis on monogamous heterosexual happy endings, or refuting them altogether in favour of homosocial bonds. Moreover, their marketing and promotional material emphasised their 'male address'. *Doghouse* and *Lesbian Vampire Killers*, for instance, were both *promoted as* laddish comedies, carrying endorsements from *Zoo* and *Nuts*, respectively,[24] and both had mainstream cinema releases with mediocre box-office returns.[25] As Steve Chibnall has suggested of the late-90s/early 2000s gangster film trend (similarly berated by the critics for its laddish allusions), a 'greater success on video is . . . suggested by each films' lack of cinematic spectacle and elaborate special effects best appreciated on the big-screen, and the masculinist subject matter which renders these films problematic as "date" movies' (2009: 377). Indeed, it is arguable that *Doghouse* and *Lesbian Vampire Killers* specifically refuted any 'date movie' potential by not replicating the 'rom-com' elements of *Shaun of the Dead* and therefore being set apart from its monogamous ideals. Through being aligned, in many ways, to contemporary lads' weeklies whose readership figures were decreasing during the decade (Ponsford 2009), *Doghouse* and *Lesbian Vampire Killers* presented the 'exclusive' cult arena of the laddish fan-boy as a niche and socially peripheral endeavour.[26] Indeed, the general obscurity of other independently financed 'no-budget' horror-comedies such as *Zombie Women of Satan* and *Stag Night of the Dead*, which share crude jokes and sexual innuendos with *Doghouse* and *Lesbian Vampire Killers*, inhibited these films' saleability to a broad mainstream audience.[27] They were not fortunate to have had the kind of 'fashionable buzz' that surrounded the release of the Guy Ritchie crime film *Lock, Stock and Two Smoking Barrels* in 1998, and were never destined to be 'a cultural event' assisted by, say, the fashion industry (Chibnall 2009: 378). Rather, by mainstream standards, they were, and have remained, decidedly *unfashionable*.

Of course, such de-centralisation from a broader to a narrower audience demographic was one of the most consistent staples of the period's British horror films. As explored elsewhere in this book, many films that were produced during this era were often reliant on an audience's familiarity with the pre-texts or film cultures being lampooned. Hollows (2003: 37) has suggested that this kind of insider knowledge works to reinforce the 'masculinity of cult'. However, the ways in which the horror-comedies lampooned the conventions of the horror film also alludes to one of the central anxieties of the cult film fan: 'a potentially nerdish failed masculinity' (Read 2003: 68). As David Gauntlett has argued of lads' mags such as *Loaded*, which repeatedly looked to trivia and nostalgia for 'masculine' social-reassertion, 'this doesn't sound like a super-confident masculinity; frustrated desires and nostalgia are quite the opposite of a thrusting agenda' (2008: 180). Textual analysis of the less-popular *Lesbian Vampire Killers* and *Doghouse* – that were repeatedly positioned by the media as being inferior to *Shaun of the Dead* – will illustrate how this knowingly 'failed'/'insecure' masculinity is presented within each of the films via their preoccupation with horror film subcultures.

HEAVING BOSOMS AND DIAPHANOUS NIGHTGOWNS: *LESBIAN VAMPIRE KILLERS*

'Even dead women would sooner sleep with each other than get with me, it would appear' (Fletch, *Lesbian Vampire Killers*)

'He's like a little kid in the playground with all his favourite toys round him' (MyAnna Buring discussing Phil Claydon, director of *Lesbian Vampire Killers*)

The laddish preoccupations of *Lesbian Vampire Killers* are worn on its sleeve, both as a means of indulgence and critique. The film sees two best friends, Jimmy and Fletch (played by real-life comedy TV duo Mat Horne and James Corden), travel to Cragwich, a fictional location in rural England, in the hope of mending Jimmy's (recently) broken heart (the presumed solution: 'loads and loads of fanny'[28]). Upon their arrival, it becomes apparent that the town – anachronistic in its period mise en scène, evocative of Hammer's most famous horror films – is plagued by a curse, which has every female virgin turn into a lesbian vampire on her eighteenth birthday. Jimmy and Fletch must unite with Lotte (MyAnna Buring) and the vicar (in echo of Peter Cushing's Van Helsing roles, played Paul McGann) to defeat the vampires, and save the world in the process. As mentioned above, the film was generally met with disdain and/or annoyance by critics, some of whom simply lamented the fact that it was, in the words of *The Times*'s James Christopher, 'profoundly awful',[29] with a

Pink News poll hailing it as 'the worst film of 2009' (Anon. 2009b). Others, however, suggested that its failings went beyond its paracinematic characteristics, and that the film constituted a vicious attack on homosexuality and femininity (Hammond 2009: 68).

However, crucial to the ironic tone of *Lesbian Vampire Killers* was precisely the fact that it made no bones about its own perceived 'offensiveness' and the broad brushstrokes with which it painted its women, its men and contemporary attitudes to sexuality. Being laddish in its tone and aware of the genre within which it operated, it worked to exacerbate and satirise any anticipated negative perceptions from the press and radical feminists. James Corden, in an interview on the film's DVD, affirms its self-awareness and low humour, by shamelessly describing it as '*Shaun of the Dead* – with tits'. This flippant statement, while being vulgar and politically incorrect, underscored not only how the films were similar – in that they both spoofed horror conventions and starred TV personalities – but also alluded to the key difference between them: namely, that *Lesbian Vampire Killers* had a more concentrated cult/laddish address than a romantic comedy, and resultantly more of a limited commercial appeal.[30] However, the film's focus on 'tits', and its jokes about 'lesbians', were not the only ways that the film went about aligning itself with the marginal masculinity of cult mentality. This was also achieved through the cult pre-texts that it lampooned.

As Wright had done with *Shaun of the Dead*, Claydon offered a series of references to 1980s cult films, including nods to *An American Werewolf in London*, *Evil Dead II* (Sam Raimi, 1987) and *Ghostbusters* (Ivan Reitman, 1984). The most pronounced allusion, however, was to the 'lesbian vampire' films produced by Hammer Films in the UK in the 1970s. Whereas *Shaun of the Dead* took inspiration from highly regarded and politically charged American horror productions of the same era, *Lesbian Vampire Killers'* Gothic setting, and its deployment of an ominous country cottage, a menacing inn, a vengeful priest and care-free youths, as well as its mild eroticism and audacious title, harked back to a comparatively embarrassed era of British cinema when 'horror was either blending with, or losing ground to the sex film' with productions such as 1971's *Lust for a Vampire* (directed by Jimmy Sangster) (Hunt 1998: 144). Moreover, its low production values, hinted at by its overuse of computer-generated imagery (CGI) for wide-angled shots of the woodland (thus emphasising the small studio space), and the occasional exposure of film set at the edges of the frame, echoes the hurriedness and 'rather papery . . . sets' that films such as *The Vampire Lovers* (Roy Ward Baker, 1970) have since been accused as having (Rigby 2002: 172). To compensate for these factors – that were one of the many results of having a low budget and six-week shooting schedule – the final product evidenced awareness of (what may be perceived as) its shortcomings, by emphasising its limitations and revelling in its artifice. After all, in terms of box-office projections, Hammer was an odd choice of company to send-up in a mainstream theatrical film, especially when one considers that, when Claydon's film was in production, Hammer had not made a film in thirty years. However, an examination of the production history of *Lesbian Vampire Killers* offers potential reasoning for this.

Originally, the filmmakers were little concerned with amassing mainstream success (Claydon 2010). In fact, *Lesbian Vampire Killers* was intended as a film with a marginal cult appeal that could have happily sat alongside any number of obscure no-budget horror films on any horror fan's DVD shelf. Yet, the film garnered an unprecedented level of mainstream visibility during its production, due to the rising star profiles of Horne and Corden on television. As *Lesbian Vampire Killers* was shooting, Horne and Corden were becoming well known for their roles in the increasingly popular, and recently BAFTA-winning, sitcom, *Gavin and Stacey* (2007–10). One may assume that, had *Gavin and Stacey* been as successful prior to the production of *Lesbian Vampire Killers*, more could have been done in the script to, perhaps, tone down the allusions to classic Hammer, and to make more overt allusions to Horne's and Corden's televisual characters (as per *Shaun of the Dead* and *Spaced*, for instance). However, since the film's original script was written long before Horne and Corden were even associated with the project, its niche cultish allusions – that would likely have been lost on most mainstream audiences – remained intact. Indeed, beneath the subsequent marketing gimmicks that made the most of Horne's and Corden's newfound celebrity (see Figure 4.1), remained the indulgent and nostalgic direct-to-DVD-style film that the creative team had always intended to make. As Claydon has argued, the film was written, not as a crowd-pulling vehicle per se, but, rather, 'with the intention of "let's just write a film that *we* would want to go and watch if we were 15 again"' (Claydon 2010; emphasis in original).[31] And, since the fifteen-year-old males who ended up being the primary audience for *Lesbian Vampire Killers* would not necessarily have been familiar with Peter Cushing's Van Helsing in the same way that they would have been with, say, *Shaun*'s zombies,[32] the lampooning of Hammer worked as an unanticipated mainstream trump, because *Lesbian Vampire Killers* was a commercial film that uneasily straddled the gendered insider/outsider mentality of genre/cult film fandom (Jancovich 2000; Hollows 2003: 36–7). In other words, a film that was designed for the 'insiders' (the cult film fans who would understand the references) resultantly ended up alienating the 'outsiders' (the feminised mainstream audience and feminist detractors of the film), despite it never have being intended to attract that wide an audience in the first place.

Lesbian Vampire Killers relied on a number of in-jokes relating to its source material and horror film fandom. Resultantly, the ways that Jimmy and Fletch are presented in the film can be aligned with nerdish/laddish fan types, in

Figure 4.1   The commercial and critical success of their sitcom, *Gavin and Stacey*, led to Horne and Corden receiving star-billing on one of the posters used to advertise *Lesbian Vampire Killers* in the UK. © 2009 Alliance Atlantis Releasing Limited T/A Momentum Pictures.

that, like the film itself, they do not quite fit with contemporary mainstream thought, and thus, through their haphazard and vulgar personas, invite ironic, unattractive and deliberately self-deprecating parallels with Claydon and the film's screenwriters, Paul Hupfield and Stewart Williams. Jimmy and Fletch, thus, are socially awkward misfits who are, to many, annoying, and, as the epigraph to this section alludes, unsuccessful with women (due, in part, to their perceived sexism). *They* are the butt of the joke, not the lesbian vampires, and they appositely personify the 'insecure' lads' mag readers that Gauntlett discusses. To quote the original poster for the film (see Figure 4.2), they are 'no-hopers' who, like New Lads and cult fans of paracinema, revel in and have fun with the outmodedness and controversy of the politically incorrect. As though an extension of the director's and writers' creative visions, they are literally transported to a Hammer-esque land of 'big, heaving bosoms and diaphanous nightgowns' (Claydon 2010) where such opinions get the better of them, and their insecurities unfold.

Lesbian Vampire Killers' 'provocations' – that are less provocative if we

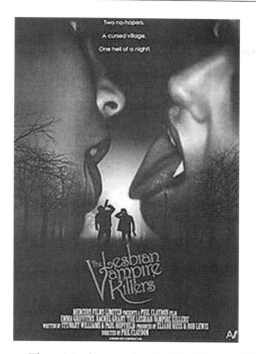

Figure 4.2   No-hopers: The original poster for *Lesbian Vampire Killers* was used to attract funders prior to the involvement of Horne and Corden. © 2009 Alliance Atlantis Releasing Limited T/A Momentum Pictures.

consider the original audience for the film, who would likely be more aware and attuned to the conventions and era of cinema that were being satirised – seep through the film in a way that seems to assume that, in its mainstream context, the film will not always be read as an ironic genre parody, which identifies the excesses and silliness displayed by Hammer films such as *Lust for a Vampire*. Several of the film's detractors acknowledged the self-reflexivity (Hunter 2009; Robey 2009; Tookey 2009), but it was largely agreed that the film was written in bad taste, and that it lacked 'genuine affection for the source material' (Hammond 2009: 68). Moreover, few were able to break away from the opinion that the film was in some way dangerous in its representation of women and that it simply fortified 'lesbian fake fantasies [that men] see/read in magazines' ('Ms Farrah Lalloo', The Angry Lesbians, n.d.), despite that the strongest character in the film is a woman, and once the vampire curse is eventually lifted, all of the women turn out to be lesbians anyway (and are *still* unwilling to 'score' with Fletch, who remains the butt of the joke once again). Indeed, one of the film's central gags is its lampooning of the stereotypical male presumption that, if a woman does not want to have sex with them, she *must* be a lesbian. In this instance, this stereotype is used to poke fun at hypermasculine arrogance.

Claydon, Hupfield and Williams were clearly aware of the ways that fans of the horror film are typically perceived. Claydon often refers to his own genre fandom on the film's UK DVD commentary and the immaturity typically associated with it. The team also clearly anticipated the negative ways that the film would be viewed in some critical circles. To some extent, then, it could be suggested that Claydon and the writers sought to deliberately subscribe to the widely felt prediction that the film would indicate the living out of a perverse childhood fantasy, or, as one angrylesbians.biz petition signee somewhat awkwardly phrased it: 'Mindless boys using their penis-sensation obsession for creativity' ('Mrs Jessica Praveen Menon', The Angry Lesbians, n.d.).

In anticipating criticisms such as this, the creative team positioned *Lesbian Vampire Killers*, and its cult allusions, firmly in the sights of those critics likely to react. For example, in one instance, when Jimmy accidentally 'invites' the vampires into his cottage by exclaiming, 'It's not like I am going to say, "Come on lesbian vampires, come into my cottage!"', he attempts to revoke the invitation by using the oft-used 'defence' of the New Lad: 'I was being ironic' (Genz and Brabon 2009: 102). Moreover, the film repeatedly descends into overt, and quite deliberate, Freudian territory, as though to allude to the theoretical and ideologically wired excesses imposed on the genre by psychoanalytic feminist film theory. This is particularly evident when Fletch pretends to be a Jedi Knight (in direct echo of Claydon's admitting to owning a light sabre and having it mounted on his living-room wall), alongside the only weapon powerful enough to defeat the vampire – the penis-like 'Sword of Dieldo' – only to be emasculated when he is interrupted by a sexually forward, eighteen-year-old, lesbian vampire: 'Erm, no I wasn't, erm, doing *Star Wars*.' Again, the audience is directed to laugh at Fletch's nerdish, failed masculinity, and, in the process, Claydon's parallels to the 'neurotic' filmmaker, said to be 'obsessing and addictively playing with [his penis]' ('Mrs. Jessica Praveen Menon', The Angry Lesbians, n.d.).

Fletch's (and Claydon's) *Star Wars* fantasy, and the emasculation that this causes, resonates throughout the film. Indeed, 'impotence', and the reality of being unable to 'perform' when necessary, is another one of *Lesbian Vampire Killers'* running gags, and repeatedly functions to allegorise typical feminist criticism of lads' magazines, and subsequent criticism of cult film fandom. For example, at the beginning of the film, when we first meet Fletch, he is immediately sacked from his job as a children's party clown by his sexy and assertive female boss. He also repeatedly fails to 'score' with women despite his best efforts, or even appeal to the desirable virgin of the tale, Lotte, who he aims to deflower during their 'end-of-the-world' scenario as the vampires surround the cottage. Moreover, later in the film, when he swings a condom filled with holy water with confidence (in recollection of a gun-slinging cowboy), it pops *prematurely in his hand*, and he is forced to run away from the sexually confident vampires in embarrassment. (By this point he has already come clean with the vicar and admitted that the reason why he brought so many condoms in the first place was not because he truly anticipated having sex, but, rather, he and Jimmy were due to have a water-bomb fight.) Moreover, Jimmy, despite being the conventional hero figure of the narrative, is repeatedly unable to personify the Knight in Shining Armour and fulfil stereotypical 'hero' duties, such as running and breaking through locked doors. In fact, he is repetitively upstaged by Lotte, who can open the doors with one kick ('I must have weakened it,' Jimmy bashfully exclaims). Indeed, Jimmy's 'impotence' is fully allegorised when the only way he can open a door is with the assistance of *a long piece of hard wood*.

Lesbian Vampire Killers, then, for all the criticisms it has received (and all the poor jokes that it makes), remains an intriguing examination of the classic British horror film and surrounding fan cultures. Claydon, by presenting himself as a fan in the paratextual material that accompanies the DVD, complicates any straightforward reading of the film as an exercise in sexism. At once engaging with, and enjoying, cult films of the past, the film works to expose and critique the ways and means by which male cult fans have been theorised, and how cult films have been appropriated for mainstream consumption. Through being a self-aware film, it serves as a trump of the conventional cinematic mainstream, upholding what many perceive to be the cult of masculinity, but also criticising it, opening itself up to a variety of readings (but mostly beating us to it).

PISSED-OFF, MAN-HATING, FEMINIST CANNIBALS: *DOGHOUSE*

'Not very "P. C." is it?' (Neil, *Doghouse*)

Jake West's *Doghouse* was released in cinemas within three months of *Lesbian Vampire Killers* in the UK, and was expectedly subjected to a number of comparisons by reviewers. The main one was that, while the film seemed to be striving to be the next *Shaun of the Dead* by pitching a group of city lads against a village of zombies, it instead – and to the film's supposed detriment – ended up 'being another *Lesbian Vampire Killers*' (Powlson 2009: 21). In adopting a similarly low-cultural status to Claydon's movie due to its laddish sensibilities, *Doghouse* was a successful realisation of the niche appeal that *Lesbian Vampire Killers* would likely have had in its original direct-to-DVD incarnation. Unlike Claydon's film, which, as we have seen, signified an uneasy straddling of the cult/mainstream audience, *Doghouse* had a smaller theatrical run but its audience firmly in its sight: the profoundly male fan base of lead actor Danny Dyer, and the profoundly male audience of the low-budget horror film.

Dyer, whose most prominent work was in partnership with *enfant terrible* Nick Love, had a controversial and highly marketable public image specifically within the British DVD market (Falk 2012; Godfrey and Walker 2015), while director Jake West was known among British horror audiences for his cult debut *Razor Blade Smile* in 1998, his gory comedy *Evil Aliens* in 2005 and his subsequent work with his cult film/documentary production/distribution company Nucleus Films.[33] This marriage, I contend, allowed West, alongside screenwriter Dan Schaffer (who was known in cult circles for his horror comic series *Dogwitch*), to parody the assumptions generated by those stereotypes associated with the masculinity of cult and the cult of masculinity. By positioning *Doghouse* as a 'battle-of-the-sexes' story, in which a group of thirty-something lads fight against what Dyer's character terms a group of 'pissed off man-hating, feminist cannibals' (or 'Zombirds'), West and Schaffer offered up a narrative that worked to provoke criticism, while also offering some of its own.

Similar to *Lesbian Vampire Killers*, *Doghouse* has a pronounced and direct address to fans of cult and horror cinema. Indeed, at the time of its release, the film had much in common with the majority of other horror films being produced in the UK: low commercial aspirations, 'video nasty'-type allusions and an emphasis placed on 'male appeal' through visceral visual effects and crude jokes.[34] Yet West and Schaffer, despite being aware that the material chimed with many laddish stereotypes – such as a 'boyish gang mentality' (Whelehan 2000: 64) – were also cautious not to completely homogenise the men of the story.

One way of doing this was to disperse unique character quirks among the group: Neil (Danny Dyer) is the typical laddish chauvinist; Matt (Lee Ingleby) is a nerdy comic-book geek; Vince (Stephen Graham) is a broken man going through a divorce; Mikey (Noel Clarke) has a hard exterior but is the most wimpish of the group; Graham (Emil Marwa) is a 'cockney hard man' but is also against stereotype and openly gay; and Patrick (Keith-Lee Castle) is having a mid-life crisis (and listens to therapy tapes to cope with his insecurities). Whereas the group are shown to all have laddish vices (they all have the *Match of the Day* theme as their ring tones, and prioritise the pub over anything else), West avoided pandering to stereotypes too much, by not fully casting male actors only associated with, say, direct-to-DVD action cinema (as would later happen with subsequent Danny Dyer vehicles such as the horror films *Devil's Playground* and *The Last Seven* (Imran Naqvi, 2010)). After all, for all that Danny Dyer (rarely taken seriously by the press)[35] leads the company and can thus be read as the film's central 'star draw', other central roles in the film such as those of Noel Clarke and Stephan Graham – of *Kidulthood* (Menhaj Huda, 2006) and *This Is England*, respectively – hint towards a more 'serious', varied and credible market than the disparaged low-budget crime/hooligan/horror crowd. As West argues in the documentary that accompanies the UK DVD release, the casting of Dyer was seen as an opportunity to utilise his 'hard-man' persona, and to thus parody how the media frequently portrayed him as 'Jack the lad' following his most famous role as a football hooligan in *The Football Factory*, and his job as agony uncle for *Zoo* magazine. Dyer's character Neil, thus, is referred to by the lads as a 'throw back' who 'hasn't evolved properly'. By the same token, the lads also jokingly refer to him as the 'misogynist Neanderthal arsehole we all know and love', as if self-reflexively hat-tipping Dyer's fan base (who have remained loyal regardless of the critical response to his films) and to vocal film critics who 'love to hate' him.[36] Thus, by utilising Dyer's media persona similarly to how Whelehan defines the conventional New Lad – as 'part soccer-thug, part lager-lout, part arrant sexist' (2000: 58) – and by figuring this personality within a B-movie horror film narrative alongside other male 'types' and character actors, West exploited audience and fan knowledge to subvert expectation and underscore the film's ironic, jovial intentions.

Doghouse is thus centred on two parallel journeys: the literal journey for the lads from city to country (that resonates with countless seminal horror films from *The Texas Chain Saw Massacre* to *The Evil Dead*),[37] and also the journey for the audience, from expectation to subversion. Along the way, cult cinema, its audience, and associated stereotypes, are affectionately acknowledged and lampooned.

West is quick to establish the kinds of ways that *Doghouse* is going to engage with horror cinema formalisms and surrounding masculinist discourses. The first way this is achieved is by establishing that *Doghouse* is a 'Jake West' film in the opening credits, and that he, as director, is in firm control of the proceedings, and that the audience should be familiar with what this means. West literalises this element of 'control' through the use of the hired bus that takes the cast to the village of Moodley, where the women are said to 'outnumber the men 4:1', and where the lads hope to 'pull', get drunk and help Vince get over his recent divorce. Across the side of the bus, 'West Tours' is emblazoned, followed by 'private hire', as though to suggest that a particularly niche (cult?) experience awaits both lads, and the equally willing spectator (see Figure 4.3).

Indeed, Moodley itself is, in many ways, positioned as a metaphor for the obscurity and exclusivity of cult film fandom's male saturation. It is 'off the beaten track' and, as Patrick laments, is 'in the middle of fucking nowhere'. Crucially, it is geographically *and* figuratively far away from London and the mainstream mode of thought that the city represents. Indeed, back in the city, women dominate and carry out traditional male roles (they are the butchers,

Figure 4.3   West Tours: Jake West, the director of *Doghouse* and a number of other horror movies, hints to audiences that they are about to embark on a familiar journey.

the taxi-drivers, the pub landlords). Moreover, each one of the lads is shown to be in a tumultuous relationship with unreasonable and demanding spouses (including the boyfriend of Graham, who is overtly camp; 'No girls allowed!' Graham exclaims, as he leaves for Moodley). With all its promises of sex and booze, Moodley is initially positioned as a space of male escape – a place where male dominance and control can temporarily prevail beyond the rules of a 'progressive' society that has increasingly marginalised men. It represents a space where the lads will be able to call the shots, and successfully obtain the pleasures that the city/contemporary mainstream society will not permit. Indeed, Neil confiscates all of the lads' mobile phones at the start of the trip, so that their partners back in London cannot contact them and spoil their good time. As Neil exclaims: '"Getting away from it" does not include spousal abuse via T-Mobile.' The lads literally become unreachable from the social mainstream and – as far as this film is concerned, at least – its matriarchal associations.

However, this inaccessibility is not, it turns out, as desirable as the lads initially had hoped. As considered earlier in this chapter, one of the most prominent ideas in Hollows's theory of the masculinity of cult is the exclusion of women, and an overpowering 'hardness of cult' that guarantees limited/ no female involvement. Moodley, however, functions as a subversion of this, whereby the anticipated 'loose women' that Neil desires and expects there to be – who could quite easily be read as the typically objectified women of cult cinema and fanzine culture – have mutated into the personification of castration anxiety. Shrieking, monstrous and savage the so-called Zombirds of the film are, for the purposes of the narrative, a concentrated dose of radical feminism. They have infiltrated the male space, and are seeking to punish the men for their social wrongs.

One of these 'wrongs' is 'fandom' itself, and is realised through the character of Matt, the only character in the film not shown to be in (or to ever have been in) a sexual relationship. Expectedly, he is typed as the 'nerd', 'geek' or 'anorak' typically associated with horror film fans (Cherry 2002: 44), and is introduced to the spectator defending the merits of a comic book to a twelve-year-old boy in the comic store where he works. He resonates with the confessed fan identities of both West and Schaffer as both a comic book nerd (Schaffer is a recognised comic-book writer and illustrator) and horror fan (the comic book he defends is an adaptation of *The Evil Dead*), while his virginal aspects are drawn on to generate humour. For instance, a life-size mannequin of a bride is displayed in the shop window, which the twelve-year-old mockingly refers to as his 'missus', and that prompts Matt to throw the boy out of his shop. That Matt's only contact with a woman is presumed to be a mannequin symbolically dressed in wedding whites, suggests, first, that his fandom is a turn-off to 'real' women, but also, that his idea of womanhood and relationships is bound to notions of patriarchal submission that the static, expressionless bride, symbolises. Certainly, the threat of female rejection of the fan that Matt embodies is hinted at later in the film when, upon first arriving at Moodley, he glances in a shop window and notices that mummified penises are being sold alongside the contemporary British horror cult item the *Best Of Weird World* videotape, which is a reference to the fictional TV show *Weird World* that features in Jake West's *Evil Aliens*. The implication is that cult film fan practices and intertextuality are somehow bound to, or can successfully be overcome by, castration/female control.

This is not to suggest that the film is setting out to condemn fannish behaviour. Indeed, part of the 'fun' of *Doghouse* is the acknowledgement that certain male and female stereotypes are being parodied, but also, that the audience's textual desires are going to be indulged. Indeed, towards the end of the film, as Matt and Vince take cover from a gang of Zombirds in a toyshop, the audience are invited to appreciate fandom vicariously through the characters. In one instance, regardless of the life-threatening circumstance he faces, Matt becomes immediately preoccupied with a boxed, and highly collectable, action figure from his youth, as though reminding the audience of the pleasures and importance of cult nostalgia. Indeed, Matt's and Vince's guarding of the toyshop would imply that fandom is *worth* defending – in this instance, with a toy light sabre brandished by Vince – even if it does occasionally distract from the more pressing social concerns beyond it. Moreover, the general horrors that unfold for all of the lads in Moodley, which includes fingers being cut off, heads exploding, disembowelling and people being shot, are also factors of visceral horror cinema and special effects that command great interest, discussion and adoration among fan audiences (Jancovich 2008 [2002]: 155). As such, the gender binary of the film is subverted, as it is presumed that the men in the audience will enjoy seeing their supposed comrades being killed off and/or attacked in a variety of gory and technically impressive ways.

Perhaps the ultimate subversion of this comes through the casting of scream queen Emily Booth as the scissor-wielding, ex-hairdresser Zombird, The Snipper. A former glamour model who would come to be known among horror fans as an attractive, knowledgeable horror enthusiast and media personality, Booth usually appeared in British horror films in an erotic capacity, and was often featured in sex scenes (as in *Pervirella*, *Cradle of Fear* and *Evil Aliens*). In *Doghouse*, however, The Snipper is the ultimate grotesque subversion of Booth's cult identity. Part of the fun is recognising that the repugnant Snipper *is* in actuality the beautiful Emily Booth, and that her traditional natural glamour has been surrendered for – in terms of the horror fan spectator, the presumably more satisfactory – special effects make-up. To this end, the casting of Booth works as a hat-tip to the ways that laddish fanboys are often framed as being driven by phallic urges, but that, as earlier in the toyshop, fandom (and male sexual incompetence) will always be prioritised.[38] Indeed, by the end of the film, when the remaining lads recognise that they will never be able to destroy the Zombirds (and all that they represent), the lads instead run from them, with beaming smiles on their faces. The lads recognise that, while they came to Moodley for booze and sex, they, like the supposed fanboy spectator, are happy to count their blessings, reject responsibility and revel in the gory horror instead (Figure 5.3).

At this point, it is important not to understate that *Doghouse*, for all its sophistication, will never appear all that ironic and self-aware to everyone. However, this is not to understate the refined way it navigates horror film culture, and the stereotypes of masculinity that are associated with it. *Doghouse*, thus, is a testament to British horror in the early twenty-first century: a genre that knew its audience, and could afford to push boundaries in a way that, as *Lesbian Vampire Killers* proved, would not always work in the mainstream. Because it had its core audience in its sight, *Doghouse* had artistic licence to exacerbate critiques that were very close to home, and have fun with the genre and a culture that has been condemned for its exclusivity. In doing this, the film could comment on its own niche, and, in doing so, make fun of itself, its audience who enjoy it, and those who cannot stand it.

Conclusion

By textual analysing notable horror-comedies *Shaun of the Dead*, *Lesbian Vampire Killers* and *Doghouse*, this chapter has considered how fan stereotypes, and the critiques that have been aimed at them by the academy elsewhere, were satirised and parodied in British horror cinema after 2000.

The stereotypes that surround such discourses were shown to be linked to the New Lad of the 1990s, which has subsequently been read in relation to cult film practises that are gendered masculine, to the ultimate exclusion of women. I have argued, through a detailed consideration of those theories that have surrounded fan culture in the past, and have lambasted the so-called 'masculinity of cult' and 'cult of masculinity' associated with this, that British horror-comedies offered sophisticated critiques of fans, horror filmmakers, the genre's limited male audience and the criticisms that the genre had been seen to face at the turn of the millennium. But rather than claim that films such as *Lesbian Vampire Killers* and *Doghouse* simply sought to affirm these stereotypes, I have also revealed how the films were willing to satirise their own low-cultural status. *Shaun of the Dead*, I suggested, did this in a way that suppressed its cultness, through its appeal to a broader audience base, and its romantic-comedy narrative. *Lesbian Vampire Killers*, however, was revealed as a film that trumped the mainstream expectation that *Shaun of the Dead* had created, managing to retain all of the niche jokes, gags and satire of its original incarnation as a low-budget, direct-to-DVD movie. Finally, *Doghouse* was shown, through the utilisation of cult actors such as Danny Dyer, and more respectable actors such as Stephen Graham and Noel Clarke, to provocatively kick against those dismissive of marginal cult films, and subvert expectation. More, by casting the likes of Emily Booth, and by being very self-reflexive in terms of its allusions to cult films and fan cultures (specifically through the character of Matt), its makers were prepared to acknowledge and critique their own shortcomings and insecurities.

NOTES

1. As Blake argues 'Sarah [in *The Descent*] has been rendered truly monstrous' (2008: 182), which is a reading also shared with James Rose (2009). Moreover, G. Christopher Williams (2007) has suggested that *28 Days Later* is profoundly neo-liberal in its representation of women, and that Boyle, in trying to make the character of Selena strong in the main narrative of the film, renders her a 'mother' figures in the final moments, thus making any radical comment redundant.
2. Statistics are provided for UK audiences, below.
3. It should be noted at this point that, as Gauntlett perceptively discusses, men's life-style 'magazines differ quite a lot: *Loaded* celebrates watching football with a few beers, for example, but the *Men's Health* reader would forgo the drink, and play the game himself. *FHM* encourages quality sex, but *Nuts* and *Zoo* might be more interested in quantity' (2008: 170). Nevertheless, a stereotype of the lad haunts society and post-feminist literature, while Gauntlett, regardless of his accuracy, remains in the minority.
4. Whelehan argues that what she calls 'the new irony makes it difficult to object to anything' (2000: 68), continuing, that, 'as long as the message is intended as a "joke" no one can touch you for it' (69).
5. Johannes Roberts has discussed the communal nature of British horror filmmakers, and the advice they are happy to give one another when approaching different

projects: 'That's the good thing about horror people: they are, by and large, very nice people' (Roberts 2010b).

6. For a discussion of 'feminised' mainstream 'cults' see Click (2009) and Bode (2010).

7. David Pirie does not discuss horror-comedy. Moreover, Blake does not acknowledge *Shaun of the Dead* as a horror comedy, but groups it with other films, as if its humour does not in any way alter its audience address or tone.

8. Consider *The Descent*, *28 Days Later* and *The Devil's Chair* as solid examples of this.

9. The self-aware tagline for *Loaded* is 'for men who should know better'.

10. The first UKFC statistical yearbook discussed films from 2002, although it was not until a year later, in the 2003/4 book, that they started to consider genre preference by gender (see UKFC 2004: 41).

11. I am taking into account films such as *The Mummy: Tomb of the Dragon Emperor* (Rob Cohen, 2008) and *Hellboy II: The Golden Army* (Guillermo del Toro, 2008), which the UKFC classify as action-led films, but that also contain elements that would be familiar to a horror-going audience (2009: 116). The same can be said of the werewolf/vampire film *Underworld*, although it could also be easily placed alongside films such as *X2* (Bryan Singer, 2003) and *The Matrix: Revolutions* (The Wachowski Brothers, 2003): films that are also described as 'action-led' with a 69 per cent male audience share (UKFC 2004: 41). This is also true of Spielberg's remake of *War of the Worlds* (2005), and Peter Jackson's *King Kong* (2005) remake, whose UK audiences were made up of 60 per cent male and 62 per cent male, respectively (UKFC 2006: 54).

12. 'Action-led' was the UKFC's – and is now the BFI's – preferred turn of phrase when referring to traditionally 'male' genres like the action film, the thriller, science-fiction and horror.

13. *Dodgeball* (Rawson Marshall Thurber, 2004) was another.

14. Romantic comedies continue to be targets for feminist critics, although they remain most popular with female audiences. Hilary Radner (2011) discusses these issues at length in her book *Neo-Feminist Cinema: Girly Films, Chick Flicks and Consumer Culture*.

15. On the directors' commentary to the UK DVD, Wright and Pegg list a multitude of films as inspirations, including *Dawn of the Dead*, *Zombie Flesh-Eaters*, *Halloween* (John Carpenter, 1978), *An American Werewolf in London* (John Landis, 1981) and *Army of Darkness* (Sam Raimi, 1992).

16. *Samhain* was a rival fanzine to the more popular *The Dark Side* in the UK in the 1990s. *Scream* and *Shock Horror* are newer publications, having risen from the ashes of the recently cancelled *Gorezone* (not to be confused with the American *Fangoria* spin-off of the same name).

17. A parallel can be drawn here between horror and British 'hooligan' film. As Rehling argues, 'most films target the youth markets, well versed in postmodern culture and less versed in the labor movement, a strategy that proved to be a winning formula with *Trainspotting* (1996) and gangster films like *Snatch*' (2011: 163).

18. It is not my intention to presume that all horror fans are of this laddish ilk: this would be reductive. As for evidence to the contrary, in a public discussion that broke out online regarding *Gorezone*'s alleged 'sexism', one reader said, 'I don't like that you assume that all horror fans want to see bikinied up girls flaunting it around. I'm a red-blooded male gorehound who loves the ladies, but when I pick up a horror magazine I want to read about what gory flicks are coming soon and about classic genre flicks that get our jugulars pumping' (Carruthers 2010).

19. In spite of *Gorezone*'s proclamation on its cover that it is '*Vogue* for horror fans', thus pertaining to a certain 'highbrow' sensibility.
20. The petition read: 'I'm saying no to the movie: "Lesbian Vampire Killers". A movie shamelessly catering to men's girl-on-girl fantasies' (The Angry Lesbians, n.d.).
21. Until 2013 *The Dark Side* offered low-budget producer Jonathan Sothcott (the owner of Black and Blue Films, who produced hybrid horrors with a certain laddish appeal – see Chapter 2) a regular column every month, while *Gorezone* featured a column by Nigel Wingrove, owner of British horror video label Redemption films (and affiliates Jezebel, Purgatory and Salvation).
22. This release strategy is discussed in some detail in Chapter 2.
23. Titles appeared with some immediacy, including *Killer Bitch* (Liam Galvin, 2010) and *Big Fat Gypsy Gangster* (Ricky Grover, 2011).
24. The theatrical trailer for *Doghouse* displays a positive review by a *Zoo* critic, and the UK DVD cover for *Lesbian Vampire Killers* shows *Nuts* having given the film 'four stars'.
25. *Doghouse* was released in ninety-nine cinemas and grossed £56,500. *Lesbian Vampire Killers* was released in 362 cinemas and grossed a disappointing £1.5m (http://imdb.com/pro).
26. A lot of this has to do with the rise in popularity of the Internet, although Horvath *et al.*'s (2012) recent study, which seeks to bogusly align the rhetoric of lads' mags with rapists' testimonies, unusually draws examples from the magazines themselves, not their online content.
27. *Zombie Women of Satan* in particular strives to target the highly niche market of those who regularly attend Burlesque and Cabaret Clubs. Moreover, the film has a particularly localised appeal to the North East of England. Warren Speed, the director, is local stand-up comedian in the Durham area, and is the owner of the Burlesque Club where a lot of the film was shot.
28. In the interest of clarity, 'fanny', in the British context, is a slang term for 'vagina'.
29. So negative was the response to the film that *BBC News* collated some of the most severe on its website, along with the only positive press review from *The Sun*'s anonymous reviewer, The Sneak (see Anon. 2009a).
30. As one petition-signee argued: 'James Corden is a talentless pig, I have always thought and known this and this film plainly confirms my suspicions' ('Mr. Phil Brand', The Angry Lesbians, n.d.).
31. They effectively did the opposite to what the original producer, Vic Bateman (before he left the project), had advised his directors in the past: 'Make films for an audience, not for yourself' (Bateman cited in Waters 2006).
32. This was made clear by Hammer's decision to use Myspace as a spring board for their re-launch – with the web serial *Beyond the Rave* – rather than securing *Lesbian Vampire Killers* for distribution as it has originally planned (see Jones 2010 and Chapter 6).
33. West had made a name for himself providing special features for various DVD distributors. His best work up to this point was, perhaps, his documentary about the making of the *Phantasm* (1979–98) franchise, *Phatasmagoria* (2005), which was included in the US and UK box set from Anchor Bay Entertainment.
34. In her analysis of female audiences for horror cinema, Brigid Cherry recognises that 'gore' is one of the main aspects of the genre that puts women off (2002: 181–2).
35. For a discussion of Danny Dyer's presence in exploitation cinema and the typical press reaction to his work, see Hunter (2013: 160–1, 170–5) and Godfrey and Walker (2015).
36. British film critic Mark Kermode, for example, has rarely said anything complementary about Danny Dyer on his BBC radio review show. In fact, Kermode is

well-known for his high-pitched grotesque impersonation of Dyer, which has encouraged Dyer to respond in his autobiography, and accuse Kermode of elitism and class-bashing (2010: 236).
37. I further explore the city/country binary in relation to the hoodie horror cycle in Chapter 5.
38. Indeed, in the lead up to the release of the film, Booth's reputation as a cover girl for the lads' mag *Front*, and surrounding horror fanzines, was deliberately circumvented on the cover of *Gorezone* magazine, where she appeared in full Zombird make-up.

5. HEARTLESS HOODIES

From 6 until 10 August 2011 several English cities endured what is thought to have been the most significant social riots since those of Brixton, Birmingham and Toxteth in 1981, and Broadwater Farm in 1985 (Bloom 2012: 101). Beginning as a protest in Tottenham in response to a supposed race-related fatal police shooting of an alleged gang member, the initially peaceful demonstration soon spiralled into attacks on officers by gangs and opportunists. Rioting, violence and looting rapidly spread through England: first within the surrounding boroughs of London, and gradually throughout the Midlands (Tyler 2013: 179).[1]

Whereas some have recognised that the 'August Riots' were 'political' and that they symbolised the plight of 'disenfranchised young people' in poverty-stricken areas (180), for others they represented a climax to already prevalent anxieties regarding alleged ruptures in the UK's social and moral fabric. Indeed, since 2004, the media and the government had frequently lamented what was purported to be a rise in street gang culture and 'knife crime'. These phenomena were typically framed as results of the negative attitudes and anti-social actions of what right-wing scholar Charles Murray (1990) once recognised as a burgeoning 'underclass', which Imogen Tyler has summarised as 'an adjunct class divorced from the body politic proper' (2013: 184), and that has often been written about in terms of its excessiveness and abjection, a perceived unwillingness to work for a living, and having a taste for violence (Tyler 2013: 184). As was the case in the news reportage following the August Riots, young – largely working-class – people were often blamed for this downward turn, and were codified by the 'uniform' of sportswear and identity-concealing hooded sweatshirts.

The hooded youths in question – or 'hoodies' as they came to be known – and the threat of social disruption that they signified, were said by the press, the government and others to be products of 'broken Britain'.[2] According to Conservative Prime Minister David Cameron in the wake of the Riots, 'broken Britain' constituted a country divided by conflicting morals, where 'people [show] indifference to right and wrong ... people with a twisted moral code. . .people with a complete absence of self-restraint' (Cameron cited in Stratton 2011). If such rhetoric were to be believed – and this kind of attitude was certainly prevalent across the entire media spectrum – Britain had entered a period of unruliness and terror, and was desperately in need of repair.

This is the social context from which the films of this chapter, the 'hoodie horror' cycle, emerged. From about the year 2008, hoodie horrors such as *Eden Lake*, *Heartless*, *Cherry Tree Lane*, *F*, *Community*, *Comedown* (Menhaj Huda, 2012) and *Citadel* (Ciaran Foy, 2012) would allegorise social anxieties surrounding the perceived 'decline' in respect and morality of British young people, by presenting hooded youths of the underclass as monstrous antagonists. An exception to the rule was Joe Cornish's science-fiction comedy *Attack the Block*, in which the hoodies are 'goodies' (Virtue 2011). Yet, in most cases, hoodie horror films were deliberately inflammatory, and would often evince a moralistic binary similar to that purported by politicians and the news media between feral hoodies and the well-to-do middle classes. In other cases, films presented hoodies as symbols of rifts within an otherwise 'good' working-class community. However, irrespective of narrative specificities, the hoodie figure was always demonised (and in some instances would be quite literally portrayed as 'demonic'). The films in question, therefore, have prescient social resonances that are worth unpacking and examining in some detail.

This chapter therefore examines the hoodie horror cycle in light of its engagement with hot-button social issues in the lead up to the August Riots. First, the chapter will locate the cycle amid other trends in British popular cinema. Second, it will move on to examine the specific ways that hoodies were represented in hoodie horror films, and question what the implications of these representations are in regard to the ways that the contemporary working classes have been portrayed in the national media. Finally, the chapter will examine the settings of a number of hoodie horror films, to show how specific locales have been invoked across the cycle to convey the supposed pervasiveness of monstrous youths in the real world.

HOODIES AND CONTEMPORARY BRITISH CINEMA

Unemployment. Social deprivation. Youth gangs. Crime. Domestic violence. Inner-city council estates.

Throughout the 1990s, 2000s and 2010s such things were regularly invoked in news reports about the underclass. But these elements were also a stone's throw away from many British films. Indeed, the disenfranchised working-class bodies that populated the daily news in many ways complemented what Claire Monk (2000b) has termed the cycle of 'underclass films' of the 1990s, such as *Trainspotting* and *Twin Town* (Kevin Allen, 1997), which 'drew their subject or subtext from the problems of unemployment and social exclusion' (Monk 2000b: 274), as well as 1980s/1990s British social realism that, as John Hill has noted, focused on 'unemployment and poverty', 'the frailty of the family' and 'petty criminality, alcoholism and domestic violence' (2000a: 252–3). Yet, whereas Hill has noted that films of the social-realist tradition are typically sympathetic to the social context of their working-class pro-tagonists, and that 'familial conflicts are not simply [portrayed as] the result of personal and moral shortcomings' (2000a: 253), the hoodie horrors were often discussed by the press as lacking a sympathetic outlook for their protago-nists (Graham 2009). Unlike the kinds of films that Claire Monk identifies, the hoodie horror films were never *celebratory* of underclass life; nor were they marketed, à la *Trainspotting*, 'to suggest an affinity with young British style and creative culture' in any positive sense (Monk 2000b: 276). Instead, the marketing of hoodie horror films typically used the style of the hoodie to underscore the disparity and otherness of underclass youth, presenting hooded figures in a variety of intimidating ways (some of which I consider, below). Indeed, for all that the hoodie horror films hat-tipped social realism, many would take their lead primarily from apocalyptic press reportage in the wake of broken Britain,[3] and would thus resonate less with the films of Ken Loach and more with contemporaneous 'end-of-the-world' horror and science-fiction narratives such as *28 Days Later* and *Monsters*, or older monstrous youth films such as *The Omen* (Richard Donner, 1976) and *Village of the Damned* (Wolf Rilla, 1960). Yet, whereas the horrors of these films were alien and oth-erworldly – rage-infected zombie creatures, extra-terrestrials, the Anti-Christ and well-spoken alien children, respectively – the hoodies, due to their media currency, embodied a threat that was positioned as being much more tangible and in closer proximity. Indeed, as the tagline for the film *Community* read: 'the horror is coming to your neighborhood'.

Below, I discuss in more detail the ways that hoodie horror films sought to merge social realist and horror film iconography, while also considering how the fusing of 'realism' with 'horror' affected the cycle's perceived ability to make informed social comment. However, at this point, it is worth discussing briefly why hoodies, as ubiquitous media constructs, were deemed fitting for the milieu of a horror film, and how their presentation differed from their 'realist' counterparts.

HOODIES AND HORROR CINEMA

> These days, the scariest Britflick villain isn't a flesh-eating zombie, or an East End Mr Big with a sawn-off shooter and a tattooed sidekick. It is a teenage boy with a penchant for flammable casualwear. (Graham 2009)

The term 'hoodie' entered the British vernacular in light of growing class antagonisms surrounding the phenomenon of the 'chav' in the early 2000s. 'Chav' has been defined as 'an insulting word exclusively directed against the working class' (Jones 2011: 2) and, as Hayward and Yar recognise, it 'has always been connected with communities who have experienced social deprivation in one form or another' (Hayward and Yar 2006: 16). In the 2000s, the image of the 'chav' was appropriated in popular film and TV as grotesque, and was said to trigger feelings of disgust among the middle classes. This reaction, Imogen Tyler has noted, was 'intimately bound up with, and authorized by, comedy and the community forming power of laughter' in TV shows such as *Little Britain* (2003–6) and *Shameless* (2004–13) (2008: 30; see also Baker 2009), and in British comedy cinema, such as *Sex Lives of the Potato Men* (Andy Humphries, 2004) and *Fat Slags* (Ed Bye, 2004) (Hunter 2012: 167–8). The term 'hoodie' functioned similarly to 'chav' in press discourse, but was typically directed more towards working-class *youth* instead of the class in its entirety (Bawden 2009a). Furthermore, while 'chav' was used mostly to *mock* the working class, 'hoodie' was employed in the media to generate *fear*. According to research carried out by Echo Research Inc (Bawden 2009b), 'hoodie' was the fifth most popular word used by journalists to describe young boys in reports that were 'unrelentingly negative' (alongside the other disparaging terms: 'yobs', 'thugs', 'sick', 'feral', 'louts', 'heartless', 'evil', 'frightening', 'scum', 'monsters', 'inhuman' and 'threatening'). As Owen Jones would later explain, '[n]othing sums up the blight of anti-social behaviour in the minds of many than teenage gangs wearing hoodies and loitering menacingly on street corners' (2011: 212), while Joanne Turney would note, that

> the hoodie . . . appears to represent a clear distinction between wearers and the moral majority; it became a sign of attitude and conformity to social stereotypes surrounding the problem of youth, but more importantly a signifier of moral decline, ASBO [Anti-social Behaviour Order] culture and a general social downward turn. (Turney 2009: 126)

Significantly, 'hoodie' would be employed by the media not just in reference to the garment of clothing (the hoodie itself), but also the person wearing it. Therefore, it was not uncommon for wearers of hooded sweatshirts to be referred to *as* 'hoodies' in media discourse, as means of anonymising and homogenising groups of disenfranchised young people and to emphasise their non-human otherness. As the *Sunday Express* reported on 30 March 2008:

> Gangs of hoodies are bringing terror to our streets, menacing communities, instilling fear and putting at risk the peaceful way most of us want to be allowed to live our lives. (Murry *et al.* 2008)

The responses that the hoodies in question were deemed to evoke here – especially in terms of the *Express* report – would seem to *demand* comparisons with the audience of the horror film and how, as a 'body genre' (Williams 1991), horror is thought to command corporeal reactions that are triggered by the instilling of emotions such as fear and disgust in the spectator (Carroll 1990: 24–7). Hoodies were thus posited in news reportage as uncanny and 'impure' monsters not unlike ghosts, werewolves or vampires – that as Noël Carroll has it, offer a collusion between the 'living *and* dead' (1990: 43; emphasis in original). After all, it was not uncommon for the hoodie to be used in reports to signify death itself, as journalists drew parallels with the Grim Reaper and the Four Horsemen of the Apocalypse (McLean 2005). Moreover, the moral binary advanced by the news media at this time, between good/evil and us/them, recalled countless folk tales, as well as modern horror stories and films, with hoodies being portrayed in an array of antagonistic and terrifying ways. It was only a matter of time before the horror producers would jump on the hoodie band wagon.

Towards a hoodie horror cycle

As with any film cycle, hoodie horror films are difficult to neatly collate, and when attempting to do so, one must allow for considerable generic overlap. After all, for all the term's ubiquity in film criticism, no 'hoodie horror' film is the same, and the term has been employed to describe films as disparate as coming-of-age movies such as *Summer Scars* (Julian Richards, 2007); revenge thrillers such as *Harry Brown* (Daniel Barber, 2009); films that simply have young working-class protagonists such as *Donkey Punch*; films in which *middle-class* children are the threat, such as *The Children* (Tom Shankland, 2008); and films like *The Reeds* (Nick Cohen, 2010), *Travellers* (Kris McManus, 2011) and *Outcast* that do not engage with the threat of hoodies at all, but rather a fear of gypsy culture (a culture that has mediated mythos, and associated prejudices, all its own).[4]

In spite of the hoodie horror cycle's lack of coherence, its beginnings can be comfortably traced to the mid-2000s, and the release of the controversial art film *The Great Ecstasy of Robert Carmichael* (Thomas Clay, 2005). This film was widely reported on by the press upon its release in 2005 because of its final scene, which depicts – over a thirteen-minute static shot – the brutal rape and murder of a middle-class couple by a trio of working-class boys.[5] The same year, another controversial 'working-class' film, the violent hooligan opus *The Football Factory*, was released, in which lead actor Danny Dyer (who also featured in *The Great Ecstasy of Robert Carmichael*) is plagued by nightmarish visions of his teenage – and hooded! – former self. However, while both of these films had visibility at home and in international markets, none had an obvious impact on the horror genre per se: *Great Ecstasy* remained a curious – if unpleasant – one-off, while *The Football Factory* comparatively started a cycle of successful football hooligan films (see Rehling 2011).

The British hoodie horror cycle, thus, owed more to the themes and style of the 2006 French/Romanian horror film *Ils* (Xavier Palud and David Moreau). With a plot similar to the hoodie horror *par excellence*, *Eden Lake*,[6] *Ils* tells of a school teacher and her husband who are terrorised by shadowy figures who are revealed, in the film's closing moments, to be wayward youths.[7] This film is significant to the genesis of the hoodie horror cycle because it was released amid a boom in new European horror films such as *Haute Tension* and *Calvaire*, which James Watkins (the director of *Eden Lake*) and Johannes Roberts (the director of *F*) would go on to cite as having inspired them (Jones 2009; Walker 2011). Yet, the British films that were produced in the wake of *Ils* differed from the French/Romanian film in two main ways. First, British hoodie horrors tended to establish from the outset that youths were to be the source of the horror: signified, for example, by a teacher having a bust up with a student in *F*, or by the protagonists listening to news reports about youth run wild, as in *Eden Lake* and *Heartless*. Second, in the trailers and advertising campaigns of many hoodie horrors, such as *F* and *Cherry Tree Lane*, the iconography of the menacing, hooded teenager, is made very apparent, and is in fact presented as a central marketing device. Comparatively, the UK quad for *Ils* focused mostly on shadowy figures and a close-up image of a frightened woman's eye and was, as a result, far more ambiguous. One can determine that partial reasoning for the hoodie being so central to the marketing of the British films was to capitalise on its contemporaneous cultural resonances (see Figure 5.1), which would attest, at least in part, to the currency of the stereotype in the popular imagination, and the power it was deemed to have by marketers in capturing the then-perceived interests of British filmgoers.

As a means of assessing the role and presentation of hoodies in hoodie horrors, the section that follows will take a close look at some specific examples. In the first instance I will consider the similarities in presentation in the

Figure 5.1   'No escape': a hoodie waits menacingly outside of a middle-class home in the UK quad poster for *Cherry Tree Lane*. © Metrodome Distributors Ltd.

films *Heartless* and *F*. Both films were released at about the same time and have rich stylistic and thematic parallels that are worth scrutinising. Following this I will consider the very different ways that the hoodies are portrayed in *Eden Lake* and *Cherry Tree Lane*.

REPRESENTING HOODIES

'Visual shorthand for "Broken Britain"': *Heartless* and *F*

In *Heartless* and *F* young people are presented as the catalyst that leads to the psychological downfall of the leading male characters. Thus, by pitching evil anti-social hoodies against morally sound and decent people, both films reflect contemporary concerns about broken Britain. So, in *Heartless*, the lead character Jamie (Jim Sturgess) is a likeable young photographer living in London's East End who faces daily humiliation from a gang of hoodies who torment him about the unsightly birth mark that covers half of his face. Throughout the film, as an assumed direct consequence of such torment, Jamie is plagued by psychological imaginings of feral hooded gangs, who have monstrous faces and razor-sharp teeth (see Figure 5.2). Similarly, in *F*, the main character Robert Anderson is a schoolteacher in North London who has to deal daily with obnoxious pupils. In the opening scene he is attacked for awarding one of them the 'F' grade of the film's title, which leads to Anderson being

Figure 5.2   A feral hoodie from *Heartless*.

suspended from work (the school wants to avoid a lawsuit from the pupil's parents). For the remainder of the film, his anxieties about being attacked again are literalised when he must defend his wayward daughter from a gang of murderous hoodies who break into the school after hours. In both films, the demonic hoodies pertain to the psychological 'demons' that torment Jamie and Anderson and, as such, can be read as signifying much broader (and reactionary) social concerns about young people.

For all that the films unquestionably seek to 'Other' the hoodies, their representations are, at times, conflicting. That is to say, there are moments when the hoodies are humanised (to some degree) and presented as typically troublesome, wayward kids who loiter in the streets, disrupt class and who shout, swear, play music too loud and consume alcohol under age. These representations may ring true as 'monstrous' in some sectors of British society, but these are not images of monstrosity comparable with, for instance, the crawlers in *The Descent* or the Zom-Birds in *Doghouse*. Rather, it is precisely the prosaic typicality – that is to say the *familiarity* – of the youth in these films that lends such depictions tangibility, against which later images of supernatural monstrosity can be played out. In *F*, for example, the school's night staff first approach the hoodies' invasion of the school as nothing more than childish tinkering that can be combated with banal, everyday expressions such as 'Some of you children don't deserve to be in school', 'I've had it with you fucking kids!' and empty threats like 'You are in so much trouble!' Similarly, during one scene in *Heartless* an elderly man shouts out of his window to a gang listening to loud music, 'Turn that bloody music down! Don't you have any respect?' Through their facileness these instances underscore the commonplaceness of the hoodie subject, while also pointing towards society's inability to counteract it. The aforementioned scene in *Heartless* presents this implied normalcy perfectly. The kids are first captured in a long-shot so that their faces remain obscured, and, for the remainder of the scene, they remain off-screen. Only the faint sound of rap music and jovial banter is heard. The director Philip Ridley's creative decision to not focus on the gang emphasises the supposed cultural familiarity of the hoodies' behaviour. The gang of youths would not appear to *require* any characterisation at this stage because, it is implied, we already know what/who they are, and what behaviour to expect of them.

It is therefore of no little significance that, at the end of *Heartless*, the revelation is that the majority of the narrative has been an elaborate dream, and, crucially, that Jamie's imaginings have been directly influenced by a news item reporting gang violence that he watched early in the film. The news item in question reports the murder of a father and son by 'a gang of youths wearing hoods'. An interviewee at the scene explains how, a 'gang of kids came out of nowhere, setting the father and son on fire', and that they 'sounded like a bunch of wild animals . . . They were wearing these masks, these demon masks.' This dialogue evokes real-world reportage that claimed Britain's moral decline was being symptomatic of, to quote one journalist, 'wild packs of yobs' (Collins 2008: 5) and, to quote another, 'feral youths . . . running wild like a pack of wild animals' (Broadbent 2006: 9). Indeed, the hoodies that Jamie envisages for the rest of the film move in packs, shriek, and have sharp teeth like wild animals. They are, as Imogen Tyler has characterised the news reportage of the August Riots, '[f]rightening, surreal and carnivalesque' (2013: 180). And they are also – as was common in media reportage – positioned as a product of a society with weak family ties (see, for instance, Ware 2009). As the reporter in *Heartless* comments, 'Violence is their mother . . . Their father, chaos.' The hoodies in *Heartless*, by being aligned with ideas of a ubiquitous monstrosity, can therefore be construed, as journalist Fiona Bawden has argued of image of the hooded youth, as 'visual shorthand for "broken Britain"' (2009a: 2).

F is very similar to *Heartless* in the sense that the writer/director Johannes Roberts refrains offering hoodies detailed characterisation beyond their hooded garb and animalistic traits. As with Ridley's film, the hoodies of *F* possess a supernatural quality and are typically photographed at the edges of the frame or in the background, out of focus, or in long shots, lurking in the shadows. Significantly, their faces are fully blacked out, which works to personify their assumed lack of morals and compassion and, specifically, their identity, as the hoods obscure both their sex and nationality. They are invasive (they break windows, smash through doors), form a homogenous mass (they move in packs and are indistinguishable from one another), and, to borrow recent terminology used by journalists when describing the hoodie moral panic, they are presented as 'evil', 'frightening', 'inhuman' and 'threatening', and since their identity (and species) is never confirmed, they are also conveyed as 'monsters' (Garner 2009: 13). This is particularly clear in one sequence when a librarian proceeds to investigate a noise heard off-screen, and the hoodies are shown to be *crawling*, animal-like, over the bookshelves.

The hoodies, as they are portrayed in both *Heartless* and *F*, can be understood in relation to common theoretical notions of social stereotypes. Richard Dyer, in his highly influential essay on the topic, suggests that 'the effectiveness of stereotypes resides in the way they invoke a consensus ... as if these concepts of these social groups were spontaneously arrived at by all members of society independently and in isolation' (2009 [1993]: 209). Continuing, he explains that the 'consensus invoked by stereotypes is more apparent than real' and that 'stereotypes express *particular definitions* of reality, with concomitant evaluations, which in turn relate to the disposition of power within society' (ibid.; my emphasis). The ground for 'consensus' within *Heartless* and *F* is realised through the 'sign' of the hooded sweatshirt itself, the stigmatic meaning it has been ascribed in popular media (in this instance, the meaning-making 'power' in question) and how this functions when presented in the films. The hooded sweatshirt is the signifier *par excellence* of terror and fear in the diegetic, and the extra-filmic, world.

'Thoroughly credible': *Eden Lake* and *Cherry Tree Lane*

In terms of narrative, style and plot, *Eden Lake* and *Cherry Tree Lane* are the hoodie horrors that are the most similar to each other. In the former, our protagonists Jenny (a schoolteacher played by Kelly Reilly) and Steve (Michael Fassbender) leave their home in the city for a relaxing weekend at one of Steve's previous holiday destinations, Slapton Quarry. Their trip significantly occurs days before the quarry is due to be redeveloped into the desirable 'gated community' of 'Eden Lake'. When they arrive, they are disturbed by a gang of hoodies from the local village, who torture, and then murder, Steve. *Cherry Tree Lane*, comparatively, sees the home of a middle-class couple, Christine (Rachael Blake) and Michael (Tom Butcher), invaded by a gang of hoodies seeking vengeance on behalf of their ring-leader's cousin, who was supposedly reported to the police by the couple's son, Sebastien (Tom Kane), resulting in a jail sentence. The film sees the hoodies torture both parents, while they await Sebastien's return. When he eventually arrives home, the hoodies kill him.

The supernatural elements that characterise the hoodies of *Heartless* and *F* are not apparent in *Eden Lake* and *Cherry Tree Lane*. The symbolic hooded sweatshirt is also not a central feature of either of the films. Rather than relying simply on connotative iconography,[8] *Eden Lake* and *Cherry Tree Lane* instead home in on the personalities of said 'feral youth' and more overtly consider the social backgrounds that shaped them. So, in *Cherry Tree Lane*, the hoodie's home invasion and subsequent bloodshed is a *direct consequence* of the criminal activity of the gang-leader's cousin. And in *Eden Lake*, we in one scene witness one of the hoodies' fathers using threatening language towards his son, while appraising a fist-shaped hole in the plasterboard of his living-room wall – the implication being that domestic violence is a regular occurrence in the household and is partly to blame for the hoodies' waywardness.

There are also elements of peer pressure shown to account for the hoodies' behaviour in both films. In *Eden Lake* gang-leader Brett (Jack O'Connell) coaxes everyone but himself to 'have a dig' at cutting Steve (who the hoodies have tied to a tree with barbed wire) with a rusty knife. Similarly, in *Cherry Tree Lane* Rian (Jumayn Hunter) instructs fellow gang-member Asad (Ashley Chin) to 'cut' Michael, who is bound and gagged on the floor, irrespective of the fact that it is supposedly Rian's family member that the gang are there to avenge.

The way that the youths are presented – as unruly and aggressive yet with identifiably human qualities – has led certain critics to compare them with wider trends in British social realism. Chitra Ramaswamy of *The Scotsman*, for instance, argues that

> there are moments in *Cherry Tree Lane* of senseless violence and moments where nothing much happens at all. [Paul Andrew Williams] shot the film quickly, in just two weeks, and did a lot of improvisation work with the unknown cast. All of this adds to its gritty realism. (Ramaswamy 2010: 38)

The term 'realism' is employed here in a way typical of much writing on British cinema: focusing on the unknown actors (they don't have the allure of fame of major stars),[9] and, crucially, the film's working-class themes. As John Hill argues:

> Within the British cinematic tradition, [realism in cinema] has generally involved the working class. In so far as the working class is neither more nor less 'real' than other social groups, the idea that realism is linked to the representation of the working class derives in part from context, and specifically the perceived absence of (adequate) representations of this group within the dominant discursive regimes. (Hill 2000a: 250)

Certainly, the director Paul Andrew Williams utilises stylistic elements that one would typically associate with realism. For example, long takes, which have been said to 'create more real-time equivalence' in realist films (Hallam with Marshment 2000: 43), are used. So too are close-ups, which are traditionally said to 'accentuate the characters' feelings of isolation and alienation' (215). Indeed, long close-ups capture the facial expressions of the gang, purportedly hinting at their inner emotions and thereby their human, non-monstrous, qualities. For example, in a scene when it is revealed that Asad has difficulty reading, the camera lingers on his despairing and embarrassed facial expression as he reacts to being made fun of by Rian. Similarly, it is implied that Rian, from the lingering close-ups and his expression of uncertainty throughout the film, perhaps feels somewhat out of his depth having broken into the house, and having (it is implied) raped Christine. However, while these stylistic devices are used throughout, it would be foolish to describe *Cherry Tree Lane* as an all-out social-realist film. For the most part, it strays from the vérité style that typically characterises gritty 'documentary realism' (Hallam with Marshment 2000: 106), opting instead for harsh colours (mostly blues) and tempered Steadicam sequences over a more spontaneous, documentary mode. In fact, one may argue that it owes more to Stanley Kubrick than it does to Ken Loach. The film is therefore perhaps best understood as an exercise in stylistic hybridity, drawing as it does on social-realist archetypes, but within the horror/exploitation framework of 'home-invasion/violation', as in Kubrick's *A Clockwork Orange*, 'in which the frequent threat of rape [asserts] working-class virility over middle-class repression' (Hunter 2011: 98).

Irrespective of how we phrase it, the overt, and perhaps deliberate, conflation of film style in such films has encouraged problematic readings by some critics, for whom 'cinema' and 'actuality' have blurred to inconceivable ends. A case in point is Chris Tookey (2008b), whose review of *Eden Lake* appeared in the right-wing British newspaper the *Daily Mail*. In it, Tookey commends the film for its *accurate* portrayal of contemporary British youth, downplaying the film's elements of generic convention, arguing that it is 'willing to say what other films have been too scared or politically correct to mention: the *true* horrors we fear day to day are not supernatural bogeymen or monsters created by scientists. They're our own youth' (my emphasis). He praises the film's set-up as 'thoroughly credible', in spite of it being directly lifted from a host of 'rural horror' films such as *The Texas Chain Saw Massacre* and *The Hills Have Eyes* (Wes Craven, 1977), in which middle-class city folk head off into the country, only to be confronted by savage yokels (Hutchings 2008: 272–3). If we were to use Tookey's logic, the savage yokels of *Eden Lake*, in spite of the generic antecedents, are very realistic indeed. This is a precarious position for Tookey to maintain, because just as social stereotypes are said to 'maintain sharp boundary definitions' (Dyer 2009 [1993]: 211) horror and social realism are similarly reliant on culturally acknowledged *generic* demarcations (Hill 1999: 134–7). That is to say, such designations, whether in relation to real people or films, should never – because they *can* never – be directly reflective of real life. These are factors, no less, which ensure the continued currency and repeatability of stereotypes within society, the news media and the cinemascape, and that, above anything else, bring their pretensions to veracity into question.

Certainly, the decision to cast British-cinema regular Thomas Turgoose as Cooper, the youngest and most impressionable hoodie in *Eden Lake*, was designed to set up generic expectations in the audience. Turgoose, by the time that the film was released, had garnered a moderate cult following for his sympathetic portrayal of young working-class youngsters in socially engaged realist dramas: Shane Meadows's cult hit *This is England* (2006), in which he plays a naïve eight-year-old who gets caught up in a skinhead gang; and Meadows's follow-up, *Somers Town* (2008), in which he plays a young boy who leaves his tumultuous working-class background to find friendship with a Polish immigrant (Fradley, Godfrey and Williams 2013). The producers of *Eden Lake* knowingly set out to embellish Turgoose's known persona.[10] For example, during the scene when Brett peer-pressures Cooper to cut Steve with a knife, Cooper is shown to be uncertain and unwilling, and is caught between guilt and wanting to impress his friends. As in *This is England*, Turgoose here plays a little boy, out of his depth, who has gotten in with the 'wrong crowd'. To offer another example, in a later scene, having been running from the hoodies all day, an adrenaline-fuelled Jenny mistakenly stabs Cooper in the neck with a piece of broken glass. The shock that registers with Jenny is also supposed to register with the audience. Turgoose's performance, and the familiarity of his on-screen persona as an innocent and mislead youth, is integral to this.[11]

The factors identified here complicate the critics' claims to the films' realistic credentials. It could be suggested, rather than pertaining to authenticity per se, the representations are employed to recall the perpetuation of a mythology that is *said* (by some) and *believed* (by some) to exist, similar to the ways that journalists 'point their camera at the worst possible workless dysfunctional family and say "This is working-class life"' (Toynbee cited in Jones 2011: 24). By drawing on the fears of a 'broken Britain', and by exploiting the notion of such generalisations within self-aware genre films, *Eden Lake* and *Cherry Tree Lane* revel in the same kinds of excesses as reactionary news media. But instead of pertaining to truth by vouching for the social divisions they realise, they instead make them apparent, and expose the futility – and fantasy – of such generalisations.

REPRESENTING 'BROKEN BRITAIN'

'Uncanny landscapes'

James Leggott has identified how contemporary British horror cinema is marked by 'the recurrence of stories in which individuals or groups of characters are transplanted into hostile, unfamiliar landscapes' (2008: 60). Similarly, Peter Hutchings (2004b) has recognised the longevity of 'uncanny landscapes' within British science-fiction and horror film and television. To certain varying extents, the landscapes of the hoodie horror films so far discussed correlate with the themes and ideas that Hutchings and Leggott acknowledge. For instance, we can certainly read the landscapes of the hoodie horror films as being, in all cases, landscapes of hostility and of 'dispossession and vacancy' (Hutchings 2004b: 29). However, Hutchings's argument that this 'is not a landscape where we find ourselves as modern national subjects' is not applicable to the hoodie horror film. Neither is the summation that 'it is . . . a landscape where that sense of identity is diminished or removed entirely' (ibid.). On the contrary, *Eden Lake*, *Cherry Tree Lane*, *Heartless* and *F*, through the invocation of said 'uncanny landscapes' seemingly assemble a broken Britain, where we *do* (supposedly) find ourselves as national subjects, and where identity *is* paramount. As Andrew Higson has argued, '[p]lace . . . plays an important role in defining national and local identities' (2011: 87). As such, the city (*Heartless*), the countryside (*Eden Lake*), the middle-class household (*Cherry Tree Lane*) and the school (*F*) collectively resonate with broader social concerns.

The city in *Heartless*

'London burns' (J. G. 2011)

The presentation of the city in *Heartless* is integral to the film's social commentary. Indeed, the director Philip Ridley's envisioning of an urban environment fraught with terror speaks out to the ways that inner-cities were positioned in much media reportage as being a hotbed of hoodie activity before, leading up to and during the August Riots of 2011. The film thus presents the city in two distinct ways.

The first way is geographical: the city is used as a device to nationally orientate the viewer. Shots of London skylines offer glimpses of what Charlotte Brunsdon has famously termed 'Landmark London' (2007: 21–56) – we see the banks of the Thames, the iconic Gherkin – and are employed, as in other examples of London-set British horror, as 'guarantor[s] that the story's events are being played out in relation to a real city' (Hutchings 2009a: 196). That is to say, the fact that *Heartless* is so explicitly set in London and not somewhere else, is important, and the aforementioned establishing shots are designed to create the illusion that 'we know where we are', and, in doing so, frame the horrors that Jamie encounters throughout the film within the specifically *national* context of broken Britain. But, crucially, it is not only Landmark London that we encounter. In fact, most of the urban scenes in the film are sandwiched between establishing shots of the type just mentioned, and take place in non-descript back alleys (although a discerning eye will be able to determine that many scenes were shot around Elephant and Castle). The

London that we come to know in *Heartless* is a city that lies in the shadows of commonplace touristic signifiers. It is a London not of heritage, but instead a 'Horror London' (Hutchings 2009b) where, to quote a shop owner in the film, 'the whole community's gone broken!'

The second way that the city is presented is *psycho*geographical: how we experience the city is how Jamie experiences it. It is through his eyes that the urban environment is perceived as being a horrifying, fragmented, place, and it is through his eyes that we too experience the heartless hoodies. 'Seeing' and 'believing' are therefore pertinent themes throughout the film and are made all the more important in light of the film's urban setting and the social context with which it engages. The spectator sees and thus is expected to believe (for the purposes of the narrative) the hoodies, the attacks, and beyond, similar to the way that the popular media have perpetuated crude stereotypes of the contemporary working class as supposedly accurate representations. For example, it was not uncommon in the 2000s for journalists, politicians and education policy-makers, to invoke the supposedly satirical character Vicky Pollard from the TV show *Little Britain* – an 'incurably sub-literate, sexually promiscuous, pregnant, teenage chavette' (Tyler 2008: 27–8) – as a means of 'shorthand' when referring to the contemporary working class in '"serious" debates':

> [T]he movement of this fictional figure from scripted television comedy into news media, political rhetoric and onto the streets foregrounds the disturbing ease which the chav figure shapes social perception and comes to be employed in instrumental ways. (Tyler 2008: 28)

Jamie's urban encounters with feral hoodies in *Heartless*, it could be argued, are thus designed to chime with, and bring into question, the accuracy that is ascribed to such fantasy in the extra-diegetic world.

In retrospect, the artificiality of these visions is repeatedly hinted at during the film, symbolised primarily by Jamie's passion for photography. Throughout the film, he photographs different parts of the city: buildings that were once family homes and factories that were presumably once at the core of industrial development, but are now merely shells, inhabited – so Jamie thinks – by demonic hoodies. The connotation is that society has failed the former inhabitants (the old working classes) and that the feral hoodies are products of, quite literally, broken homes. Jamie's love interest, Tia (Clémence Poésy), correlates the practice of photography with the work of Caravaggio, an artist once described by Françoise Bardon as 'realist' because his art was said to depict 'ordinary people . . . in a relationship that belongs to them . . . a relationship, above all, to the reality of which they objectively partake' (Bardon cited in Bal 2001: 41). This description can aptly be ascribed to Jamie's visions of hoodies and his photographic interactions with the urban environment that offer that link between actuality and the 'reality' in which *he* objectively partakes. The difference being, the ordinary people are no more, but have been superseded by a feral underbelly. Jamie's reality, it is inferred, is like ours, in as much as that he puts so much faith in the media (the news media/the medium of photography) that he starts to believe that demonic hoodies really exist. His photography of the city, thus, could be seen as capturing a *version of* Britain *in pieces*, embodying quite literally a 'broken Britain' by 'snapping' the urban into fragments of places and people, destruction and vacancy, that contribute to a topography, both of the city and of his psyche, when reassembled.

The countryside in *Eden Lake*

. . . escaped
From the vast city, where I long had pined
A discontented sojourner: now free,
Free as a bird to settle where I will.
What dwelling shall receive me? (Wordsworth 1979: 29)

The countryside is often promoted as being integral to the British national identity. Tourist boards boast about it, and many films that have been celebrated for their Britishness (or their Englishness) have been set there. Yet, in horror cinema, the countryside has a history of being a site of dread. *Eden Lake* adds to this trend.

The film's rural setting sets it apart from all other hoodie horrors discussed here. In fact, in a social context where the hoodie is most frequently framed as an 'urban' threat, the countryside locale works to bolster *Eden Lake*'s generic credentials. As touched on briefly above, films such as *The Texas Chain Saw Massacre* typically show protagonists travelling from the comforts of the city to then meet their horrific fate in the wilderness of the countryside. This narrative trajectory was famously described by Carol Clover in 1992 as constituting a move from civilisation to savagery, 'where the rules of civilization do not obtain' (1992: 124). In rural horror films, Clover suggested, 'People from the city are people like us' while 'People from the country . . . are people not like us' (ibid.). The arrival of Jenny and Steve to rural England in *Eden Lake* invokes a similar binary – that, in the context of broken Britain, is highly political. Indeed, a commonly shared philosophy in contemporary British culture is the idea that society is divided between *us* who are 'all middle-class', and *them*, who constitute 'a hopeless chav rump' (Jones 2011: 139).

In line with Clover's city/country paradigm, Jenny and Steve are thus people like us – or, at the very least, are presented as people we should aspire to be like. Their middle-classness is made apparent through their demeanours and material possessions. Jenny, for instance, is a primary school teacher, whose caring nature is conveyed in the first scene when she is shown playing 'peek-a-boo' with her obedient class, while Steve drives a large – and presumably very expensive – Land Rover, and wears 'Ray-Bay Aviators'. The hoodies, by comparison, are not like this at all, and the countryside they inhabit, by extension, is coded as a working-class domain, home to a 'threatening rural Other' (Clover 1992: 124; see also Murphy 2013).

Early in the film, it is revealed that a wooded area in the vicinity of the hoodies' village is due for imminent redevelopment into 'Executive Homes'. The signage describes 'a secure gated community of fifty superior new England homes . . . with 300 acres of private woodland'. The language employed is telling of the film's social context. The promised 'gated' community of 'new England homes' is a decidedly post-apocalyptic conception, with the implication being that a *new* England, locked away from the threatening hoodie culture of the old, is desirable among a wealthy class. The old Britain, it is implied, is broken beyond repair, and 300 acres of private woodland, gated and protected, is one means of escaping its horrors. The hoodies' disdain for this development is conveyed through graffiti spray-painted on to the back of the developers' sign that reads 'fuck off yuppy cunts'. On the face of it, the graffiti is yet another generic device: in rural horror films it is very common for the city folk to be confronted with a warning that they wilfully ignore, or mistakenly take a 'short cut' that leads them to their death. The warning in *Eden Lake*, however, carries additional, and specifically national, connotations. 'Yuppy' is a term with considerable bearing on contemporary media discourse, and, in this context, can be connected to the 1980s when the neo-liberal ideology of Margaret Thatcher is said to have promoted the plight of the 'individual' over class 'solidarity'. As Owen Jones has argued, working-class 'communities were, in some cases, shattered, never to recover; and [their] values, like solidarity and collective aspiration, were swept away' (2011: 10). The developers in *Eden Lake* embody this conservative ruthlessness – the prospective home owners have the money, and therefore the right, to bring in the machinery and 'sweep away' what was there before. Jenny and Steve are extensions of this because they ascend from the developed city. They stand in direct opposition to the savage, working-class, horrors that they witness and experience. Although they are not directly part of the 'Eden Lake' woodland redevelopment, their being there for leisure in the first place is tantamount to trespassing. They, like the developers, do not heed the warning, and face the bloody consequences of venturing where they are not wanted.

The countryside has been read against ideas about sexual promiscuity and fertility in assessments of British occult horror films of the 1970s such as *The Blood on Satan's Claw* (Piers Haggard, 1971).[12] It should seem fitting, then, that, in *Eden Lake*, the countryside is the home to the working class, who are frequently accused in the press of 'excessive reproduction' and bad parenting (Tyler 2008: 30). The name of the village where the hoodies live, Redcott, plays with this implication. Indeed, we may well read 'Redcott' itself as 'bad parenting': 'Red-' conjures up images of both birth and horror – from blood, to abortion, to murder – while '-cott' (cot) evokes, quite simply, a baby's bed. The negative connotations are clear: the kids from Redcott Village are at once a bloody nuisance with a blood lust and there are lots of them ('excessive reproduction'), and they lack proper parental (that is to say, moral) guidance.

'Bad parenting' is a recurrent theme of much recent British cinema, and the countryside often features in films as a place where the young working class 'play, in flight from a home environment that is posited as traumatic' (Leggott 2004: 168). In *Eden Lake*, the woodland that lies beyond Redcott village where the hoodies' horrifying acts take place is also a site of youth transcendence. Yet the violence experienced at home is re-enacted in the countryside, rather than 'escaped' from. The final scene of the film see's Brett's father peer-pressure the other parents into murdering Jenny, after it is revealed that the young Cooper has been killed. This moment contextualises the way that Brett coerces Cooper and the others during the woodland sequences earlier in the film. The implication is that violence is a domestic staple of the working classes in broken Britain – an incurable symptom. Therefore, the country woodland, far from being an idyllic escape, is merely a genealogical extension of the homestead horrors. In fact, the countryside is a metaphor for broken Britain itself. Here, the working class live carefree and uncivilised. They drink excessive amounts of alcohol; the men beat their wives; their children commit horrific acts of murder; and, concurrent with reactionary media discourse, the middle class are unable to keep a handle on them in spite of supposedly 'knowing better'.

The middle-class household in *Cherry Tree Lane*

'I realised this wasn't an attempted burglary. It was an invasion.' (Cole cited in Smith 2011: 9)

According to Owen Jones, the class divide in Britain has never been so apparent and never have the middle classes felt so removed from the 'dumping ground' that is the modern-day, inner-city, council estate (2011: 35). The middle-class household, thus, has adopted a somewhat sacred aura in the era of the hoodie. Indeed, in the immediate aftermath of the August Riots, right-wing newspapers were keen to take a stand against members of 'the mob' who had 'invaded' and burgled houses in London's wealthy Notting Hill area. The *Daily Mail* actually published a story billed as 'One *middle-class* mother's terrifying account of the . . . Day the mob came crashing through my door', lamenting how it 'wasn't just shops and businesses which were attacked during the rioting – individual households in some of London's most expensive streets were targeted too' (Smith 2011: 9; emphasis added). The binary between the faceless hooded mob and the privileged couldn't have been clearer, and it was precisely these kinds of fears that *Cherry Tree Lane* explored upon its release in 2010.

Perhaps the most obvious way that the film chimes with these issues is through the title itself, which operates as an intertextual hat-tip to one of the most iconic envisionings of upper-class family life ever committed to film, Walt Disney's *Mary Poppins* (Robert Stevenson, 1964), where Cherry Tree Lane features as the name of the street where the well-to-do Banks family lives (Williams 2010). The employment of something so saccharine and innocent within a horror film works to deliberately upset the upper-class idealism of the Disney movie. Indeed, in *Cherry Tree Lane* it is not a magical nanny being welcomed into the home, as in the Disney film, but rather a gang of feral hoodies who *break in*.

The infiltration of middle-class domesticity is anticipated in the film's opening shot. A saucepan is shown centre frame, simmering, and then eventually boiling over. The metaphor is clear: the threat of broken Britain is bubbling beneath the surface of normalcy, eventually to be fully realised when the hoodies eventually arrive, and middle-class complacency shatters.

The bubbling saucepan also alludes to the existent frictions within the household. The stark mise en scène of bright blues in the living room and greens in the bedroom suggest a Sirkian veneer of 'garish colours' (Klinger 1994: 17) that superficially mask internal frictions. The married homeowners, Christine and Mike, are introduced to the spectator through conversation that has little context, and, as a result, little meaning to the spectator. For instance, when we first hear Christine's voice, it is muffled: her words are unintelligible as she has a phone conversation, out of focus, in the background of the shot. And, when Mike arrives home from work, they discuss each other's days, little of which has any bearing on the narrative, beyond the parameters of the day-to-day small talk that is here symbolising middle-class life, as though all that is truly significant in determining their characters is the mise en scène's evocation of privilege, and the cursory references to 'the office' and 'business trips' that they drop into conversation. Furthermore, Mike, unable to sustain a conversation with his wife (who seems at all times irritated and disinterested), is repeatedly drawn to transient pleasures of alcohol and television instead. The implication is that the stereotypical middle-class home is perhaps not as idealistic as one would have assumed.

That middle-class existence is symbolised mostly by the couple's material possessions in turn – and expectedly – exemplifies what they truly lack: namely, solid familial bonds. Indeed, when the hoodies break in, and tie them up, they are repeatedly mocked for owning things that would attest to their sophistication in other circles, such as their collection of 'foreign' (art) films on DVD ('Where are all the "18s"?' Asad asks). And when Rian angrily asks for cash, to find that Michael only has numerous credit cards, he asks Christine for the pin numbers, only to discover that she herself does not know them. 'He don't tell his own wife the numbers for his cards!' he expels, reifying the family divisions within the homestead, while simultaneously emphasising the strong bonds that exist between Rian, the cousin he is avenging, and the other gang members who stick by him.

There are repeated examples of the hoodies drawing distinctions between themselves, their families and the middle-class couple. Yet, there is still a pervading sense that they yearn for the empty promises of a middle-class life. For instance, Rian compares his mother to Christine, concluding that his mother is in fact younger, but looks much older. Moreover, in one scene, gang member Teddy (Sonny Muslim) lies comfortably on the bed in the master bedroom of the house, holding an item of Christine's nightwear: something to constitute the maternal security he presumably lacks on the street. Asad, similarly, reveals that his father cheated on his mother, although is quick to exclaim that *he* is not that way. He makes known the strong bond he has with his mother when he speaks to her later on the phone. In this respect, the middle class are presented as subverting the traditional familial bonds that the likes of the *Daily Mail* saw to be at the cornerstones of broken Britain reparations,[13] while the hoodies provide evidence of similar familial fragmentation, but one that is framed within legitimate and corrupting social issues, such as the necessity to steal to survive, and the problems of drug addiction. As such, the middle-class household does not signify hope at all, but gloating and selfishness. Working-class life, comparably, is presented as one of inevitable desperation.

Ultimately, the middle-class home in *Cherry Tree Lane* is a site of negligence and arrogant complacency. Traditionally, the middle-class house in the modern horror film has been a site for wayward activities for youth, and, as in the 1980s slasher cycle, a place where youth ignore the traditional moral framework, partake in drugs and are punished by a masked killer in doing so (see Clover 1992). In *Cherry Tree Lane*, however, the parents are 'victimised', and 'punished' for their unwillingness to understand their son. The parents simply do not *understand* their son who is involved in the wayward activity of Rian's gang. The hoodies mock this reality, and Teddy asks the question, 'Did you know your son smokes weed?', to which Mike ashamedly shakes his head, and Teddy responds, 'Not such a good boy then, is he?' Significantly, the dinner table that they sit at in the opening scene is notably only big enough for two. This implies that they do not eat together like 'normal' families, and, by extension, exclude their son completely. In fact, their son's exclusion from the household is emphasised by the fact he is never on-screen until the film's final moments. When he does eventually arrive, he is taken upstairs and murdered off camera. It is only then that the parents manage to break free and murder the gang. But it is too late. Sabastien's murder works to symbolise the inner fractures beneath the veneer of middle-class idealism. The hoodies might now be dead, but they died together, their bonds intact.

The school in *F*

'To fix broken Britain we shall start at school.' (Cameron 2007)

On 2 September 2007, David Cameron – some three years before being elected Prime Minister – wrote an article for *The Telegraph*, from which the above quotation appears. In it, he set out a plan to remedy broken Britain. His central argument was that 'educational failure lies at' the heart of 'our broken society':

> Four in every five youngsters receiving custodial sentences have no quali-fications. More than two-thirds of prisoners are illiterate. And nearly one-third of those excluded from school have been involved with substance abuse. (Cameron 2007)

These were bold claims, not without exaggeration. Nor were they free of the scaremongering one came to expect from party leaders on this hot-button issue. And it was precisely these kinds of exaggerated fears that would come to be personified in Johannes Roberts's *F*, in which the school is shown to be a site, not of education, but of violence.

The fact that Anderson is not afforded sympathy by the headteacher or gov-erning body after he is beaten up by a pupil in the opening scene, but is rather *blamed* by them for having provoked the incident by awarding the pupil an 'F', emblematises the way that the school and young people are to be framed throughout the film. As in *Eden Lake*, the first scene of *F* initially presents the school classroom as a place of order. Anderson is in control as he hands graded work back to the pupils: his daughter and student, Kate (Eliza Bennett), smiles proudly up towards him as he hands her an A-graded paper. However, follow-ing the attack, and Anderson's subsequent decline into depression and alco-holism, Kate switches from being an Angelic model student to being the kind of promiscuous teenager that society was warned against: one who wholly disrespects her father. One may argue that Kate's transformation is a metaphor of Britain's own alleged downward decline (in this instance being seemingly symptomatic of an education system unable to cope with unruly youths, rather than the parents themselves). Her conservative look of innocence is replaced with a short skirt. She wears make-up, and her hair is worn down instead of in the girlish ponytail of the opening scene. The attack on Anderson acts a catalyst for the horror that follows, while the headteacher's unwillingness to sympathise with Anderson's emotional fragility exposes the school as being no longer a place of respect, but an environment where the staff are scared and the kids are in control.

Eleven months pass since the classroom attack. Anderson is no longer the confident teacher we saw in the opening scene (the caretaker will later confirm this: 'You look like shit'). He wanders, broken and jaded, through the corridors, staring vacantly, preoccupied by nothingness as staff members look on him with disdain. He is shot within an ethereal soft hue, and drifts fluidly in and out of focus, as if to underscore his weakened state of mind and the inebriating effects of alcohol. For him, the school is now a site of struggle. Indeed, when his paranoia becomes a reality as the hoodies attack the school and he finds himself separated from Kate, the school building itself becomes a literal obstacle course that Anderson must navigate if he is to preserve his and his daughter's relationship: he has already lost her respect, he must not lose her completely to the monstrousness of contemporary youth. The building – and the oppression it symbolises – becomes a seemingly 'impermeable labyrinth' not unlike the 'branches and vegetation that prevent the couple's escape' in *Eden Lake* (Hockenhull 2010: 220), nor the labyrinthine cave system in *The Descent* that disorientates Sarah and her potholing companions. The school's long brooding corridors enshrouded in darkness disorientate the characters, and afford the agile hoodies tight dark spaces from where they can leap and attack unsuspecting passers-by: just as such figures have inhabited the corners of Anderson's paranoid mind.

The building itself may well be read as a 'Terrible Place' of modern horror cinema: 'most often a house or a tunnel, in which victims sooner or later find themselves' (Clover 1992: 30). Yet, the traditional Terrible Place, for all its 'dreadful paraphernalia' of mummified corpses and rotting flesh (30–1), is also bound, typically, to the (unhealthy) preservation of a family unit: Norma Bates's corpse in the *Psycho* films; the corpse of Mrs Voorhees in the *Friday the 13th* sequels; or the human bodies turned into sausage meat for the Sawyer family's BBQ business in *The Texas Chainsaw Massacre Part 2* (Tobe Hooper, 1986). The Terrible School in *F*, however – as Kate and Anderson's failing relationship shows – hinges precisely on the family's absence, and the initial inability of Anderson to cope with the societal breakdown and 'culture of disrespect' that led to him being attacked in the first place. In cruel irony, as Kate herself acknowledges, detention, a traditional means of punishment and where morals are learned, is utilised by Anderson – 'a pathetic old man ... who's so afraid of his students that he has to drink a bottle of whisky before he can even step into a classroom' – to *spend time with*, not to punish, her.

Yet, whereas the forest in *Eden Lake*, the city in *Heartless* and the middle-class home in *Cherry Tree Lane* are places where each of our pro-tagonists do *not* (initially) anticipate horror to unfold, the school in *F* has already been established as a place of conflict and terror within the opening few minutes. As such, the school and the hoodies are already obstacles that Anderson knows he must overcome. In fact, the actual hoodie attack is con-strued as the logical consequence of Anderson's fears, as when the security guard, headteacher and, eventually, the emergency-services telephone opera-tor dismisses Anderson's concerns that there are kids in the building: 'It *is* a school,' the security guard patronisingly exerts. Yet, Anderson gradually regains composure as, one by one, those who disbelieved him, or have treated the hoodie invasion as everyday childish mischief, are all brutally murdered. They have let their ignorance get the better of them, and Anderson was right to be scared all along. The school in *F* thus becomes a place of learning for the *adults*. The ultimate lesson of the film is to remain vigilant against feral youth. Like the hoodies themselves, the school is left vacant and void of morality.

CONCLUSION

This chapter has illustrated how the hoodie horror film cycle reflected contem-porary anxieties about feral youth cultures that were grounded within broader class-based prejudices. It has also acknowledged the integral role of genre hybridity within these films, and their intertextual linkages to the horror film, social realism and reactionary media stereotyping. By analysing the ways that the hoodies have been represented within such films, and through an assess-ment of the locations in which they are set, I have examined how the cycle utilised media-based stereotypes to evoke images of horror. The stereotypes that such hoodies and their mise en scène evoke, whether supernatural in tone as in *Heartless* and *F*, or through more 'realist' characterisations as in *Cherry Tree Lane* and *Eden Lake*, when coupled with the films' resistance to explain away their monstrosities and ground them within a socially resonant 'broken Britain', affords the hoodie horror cycle a distinctive and significant cultural potency.

Hoodie horror films, then, provided a unique, of-the-moment insight into how the British horror film allegorically assessed contemporary society. And whereas, in the past, youth in horror films have been directly connected with alien beings (*Village of the Damned*), or the offspring of Satan (*The Omen*), the hoodie had a more tangible social grounding. Indeed, the hoodies were not as Andy Sawyer once observed of the alien children in *Village of the Damned*, '[g]olden, attractive [and] well-spoken (there are no rural accents among them)' (Sawyer 1999: 79), but were rooted within a more immediate and iden-tifiable trajectory that conflated fantasy with actuality, and, in turn, reflected a distinctive moment in British media and cinema history.

NOTES

1. Clive Bloom's *Riot City: Protest and Rebellion in the Capital* offers a detailed account of the riots and their social context (2012: 76–99).
2. It arguably first came to a head when the Bluewater Shopping Centre in Kent banned hoodies from being worn inside the centre in 2005 (see McLean 2005).
3. The *Daily Mail* would sum this up in 2005, when it was argued that 'there is a feeling that the streets, town centres and shopping malls do not properly belong to us and the hoodie [has become] symbolic of those we fear have taken over' (Anon. 2005b).
4. These prejudices arguably came to a head in the 2000s following the broadcast of the Channel 4 TV series *My Big Fat Gypsy Wedding* (2011–). For an enlightening discussion about 'anti-Gypsy discourse' – and of this programme in particular – see Richardson and O'Neill (2011). See also Tyler (2013: 133).
5. Its showing at the Cannes Film Festival prompted offended spectators to walk out in disgust at its violent conclusion (see Brookes 2005).
6. In fact, *Eden Lake* was the first film to be referred to as a 'hoodie horror' in print (Cripps 2008: 6).
7. Rightly, one media report (Midgley 2006) alluded to the fact that the feral youth problem was not unique to the UK, and neither was the demonisation of lower classes. Indeed, *Ils* has its own cultural preoccupations, and draws clearly upon anxieties surrounding the poverty-stricken Parisian suburbs (the Banlieue), where the French youth-focused film *La Haine* (Mathieu Kossovitz, 1995) is set, and where subsequent French horror films such as *Frontier(s)* (Xavier Gens, 2007) are also partially set. However, there has not been a national cycle of films comparable to the British hoodie horror film.
8. The use of the term 'hoodie' in the media did not always relate to the hooded sweatshirt. Eventually, the term became synonymous with gangs of working-class youths, whether they were wearing hoodies or not.
9. Jurmayn Hunter, who plays the gang-leader Rian in *Cherry Tree Lane*, had also had a minor, non-speaking role in *Eden Lake* as one of the hoodies, although this casting seems incidental. It was not a factor capitalised on in the marketing of the film.
10. Indeed, the other cast members were auditioned with him in mind (Holmes 2012). He also originally read for the part of Brett (*Eden Lake*, UK DVD Special Feature, 2009).
11. The fact that he has a prominent billing in the film's opening credits, despite having very little dialogue or screen-time, is testament to this, as is his billing as 'co-star' in some of the film's DVD promotion, as well as his subsequent inclusion on the covers of the third edition of *The British Cinema Book* (Murphy 2009) and the 2011 report by the BFI: *Opening Our Eyes: How Film Contributes to the Culture of the UK*. Moreover, Richard Holmes, one of the producers of the film, praised Turgoose's own awareness of how he is perceived in the public eye (Holmes 2012), and has admitted how integral he was to the film's (limited) success.
12. As Leon Hunt explains, in the film, which is about 'the return of . . . a horned god and of his worship by a female-led cult', 'youthful hormones run amok' (2002: 94).
13. As one article reported: 'Last month, one of Britain's most senior Family Court judges described family breakdown as a national tragedy and argued marriage should be promoted by the Government to help stop "social anarchy"' (Ware 2009).

6. LET THE QUIET ONES IN

Since the release of Hammer Films's *The Curse of Frankenstein* in 1957, the sobriquet 'Hammer Horror' has, for many, become synonymous with British horror cinema. Known the world over for its full-colour Gothic horror films 'set in a dislocated but quintessentially Victorian hinterland', Hammer enjoyed global box-office success throughout the 1950s and 60s with its 'distinctive generic style' (Meikle 2009: xiii). As Denis Meikle notes in *A History of Horrors: The Rise and Fall of the House of Hammer*, the company 'would live to take its rightful place second only to Ealing in the ranks of the great postwar British independents, while its legacy continues to be felt' across popular culture to this very day (ibid.). Indeed, since the 1970s, Hammer's legacy has been shaped by fanzines, books and websites specifically about the company, while film and television continues to pay homage to the 'Hammer brand' and its history through documentaries and late-night screenings.[1] This is in spite of Hammer having been largely inactive in the film world since the late 1970s, when it ceased to make features, and, after a brief stint in television during the 1980s, focused mainly on merchandising throughout the 1990s.

As I have explored elsewhere in this book, the centrality of Hammer to discourses around British horror cinema, in light of Pirie's influential 'heritage of horror' argument, has meant that other aspects of British horror history have been overshadowed. This meant, for a long time, the sidelining of the output of other notable horror production houses such as Amicus, Tigon and Tyburn (Hunt 1998: 143–7). Yet for all that Hammer offers us merely a limited insight into what may be termed the 'classic period' of British horror, Hammer was the only one of its contemporaries to see any kind of successful re-launch in the first fourteen years of the twenty-first century. For, in 2007, 'Hammer Films' went back into feature film production.[2] Therefore, while the 'heritage of horror' argument does little to aid in any assessment of contemporary British horror cinema's dynamic variety, it is nevertheless appropriate to turn academic attention to Hammer once more, and evaluate it as a company/brand that has had (at the very least, a perceived sense of) economic and cultural value to recent horror film production.

It is therefore my intention in this chapter to investigate notions of 'value' in relation to Hammer, as a means of identifying whereabouts the iconic brand sat among the many other developments in British horror that have already been discussed in this book. What should become clear is that, whereas one or two independent studios emerged in the 2000s to emulate the old Hammer, by producing British exploitation films with British cultural inflections,[3] the 'new' Hammer adopted a much more ambitious and outward-looking model that owed more to corporate Hollywood than the low-budget exploitation cinema that sealed its initial success. Hammer in the twenty-first century, aside from bolstering its company heritage in British press discourse, avoided piggy-backing on other modes of 'Britishness' that were being explored in other areas of British horror cinema (such as hoodies). Instead, the company spent most of its time producing films that either owed more to pan-Atlantic versions of Britishness of the Hollywood blockbuster tradition, or films that weren't particularly concerned with Britishness at all.

The company, as a means of reintegrating itself into the contemporary filmscape, spread itself quite thinly in terms of the kinds of films it invested in. That is to say: while its legacy hinged on the aforementioned recurrences of a 'dislocated but quintessentially Victorian hinterland', its newer films were less easily pigeonholed. For example, its return venture was a film made to be distributed online, *Beyond the Rave*. This was followed by a glossy remake of the critically acclaimed Swedish art-horror movie *Let the Right One In* (Tomas Alfredson) from 2008 as *Let Me In* in 2010, and two films made primarily for the DVD market, *Wake Wood* and *The Resident* (Antti Jokinen, 2010). Hammer's biggest success between 2007 and 2014, however, was the Daniel Radcliffe star-vehicle and ghost story, *The Woman in Black* from 2012, which was followed by another ghost story, *The Quiet Ones*, in 2014. The new Hammer was not just concerned with film production, however. As Matt Hills (2014) notes, the company also branched out into merchandising, theatre work and literature, and resultantly struggled to maintain a coherent brand identity. Central to this dilemma was the company's inability to balance its status as a heritage brand with its agenda to move forward as a film producer with current market appeal. As a result, Hammer's branding from 2007 to 2014 'oscillated uneasily between a reaction to the present and a loyalty to the past':

Despite a theoretical emphasis on coherence, as a brand, twenty-first century Hammer has been insistently self-divided and doubled. The company has hesitated over modernization and commodification of its legacy, and it has sought to hybridize or to align the two, rarely, if ever, successfully. (Hills 2014: 245)

It is the purpose of this chapter, then, to explore how Hammer's new owners attempted to reintegrate it, as a major brand, into the commercial movie mainstream, between the release of *Beyond the Rave* and *The Quiet Ones*. In what follows, I examine the factors that led to the company's rebirth, including the numerous handovers from 1979 to 2007, and the strategies subsequently employed, in light of past failures, to generate interest from the press and the public. Drawing on specific case studies, I consider how Hammer's new owners set about repositioning the company for a young audience, paying specific attention to the inclusion (or not) of the 'Hammer' name in the marketing of its post-millennial releases. This chapter will show that, while Hammer produced a number of films with varying degrees of success since its re-launch in 2007, it was by no means as central to contemporary British horror production as its legacy might have anticipated, and that its legacy ultimately proved inconsequential to its various developments after 2007.

But before our attention is fully turned to the 'new' Hammer, it is first necessary to contextualise more recent developments in the company narrative that spans the years 1979 to 2005. Considered by historians as 'the last moment of the old Hammer' (Pirie 2008: 191), 1979 saw the release of the then-company's last theatrical feature – an ill-received remake of Alfred Hitchcock's *The Lady Vanishes* (1938). It was also the year that Hammer exchanged hands for the first time since its inception in 1934. This exchange would be the first of four for the company over the next twenty-six years, and would, in many ways, denote the most tumultuous period of the company's history. The year 2005 was when the final moves were made to ease the studio back into film production, to no success, before it was sold on again – this time to Dutch-based consortium Cyrte Investments, which remains its custodian to this day.

'THE OLDEST "START-UP" IN THE BUSINESS': HAMMER FILMS, 1979–2005

One reason often stated for Hammer's demise in the late 1970s is its failure to adequately 'update' its output for a contemporary audience. The types of horror films with which Hammer's gothic horrors were competing at this time were 'modern' horror films such as *The Exorcist*, *The Texas Chain Saw Massacre*, *House of Whipcord* (Pete Walker, 1974) and *Frightmare* (Pete Walker, 1974), which were all set in a contemporary world far removed from the Gothicana that had characterised Hammer's most iconic work (Newman

1988: 25; Sanjek 1994: 196). Moreover, the gradual withdrawal of American funding from much British film production in the 1970s made it increasingly difficult for producers to commission British films – not least films that were so profoundly 'British' in tone and reputation as Hammer's Gothic horrors (see Chapter 1). On top of this, Hammer had been unable to replicate the production values that contributed to its earlier successes, as it struggled, along with the rest of the British film industry, to contend with inflation (Meikle 2009: 221; see also 207–23). As David Pirie notes, the company had lost the 'amazing cost advantage' that had, in the 1950s and 1960s, 'astonished their [*sic*] early American partners' (2008: 186).

As a result, Hammer was dissolved in 1979, and was passed into the hands of the receiver, ICI. It was then sold on to its former production accountant, Roy Skeggs, in either late 1980 or early 1981.[4] Having bought the company for £100,000 (Pirie 2008: 191), Skeggs turned Hammer to TV production in 1980, with the series *Hammer House of Horror* and, in 1984, *Hammer House of Mystery and Suspense*. Modelled on anthology series such as *The Twilight Zone* (1959–64), the series were devised to capitalise on the success of the BBC's late-night horror double bills in which the films of Hammer regularly featured.[5] In contrast to Hammer's most revered work, many of the stories featured in the shows were set in the present day, but an effort was made to retain central facets of the company's branding legacy by regularly featuring actors like Peter Cushing and Stephanie Beacham.[6] *Hammer House of Horror* and *Hammer House of Mystery and Suspense* each ran for one series, and there were plans in place in the late 1980s for another. The show in question, *The Haunted House of Hammer*, was to once more hark back to Hammer's golden age of period Gothic tales as a means of keeping the brand alive in the minds of contemporary audiences, and would feature adaptations of work by Agatha Christie, Bram Stoker and M. R. James. Originally aimed to run in conjunction with another series, *The Best of British* (that was to feature twenty-six episodes featuring edited versions of Hammer's most memorable moments), *The Haunted House of Hammer* ultimately never materialised. It seemed that the appetite for all things English Gothic was at an all-time low, with home video now offering a host of modern 'video nasties' for the delectation of televisually versed horror fans.[7]

Throughout the late 1980s and early 1990s, there were several announcements made that Hammer was to return. A feature film adaptation of Daphne Du Maurier's gothic tale *House on the Strand* from 1969 was mooted, although it never went into production (Anon. 1990: 4). What did ensue, however, was a bizarre stint in rock music for the company, where, under the branding of Hammer Films Music Ltd, it released the heavy-metal album *Hammer Horror* performed by the Newcastle-based band, Warfare. Although the album featured the endorsement of Peter Cushing and Christopher Lee (who each provided sleeve notes), the album failed to generate any real interest from metal fans, Hammer fans or the general public.[8]

Some promise was shown, however, when the company signed an agreement with the American filmmaker Richard Donner, Lauren Shuler Donner (his wife) and Warner Bros Studios, for what was reported to be a 'nineteen film multi-million dollar package' designed to rejuvenate Hammer's feature film production (Skeggs cited in Jones 1994: 19). In spite of Skeggs' failure to capture the public imagination with his gothic TV series, the Donner/Warner Bros venture hinged mostly on remaking past Hammer successes, in an attempt to revitalise the horror film market with gothic fantasy. It was thought that an injection of Hammer-style horror would be welcome following the decline in popularity of the US slasher film and the rise in popularity of costume gothics as per Francis Ford Coppola's *Bram Stoker's Dracula* (1992) and Kenneth Branagh's *Mary Shelley's Frankenstein* (1994).[9] The first Hammer title scheduled to be remade was *The Quatermass Xperiment* with an estimated $50m budget. Other, lesser-known Hammer thrillers such as the noirish *Stolen Face* (Terence Fisher, 1952) and *Taste of Fear* (Seth Holt, 1961) were also slated to be remade, as a means of riding the popularity wave of controversial neo-noirs like *Fatal Attraction* (Adrian Lyne, 1987) and *Basic Instinct* (Paul Verhoeven, 1992).

The details as to why the Donner/Warner Bros deal fell through are not clear.[10] One may have thought that the involvement of Warner Bros would have benefited a Hammer revival, seeing as though Warner Bros, as a consequence of production and distribution agreements dating back to the 1960s, owned the rights to several of Hammer's past features.[11] A reason for the failure, therefore, may be partly due to a realisation that Hammer was, at this time, very much a heritage brand with little perceived relevance to present-day cinema-going audiences. Indeed, Coppola's and Brannagh's respective re-imaginings of Hammer's most recognisable commercial properties would have proved tough competition for any company wanting to broach gothic horror again. Nevertheless, Hammer's lack of success in the feature film market gave way to a steady merchandise arm that very much celebrated the company's legacy – thanks in part to the aforementioned revitalised interest in the Frankenstein and Dracula characters elsewhere – with the *Hammer Horror* (1994) fanzine published by Marvel Comics, as well as a string of movie soundtrack reissues,[12] T-shirts and other merchandise.[13] Clearly then, Hammer existed with some degree of commercial success, being known for having *once* been a film studio. But its brand status, which was becoming increasingly diluted as the company moved away from film production, very much hinged on the nostalgic appreciation of what the company *used to do*, rather than what it was doing currently (that, frankly, was very little). This continued into the late 1990s with a celebratory documentary, *Flesh and Blood: The Hammer*

Heritage of Horror (Ted Newsom, 1994), a film season at the Barbican in London in 1996, a retrospective exhibit held at the Museum of Moving Image in London in 1997 and, finally, the release of the 'The authorised story of Hammer films', *The Hammer Story* (Hearn and Barnes 1997), which, in more ways than one, closed the book on the Hammer of the 80s and 90s.

By the dawning of the new millennium, Hammer would be sold on again. In 2000, the company was acquired by an investment consortium made up of industry heavy-hitters, including advertising executive and owner of the Saatchi Gallery in London, Charles Saatchi (Minns 2000). As with the company's earlier incarnations, the consortium – comprised of publishers, advertisers, record labels, bankers and media professionals – wanted primarily to exploit the film company's back catalogue as well as its potential in merchandising. The idea was to develop various product lines that could be advertised across age groups, from toys in cereal, to magazines and books. Again, the emphasis was firmly placed on celebrating Hammer's *past* as a viable means of going *forward*. With this in mind, the company recruited esteemed graphic artist Graham Humphreys[14] to design a logo that sought to capture the company's legacy and desired contemporary edge. The logo evoked Hammer's past by presenting the letter 'H', in a gothic font, surrounded by blood, while its more current (corporate) identity was invoked through the company name presented as though it were branded (or, 'Hammered') into a sheet of metal (see Figure 6.1). This literal 'branding' embodied the company's want to be, not merely visible, but also *permanent* – to reclaim its past reputation for resilience, industriousness and productiveness. A wide range of merchandise therefore followed suit, including *The Curse of Frankenstein* lunch boxes, *Dracula*

Figure 6.1   Graham Humphreys' Hammer logo. © Hammer.

T-shirts and *The Mummy* (Terence Fisher, 1959) satchels – all of which were designed to keep the company's heritage afresh in the minds of consumers.

In terms of future film production, emphasis was placed less on major theatrical releases than before. Indeed, it was assumed that if the company was to have the prominence in film production that its logo implied, it was to be on home-viewing media. A six-picture deal was therefore signed between Hammer and the Australian film company, Pictures in Paradise, which specialised in low-budget horror and teen dramas.[15] Hammer's role in this marriage was to oversee 'production funding and distribution' of new films over a five-year period, with sights set on the emerging DVD market (Anon. 2003: 20). The deal, however, fell through, and it was soon replaced in 2005 by another agreement, this time between the British production company Random Harvest, and the US-based Stan Winston Productions. The deal between the three factions was to create an Enterprise Investment Scheme (EIS) company[16] for the production of horror films designed to capitalise on the genre's popularity with DVD-buying audiences, and thus return to film production with some regularity. As discussed in Chapter 2 of this book, Random Harvest at this point had made the lacklustre British horror films *Octane* and *Lethal Dose: 50* (*LD50*) for the theatrical market. However, it had also succeeded in generating £18m in funds through another EIS, which is what likely made the partnership so appealing for Hammer in the first place (Macnab 2005c). Stan Winston Productions was a comparatively newer outfit, although its sister company, Stan Winston Studios, had been providing special effects for big Hollywood features since the 1980s.[17] For reasons that remain unclear, this deal also collapsed, although some of the films slated would go on to be made by other companies over the coming years.[18]

The rapidity with which Hammer seemed to be changing hands by the time it was acquired in 2007 by Cyrte Investments, led to it being referred to in industry circles, rather cynically, as 'the oldest "start-up" in the business' (Simpson 2014). As we have seen, the company had not been all that lucky in maintaining the market presence and relevance of its forbear. Yet, Cyrte's acquisition would in fact signify the rebirth that the company's previous owners had hoped for. For the first time since 1979, 'Hammer' would finally return to making films.

'The newly reborn Hammer Films makes its movie debut':
Beyond the Rave and beyond

Overseeing Hammer's redevelopment was CEO Simon Oakes and his associate Marc Schipper, who had previously worked together at 'the leading international cable company' Liberty Global.[19] Under Cyrte's proviso and Oakes' and Schipper's management, the new Hammer would not simply remain a 'custodian of an extensive back catalogue' as it had remained throughout the 1990s and early 2000s (Hills 2014: 229). Rather, the brand would be very much a multimedia entity and would produce a film for the Internet, *Beyond the Rave*; as well as films for the theatrical and DVD markets, such as *The Woman in Black* and *Wake Wood*; it would publish novels, including movie tie-ins such as *The Resident* (Cottam 2011) and original work such as *Coldbrook* (Labbon 2012); and it would also oversee a stage adaptation of Henry James's 1898 gothic ghost story novella, *The Turn of the Screw* (Hills 2014: 230). Oakes' desire to modernise the company, to 'bring the brand kicking and screaming into the 21st century' (Oakes cited in Anon. 2010a: 16), would be epitomised by his coining a new nickname: 'Hammer 2.0'. This moniker, which deliberately riffed on the trendy neologism 'Web 2.0', symbolised a true 'reboot' for an old company in the digital age and implied that Hammer's new incarnation was, unlike its previous up-starters, now in touch with the contemporary mediascape.

Yet, in many ways, Hammer 2.0 was still faced with the same problems that had confronted both Skeggs and the Saatchi consortium. With the exception of some DVD releases of classic Hammer films that were overseen by the latter, Hammer's presence in the movie marketplace was none existent. In the press, Simon Oakes would often talk of Hammer's historic legacy, and the transnational recognisability of the brand name (see, for example, Mitchell 2007a; Macnab 2008b). But in truth there was no real evidence to show how popular the 'Hammer Brand' was in the minds of contemporary film audiences or even if said audiences knew what it was. This would partly explain the branding incoherence that Matt Hills has written about – Hammer's oscillating 'between a reaction to the present and a loyalty to the past' – because the company was undergoing not only a transitional period, but also a period of trial and error as it attempted to come to terms with what may or may not work for the company going forward. Indeed, Hammer certainly had a brand, but that was all it had, and it was unclear how beneficial that brand would be to the company's future. The result, as Hills (2014) has identified, was an awkward catch-all attempt to cover all bases, with proclamations of Hammer's success in the 1950s repeatedly juxtaposed with its claimed drive to modernise in the face of new audience tastes.

This contradictoriness, which in many ways boiled down to Oakes' and Schipper's uncertainty of Hammer 2.0's relevance in the modern world, would inevitably lead to some second-guessing on their part. For example, in 2007, the company had initially expressed an interest in being the primary investor for Phil Claydon's Hammer horror parody *Lesbian Vampire Killers*, which had been in development hell since 2005. However, as I explain in Chapter 4 of this book, the deal that Hammer eventually made with Claydon failed to match what he initially believed was the company's early enthusiasm for the project. Were he to have accepted Hammer's offer, it would have further delayed the film's production.[20] Although it remains unclear why the company 'didn't fully back it' (Claydon cited in Jones 2010: 59), there is one likely reason. *Lesbian Vampire Killers* may have been thought of as too satirical of the company's legacy. After all, Hammer was, at this time, in the process of being re-established as a real industry player; funding a parody of its own iconic brand could have been a suicidal gambit. But it is also possible that *Lesbian Vampire Killers* was, perhaps, too celebratory of the political incorrectness and slump in production values that Hammer became infamous for in the 1970s.[21] After all, in early interviews, Oakes was keen to promote the world-famous *credibility* of Hammer's legacy in the *1950s and 60s* as being translatable to a contemporary, global, audience. *Lesbian Vampire Killers* was therefore arguably hat-tipping the *wrong* era: an era that marked Hammer's decrease in popularity with audiences domestically and abroad, rather than when it was in its international record-breaking prime (see Mitchell 2007b; Lowe 2008).

As far as Oakes and Schipper were concerned, then, their focus would need to be on producing films that would have a transnational commercial appeal, and that at once retained some of the elements that had established Hammer as a market-leader in the 1950s, but that also traversed any outmoded trappings. This led to the production of four films in quick succession that were all different in tone and style. The first was *Beyond the Rave* – about a clan of vampires that use illegal raves to lure their prospective victims – that was designed to generate the company a younger audience by being distributed online through Myspace.com. This was followed by the production of an occult rural horror set in Ireland, *The Wake Wood* (later retitled simply *Wake Wood*). The film is about a young family who tragically lose their daughter, yet who, with the assistance of a local cult, are able to 'bring her back' from the dead temporarily. The theme of child loss and resurrection was designed to be in-keeping with classic horror films such as *The Wicker Man* and *Don't Look Now* (Nicolas Roeg, 1972): films that, while not Hammer productions, have since become seminal examples of seventies British horror. This film was followed by a US-set thriller, *The Resident*, which starred recognisable Hollywood faces such as Hilary Swank (as a woman who is stalked by her landlord) and Jeffrey Dean Morgen (as the landlord in question). And lastly came *Let Me In*: Hammer's attempt at riding the Hollywood remake train. If these films failed to point to brand coherence and were symptomatic of Hammer's own uncertainty as to what the brand should be, what it should look like and who its core audience was, this confusion was further evident in the films' spaghetti-like production and release schedules.

Wake Wood was shot immediately after *Beyond the Rave* in 2008, but did not go on general release until 2011, after the release of *The Resident*, which was also shot in 2008 but released in late 2010, and the release of *Let Me In*, which was shot in 2009 and released in 2010. The release dates for *Wake Wood* and *The Resident* were deliberately stalled so that Hammer could focus more on the production, promotion and release of *Let Me In*; after all, *Wake Wood* and *The Resident* were more modest productions and were shot primarily for the DVD market (see below). *Let Me In*, comparatively, was always planned as a mainstream theatrical hit (Kay 2008), and was better set to attract broader audiences due to the popularity of both the book and previous film version of *Let the Right One*. These factors partly explain why *Let Me In* was often falsely promoted in the press as being 'the first film in 30 years from the rejuvenated British horror studio Hammer Films' (Muir 2010: 21). Yet *Beyond the Rave*'s omission from *Let Me In* press discourse is more curious, because that film had already been formally released: it went live on Myspace, in an episodic format, in April 2008, and was released on to DVD in September 2010.[22] It had also been featured in the press at some length in 2007 when it was first confirmed that Hammer had once again gone back into production and in 2008 when it went live online. It was also credited at the time for being 'the first Hammer horror film for 30 years' (Anon 2007; see also Mitchell 2007b), and was, generally speaking, looked towards with some degree of optimism (Jefferies 2007; Lowe 2008; Lee 2008). But by the time that *Let Me In* was released into cinemas the following November, earlier statements that had heralded Hammer's 'return' with *Beyond the Rave* were largely forgotten. The *Sunday Express*, for example, reported on 7 November 2010 that the 'newly reborn Hammer Films makes its movie debut with . . . *Let Me In*' (Fitzherbert 2010: 62), while *The Times* reported on 15 October that '[*Let Me In*] is the first film in 30 years from . . . Hammer' (Muir 2010: 21), and *The Independent* stated on 15 November that 'Hammer horror is back in British cinemas with *Let Me In*' (Macnab 2010: 20). Regional press such as the *Bristol Post* reported the film as '[marking] the return of the hugely popular Hammer Horror' (Anon. 2010b: 36), and the *Lincolnshire Echo* named it 'the first movie to come out of the studio for 30 years' (Anon. 2010c: 5). Even Matt Reeves, the director of *Let Me In*, stated in an interview that there is 'something really exciting [about] being part of the first Hammer film in over 30 years – the first Hammer vampire film of the 21st century', when his film was neither one, nor the other (Reeves cited in Driscoll 2010: 2).

There are two likely reasons why *Beyond the Rave* was overlooked in these discussions. First, Hammer was still new to contemporary audiences, the majority of which would not have seen, nor heard of, *Beyond the Rave*. After all, unlike *Let Me In* (and, indeed, lots of other horror films of the period), *Beyond the Rave* was not a $20m American remake of a foreign cult film destined for a multiplex run.[23] It was, conversely, a new script shot for £500,000 (http://imdb.com/pro), exclusively for distribution in five-minute-long 'webisodes' on a social networking site. Its modest production values, budgetary limitations and non-cinematic platform of release (and its limited audience thereof) were factors unlikely to encourage the general public to see a Hollywood block-buster. Indeed, even in the twenty-first century, when most films are viewed at home or on mobile devices and when most of a film's revenue is generated by its home video release, box office gross often remains the yardstick against which a film's 'quality' is judged.[24] If Hammer was to show the film industry and the critics that it meant business, that it was in fact a legendary company worth taking notice of once again, it would therefore have to actually generate some business at the box office first.

The likely second reason why *Beyond the Rave* was overlooked in the press discourse surrounding *Let Me In* relates simply to how it was distributed. Hammer was not all that keen on recognising *Beyond the Rave* as a *feature film* in the promotional copy for *Let Me In*, preferring 'interactive web serial' instead, so those journalists writing about the latter would unlikely have been all that familiar with the former, or were inclined to ignore it on the grounds that it was not a 'film' per se. Those who were prepared to acknowledge *Beyond the Rave* as filmic were inclined to dismiss it on the grounds of its alternative distribution method. One critic, upon hearing the news that *Beyond the Rave* would not be appearing in cinemas, stated that 'while most bad movies go straight to DVD, *Beyond the Rave* is going straight to the Internet' (Brouwer 2008). The implication was that the Internet is an inferior distribution plat-form to theatrical distribution (and, in the eyes of this one critic, even worse than DVD!). *Beyond the Rave*'s 'home-viewing' ties thus worked to reify some familiar prejudices, that 'the casual setting of the home [constitutes] a break with the quality and mesmerizing power of cinema in the motion picture theater' (Klinger 2007: 3). As far as some critics were concerned, *Beyond the Rave* was lacking the 'quality' and 'power' of theatrically released movies and therefore did not count as a 'cinema' at all.

Neil Norman's review of *Let Me In* for the *Daily Express* is notable for being indicative of this attitude. In the review he mentions both *Beyond the Rave* and *Let Me In*, but recognises the latter as Hammer's 'first film', and the former as, plainly, an 'Internet horror' (Norman 2010: 38). The vagueness of the phrase 'Internet horror', while not used to disparage *Beyond the Rave* in this context, does imply that it cannot be considered against, or in line with, *Let Me In*. The term's vagueness, which neither confirms what exactly *Beyond the Rave* is or is not, at least attests to something: that 'Internet horror' is *not* to be read as 'film', as 'feature', or, indeed, as 'worthy comeback venture'. Hammer's re-establishing as a 'brand' needed a hit if it was to gain the visibil-ity with a contemporary audience as its CEO purportedly desired. Suppressing *Beyond the Rave* as *Let Me In* was released created, for the press and the general public alike, yet another illusion of a new start for the company.

When *Beyond the Rave* went into production, Hammer believed that it was riding a wave of technological change. By using the Internet as primary means of distribution – not least the widely popular Myspace – Hammer was attempting to reposition itself not so much as a 'heritage' brand, but more as a purveyor of cutting-edge media production that had an affinity with the youth of the day. Additionally, those at Myspace believed that Hammer's involvement with the company was timely and a good opportunity for both organisations. For example, James Fabricant of MySpace Europe argued that 'Hammer's return to horror production . . . on MySpace is a phenomenal development and shows the dramatic change in how consumers want to access content', while Simon Oakes boasted about how an online release 'is perfect for a company originally born out of a culture of risk-taking and creativity'.[25] Their enthusiasm was not unfounded, either. When Hammer signed the deal with MySpace, the site had recently been bought out by Rupert Murdoch's News Corporation and was, at the time, estimated to have 30 to 70 million unique visitors each month, 'hold[ing] over 80% of all social network traffic' (Percival 2009: 10).[26] It was also believed to be a useful tool to promote new businesses to new audiences (12–13). As Sean Percival explained in his book, *MySpace Marketing: Creating a Social Network to Boom Your Business*: '[a]lthough the sheer number of MySpace users is great, the real value of marketing [through MySpace] is that you can target your key demographic so precisely' (10). It was therefore an ideal platform for Hammer to expose itself to its desired teenage demographic, and provided the company with a good opportunity to experiment with a relatively new method of content delivery.

The serial format of *Beyond the Rave* was devised by Tom and Ben Grass, owners of the 'leading cross platform entertainment producer',[27] Pure Grass Films. Before collaborating with Hammer, the company had generated a modest market presence having produced *When Evil Calls* (Johannes Roberts, 2006), 'the first made-for-mobile horror series' (Parker 2007), which was funded by the British TV station Zone Horror and made in association with the UK's leading mobile service provider, O2.[28] *When Evil Calls* was initially made available to consumers in three-minute-long episodes, downloadable from the Wireless Application Protocol (WAP) sites of all the major UK mobile phone operators. Despite a very modest budget of only £75,000, the film was successful enough to be sold to eleven territories worldwide, before being released by Sony Pictures on DVD in 2007. Although the press reviews of the film were largely negative,[29] its success and 'new' approach to the format and distribution of horror cinema proved novel enough to attract the interest of Oakes and Schipper. Indeed, Liberty Global, where Oakes and Schipper had previously worked, was the parent company of Zone Horror, so the duo were already familiar with Pure Grass's approach and vision. Oakes and Schipper agreed that releasing a horror film episodically, across an alternative media platform, was a novel way of attracting new, young and tech-savvy audiences (Grass 2011). This was especially central in the re-launch of a brand as old, outdated, and, frankly, as *unknown*, as Hammer was at the time. As Ben Grass explained to me: 'People in their forties might have heard of Hammer films, but sixteen-year-olds certainly hadn't' (ibid.).[30]

In spite of these high hopes, *Beyond the Rave* certainly was not as successful – nor, for that matter, as a good – as some fans and industry watchers had hoped (Meikle 2009: 226). Hills has suggested that 'the novelty of *Beyond the Rave* derived from its status as a web series' alone (2014: 232). Hammer's decision to put credence on technical innovation above the kinds of 'generic innovation' that its legacy rested on (246) meant that the film was always destined to be more a 'product of its techno-cultural moment' than a real game-changer (232). Certainly, the film's premise, which involves vampires using illegal raves to lure unsuspecting teenage victims, was certainly not all that innovative. However, had *Beyond the Rave* been, à la Hills, more 'textually innovative' (246), it is likely that this would have further skewed any hope of Hammer redefining itself as a strong contender in the cinematic marketplace. Hammer's legacy, as a company known primarily for its anachronistic *Dracula* and *Frankenstein* movies, limited the kinds of directions it could have taken if it wanted to remain true to Hammer's commercial essence. If the company was looking to appeal, as Hills suggests, to 'long-term fans' *as well as* the 'youth demographic' (231), counteracting people's expectations by rocking the boat too hard would not have been a wise business move. Indeed, Hammer needed a safe bet in terms of content, so a generic vampire story involving teenagers was a sensible, if unadventurous, choice. When considered in light of Hammer's failings in the 1990s and early 2000s, *Beyond the Rave* also proffered a *cheaper* means of reintroducing the company to audiences. Shooting the film for the Internet forwent many of the marketing and advertising overheads of more mainstream horror films. Having News Corporation on board also meant that *Beyond the Rave* was able to be promoted on many of the mainstream news networks and television shows under Murdoch's proviso (Grass 2011), and was, therefore, in a position to capitalise on the concurrent anticipation that surrounded, on the one hand, News Corp's acquiring of Myspace, and on the other, the anticipation surrounding Hammer's 'return' among horror fans and some industry watchers. As with *When Evil Calls*, *Beyond the Rave*'s consumer context of smartphones and mobile PCs represented a daring attempt at transcending conventional domestic viewing platforms, putting faith in viral marketing – generating 100,000 Myspace 'friends' on the official *Beyond the Rave* webpage (Grass 2011) – and good old-fashioned 'word of mouth'.

James Leggott has recognised that British horror 'films have had to compete in an international market now crowded with horror productions and therefore very different to the situation in the 1950s and 1960s when Hammer enjoyed their golden era' (2008: 58). When *Beyond the Rave* was released, the new Hammer was but one voice amid a host of other (louder) horror producers. Choosing an online serial format over more conventional means of distribution was a choice that attested to Oakes and Schipper's self-realisation that Hammer was in fact *not* the powerhouse of a brand that had thus far been assumed by its previous rights holders. They realised, irrespective of their 'contradictory approach' to the company's branding (Hills 2014), that it could *not* be successful on its name alone.

'FROM THE MAKERS OF *THE WOMAN IN BLACK*': THE HAMMER NAME IN AND OUT OF FILM MARKETING

If *Beyond the Rave* tested the water for Hammer, *Let Me In* showed that the company was capable of setting its sights much higher in terms of budget, crew and cast. A commendable international run saw *Let Me In* generate $22m at the global box office. This figure would be subsequently trumped by the record-breaking *The Woman in Black*, which generated $126m in 2012, and became 'the U.K.'s highest grossing horror film since records began' (Kemp 2012). However, in spite of these impressive figures, to what extent these films – and, for that matter, the lower-key releases *Wake Wood* and *The Resident* – established Hammer 2.0 as a *brand* with a kind of market visibility that was in anyway comparable to the old Hammer, remains open to question.

Oakes certainly tried to create the illusion that Hammer 2.0 was a major industry player in spite of its relative marginality. Just as Hammer's former CEO, James Carreras, had used various exploitation strategies 'to raise the market's awareness of [his] small, hitherto relatively unknown company' (Hutchings 2003b: 34), Oakes emulated the original Hammer's approach to distinction by investing in the company a 'degree of energy and ambition' designed to traverse its otherwise modest resources and reputation (ibid.). A key means of doing this was through mimicking the status and success of major Hollywood brands – notably the American comic-book-publisher-cum-film-producer Marvel Studios.

Marvel was, at least on paper, comparable to Hammer: it had faced financial difficulty, had in recent years been declared bankrupt (although much more recently than Hammer) and was going through a period of 'rebirth' that ran parallel to Hammer's (Johnson 2012: 1). It also had an iconic pool of commercial properties (Spider-Man, Iron Man, The Incredible Hulk and so forth) that were exploited in its subsequent films, similar to how Hammer carried historic associations with certain screen monsters. However, whereas Hammer had managed only one or two successes in the 2000s, Marvel had – of its sixteen films made since the late 1990s – produced five of the one hundred 'highest

Figure 6.2   Hammer evokes Marvel Studios with its animated ident. © Hammer.

grossing domestic films of all time' (ibid.). In other words, Marvel had the kind of market visibility and a type of highly commercial brand that Hammer was keen to (re)establish for itself. Therefore, Hammer mirrored Marvel's branding through the commissioning of an 'ident' that would prefix the credit sequences of each of its major theatrical releases. The ident was a short animated sequence, in which various poster images from the Hammer archive faded in and out before forming the company name in red lettering (see Figure 6.2). The similarities to Marvel's, which did the same kind of thing but with Marvel characters, were uncanny. Yet, as Geoffry Macnab (2010) noted in his review of *Let Me In*, such was Hammer's liminal presence and so far were the new films removed from the branding that had characterised the company in its heyday, viewers may 'register' the ident 'but [were] likely to forget it'. The implication being that, despite Hammer's best efforts, it ultimately lacked the cachet of its Hollywood contemporaries, and that it would take more than a fancy logo to reignite the brand in the twenty-first century.

If Denis Meikle's observation is true that Hammer 2.0 is simply 'Hammer . . . in name only' (2009: 226), the fact that the company name was elusive from many of the accompanying market materials for its major releases is telling of its market positioning from 2007 to 2014. Consider the UK and US posters for *Let Me In* and *The Woman in Black*. In the media, Oakes boasted about how these films recalled 'the kind of great British horrors Hammer Films started off producing, before garnering its reputation for being over-the-top' (Mortimer 2010). Yet neither materials used to promote the films featured the Hammer name in any prominent way. For example, the UK quad for

Let Me In, in contrast to some of the reviews that accompanied the release discussed earlier, makes no mention of it being 'the first Hammer film in 30 years'. Nor is its status as a 'Hammer film' all that obvious. Rather, it is promoted as 'A film by Matt Reeves, director of *Cloverfield*' with only a small Hammer logo visible, rendered grey, at the bottom of the poster. This appears to downplay the film's association with Hammer that Oakes so keenly emphasised in press interviews as being significant to his brand's development (see Anon. 2010a). Indeed, while the Hammer logo appears across other official company merchandise, often positioned centrally, in bold and in red,[31] the British poster for *Let Me In* is far removed from this sense of brand cohesion. Moreover, the positioning of 'Matt Reeves' and '*Cloverfield*' above the title in place of the company name attests more to *Let Me In*'s American connection than it being part of a tradition of 'great *British* horrors' (see also Hills 2014: 233–4). The quad for *The Woman in Black* also lacks overt connections with Hammer, save a company logo at the bottom, which appears in an even lower resolution than on the poster for *Let Me In*. In fact, the poster is mostly dedicated to an image of Daniel Radcliffe's face. In one respect, this may be seen as invoking 'Britishness' – due to Radcliffe's association with the Harry Potter franchise – more so than the poster for *Let Me In*, but any overt opportunity to capitalise on Hammer's involvement is avoided.

These examples are strikingly different to the British posters that were used to promote Hammer's horror films during the company's most prolific period of horror production in the mid-1960s and 1970s, including the poster for *Rasputin the Mad Monk* (Don Sharp)/*The Reptile* (John Gilling) (1966) double bill, which read 'From Hammer, the House of Horror', or the poster for *Twins of Evil*, which carried the legend 'Hammer Horror' in a font that was actually bigger than the film's title (Branaghan 2006: 113). Why was it, then, that the Hammer name was marginalised in the promotion of its most lucrative productions?

One theory is that Hammer's success depended less on brand recognition, and more on its acquisition of lucrative commercial properties and the casting of big name actors. After all, Tomas Alfredson's *Let the Right One In* was fresh in the minds of audiences when *Let Me In* was released, and *The Woman in Black*, as well as being a stage play with a twenty-five-year legacy in London's West End, also starred one of the industry's most recognisable faces. To pigeonhole these new releases as emerging 'From the Hammer House of Horror' would have been redundant on two counts. First, the 'Hammer brand' had not been fully re-established, so most people would have been unfamiliar with what the name 'Hammer' signified (at least in a contemporary context). Even if the audience was by some chance familiar with the Hammer of yesteryear, the company's associations with high-camp Gothicana would unlikely have registered with mainstream audiences as a reason to go and see a high-end ghost story. And, second, marketing the films explicitly as Hammer productions or as 'Hammer Horror' would have risked predetermining – or limiting – the films' demographic before they were released. As Matt Reeves has argued of *Let Me In*, part of its appeal lay in the fact that it is not simply a vampire story, but also a drama about two children who fall in love, while James Watkins (2012) argued that *The Woman in Black* is primarily 'a film about loss'. In other words, the films had more market potential than the limited horror hard-core that may have gone to see the films simply because they were Hammer productions. It can therefore be discerned that Hammer's involvement in these films, for the majority of the audience who paid to see them, and for their subsequent box-office success, was simply incidental.

It was only after *The Woman in Black* that Hammer began overtly promoting its brand in its feature film marketing, in the campaign for its next global theatrical release, *The Quiet Ones*. The UK promotional materials featured the Hammer logo more prominently than in the *Let Me In* and *The Woman in Black* campaigns, as if to imply that the company and its brand now carried some commercial weight. Some promotional materials even invoked Hammer's historical significance by carrying the strapline 'From the Legendary Hammer'. Yet, in spite of this, to what extent Hammer's name was significant to the film's appeal is questionable. The widely distributed UK quad for *The Quiet Ones*, for example, played it safe, by promoting the film as 'From the makers of *The Woman in Black*'. Employing a different strategy to the aforementioned advertisement, the quad's design team did not mention Hammer's alleged 'legendary' status, opting instead to invoke the recent commercial success that, as we have already seen, did little to promote Hammer's involvement. The box-office performance of *The Quiet Ones* testified to a perceived ambivalence regarding the Hammer brand. Grossing a meagre $8.5m worldwide (Box Office Mojo 2014), the film was clearly not in the same bankable league as a glossy remake or a major star vehicle, regardless of Hammer's visibility in its promotional materials.

If the Hammer name was largely suppressed in the marketing of its most successful theatrical features, the opposite was true of its home video releases. Indeed, Hammer's films that did not have a theatrical release, such as *Beyond the Rave*, or those that only had a brief stint in cinemas before going to DVD, such as *The Resident* and *Wake Wood*, were more overly branded as being 'Hammer' productions. For example, Hammer's UK DVD art for *The Resident* featured the Hammer logo ('HAMMER Presents'), in red, above the title, in a way that anticipated the print ads for *The Quiet Ones*. The same was also true of the DVD box art for *Wake Wood*, which adopted the same approach. But why was the Hammer name deemed more significant in the home-viewing context? One possible reason is that Hammer was, quite simply, a more powerful force in the domestic DVD market. Since the early 2000s

Warner Brothers and Studio Canal had released collectors' editions of some of Hammer's most iconic works in both the UK and America, all of which embellished the Hammer brand.[32] Once Cyrte took over in 2007, following the introduction of the Blu-ray format,[33] the company went about re-mastering some of the more famous titles and releasing 'definitive' high-definition (HD) reissues. Whereas, in the theatrical market, Hammer's name was an inconsequential factor, a 'Hammer' film was more likely to be watched for its namesake by a niche DVD market of horror fans. As mentioned earlier, Matt Hills makes the point that the new Hammer has been purely 'emulative' in piggybacking on the success of other films. Therefore, one way that Hammer could distinguish its films from others in the saturated DVD market, was to single them out as 'Hammer' productions, and thus align them with the many other past Hammer titles that were available on DVD. This context permitted more overt connections to be made between Hammer's newer productions and its legacy. For example, the DVD artwork for *The Resident* carried an image of Christopher Lee who features for only a few minutes in the film itself, but is known the world over for his role as Count Dracula in several Hammer films produced from the 1950s to the 1970s.[34] Positioning Lee as one of the stars of *The Resident*, and placing his name next to Hammer's, invariably embellishes the historical connection between the actor and the company, as well as the DVD box art for the contemporaneous reissues of other Hammer horror classics that customers may have had an awareness of. Similarly, the DVD box art for *Wake Wood* carried a quote from the *News of the World* that read 'An instant folk HORROR CLASSIC'. The invoking of the term 'folk horror' nods to Hammer's revered occult rural horror film *The Devil Rides Out*, as well as other classic non-Hammer horrors such as *The Wicker Man*.[35] Perhaps most importantly, however, the use of 'classic' in the context of a Hammer production implies a connection that Oakes and Schipper were keen to bolster all along: between the company's legacy and its inferred ability to make quality contemporary films.

In the 1950s and 60s Hammer was able to rival its competitors by, among other things, utilising its small budgets and limited studio space to 'make a film appear more expensive than it actually was'. This was one of many factors that has been said to have made the company 'distinctive' in the film marketplace (Hutchings 2003b: 35). However, as we have seen here, Hammer 2.0 played it much safer by, instead of carving its own market niche, focusing mostly on cash-ins produced for existent markets (Hills 2014: 238). With that said, although *The Resident* and *Wake Wood* were never destined for the theatrical success that graced *The Woman in Black* and *Let Me In*, Hammer's branding proved far more useful in the promotion of the former than the latter, where the films could be more easily aligned with Hammer's other output, indicating a greater sense of coherence that was not so evident elsewhere.

CONCLUSION: 'CLASSIC PRODUCTIONS FROM THE ARCHIVE'

This chapter has shown how Hammer Films re-established itself as an active film production house in the twenty-first century. We have seen how, after various stop–starts, the twenty-first century saw Hammer return to film production for the first time since the late 1970s, with films that straddled a variety of generic styles, platforms and demographics. The chapter has revealed that, while the Hammer name was able to ascertain a certain degree of visibility in the promotion of the company's home video releases, its omission from the publicity of its most successful features to date, suggests that the company's branding has mostly been inconsequential to its box-office profits. This has been in spite of the company striving to emulate the brand recognition of Hollywood heavy-hitters such as Marvel.

At the time of writing (mid-2014), Hammer's official filmography that appears on the company website makes a clear historical link between its more recent output and its earlier work. All productions, irrespective of their release date, are aligned with films that carry much more cultural and historical weight, under the banner 'Classic Productions from the Archive'. The implications of this are twofold. First, it shows an additional way that Hammer attempted to retain illusionary brand cohesion after 2007. As I have argued elsewhere, collating otherwise disparate films under a collective heading often connotes uniformity where there may be none (Walker 2014: 223). 'Classic Productions from the Archive' – in a way similar to lo-fi horror DVD series that round up cult classics from the 1970s with amateur horrors from the 2000s (ibid.) – implies that recent films like *Wake Wood* and *The Resident* are to be regarded as just as worthy as *Dracula* or *The Curse of Frankenstein*. These kinds of associations, at least to some degree, circumvent the frenetic brand incoherence that Hammer 2.0 exhibited elsewhere. What can also be discerned from this, however, is that, through making such overt suggestions of brand coherence and legacy on the company website, but suppressing such factors in the marketing of its most globally visible contemporary releases, Hammer was only truly 'Hammer' to a select few.

In terms of future developments, the forthcoming *The Woman in Black: Angel of Death* anticipates continued popularity for the company's films, if not for the company brand per se. Indeed, one of the biggest trends in the 2000s and 2010s was movie franchises based on 'Young Adult' gothic novels (à la *Twilight*), and *Woman in Black 2* may well establish Hammer as a contender in this field because of its literary associations, and the fact that the script was based on an outline drafted by the author of the original *Woman in Black* novella, Susan Hill. Hammer will also likely remain popular in the home-viewing market. At the time of writing, talks are in place to remake one of Hammer's early, less-successful, efforts: *The Abominable Snowman* (Val

Guest, 1957) (Rosser 2013). If this film gets made, it is likely that it will have a much bigger presence on DVD, Blu-ray or VoD than at cinemas, where it can share shelf space (virtual or otherwise) with other widely seen 'creature features' of recent years such as *Sharknado* (Anthony C. Ferrante, 2013),[36] and movies like *Behemoth* (W. D. Hogan, 2011), *Vipers* (Bill Corcoran, 2008) and *Sand Serpents* (Jeff Renfroe, 2009), which form part of Vivendi Entertainment's 'Maneater' DVD series. Amid this speculation, however, one thing remains certain: the Hammer name is unlikely to have any major bearing on any the company's success. As with the company's faltering status in the 1970s, what will remain essential to any profit-generation is how Hammer responds to current industry trends – not its company name, nor its legacy.

NOTES

1. Fanzines include *Little Shoppe of Horrors*; fansites include http://hammerand-beyond.blogspot.com and http://unofficialhammerfilms.com; and books include Hearn and Barnes (2007); Hearn (2009); Hallenbeck (2010, 2011); and Kinsey (2002, 2007, 2010). In autumn of 2014 the digital channel BBC4 ran a Hammer films season in the lead up to Halloween.
2. Intriguingly, Hammer's main competitor in the 1960s, Amicus Films, attempted to re-launch with the films *Stuck* (Stuart Gordon, 2007) and *It's Alive* (Josef Rusnak, 2008). In an article published in *Screen International* from 2006, it was stated that the new Amicus would look to fund original scripts as well as 'projects inspired by the catalogue' (Kay 2006b). However, the company dissolved after three years.
3. I am thinking specifically about Black & Blue Films, which cornered the UK exploitation direct-to-DVD market with films such as *Devil's Playground* and *Dead Cert*. As discussed in Chapter 2 of this book, the company's CEO, Jonathan Sothcott, created Black & Blue in the model of the old Hammer: producing low-budget genre films, in-hose, with a degree of rapidity and repeated re-casting of familiar faces (such as the lo-fi stars Danny Dyer and Craig Fairbrass).
4. Skeggs had overseen the costings on a number of productions, including *Twins of Evil* (Tudor Gates, 1971), *Vampire Circus* (Robert Young, 1972) and *Dracula AD 1972* (Alan Gibson, 1972).
5. Hutchings (2001: 2) briefly reflects on these double bills in the introduction to his book on one of Hammer's most revered directors, Terence Fisher.
6. Cushing appeared in a *Hammer House of Horror* episode 'The Silent Scream' as a mad doctor-type not far removed from Dr Frankenstein (his most famous film role for Hammer), while Stephanie Beacham, who had featured in the Hammer film *Dracula AD 1972* and other British horrors of the period, appeared in a *Hammer House of Mystery and Suspense* episode 'A Distant Scream'.
7. See Chapter 3 of this book as well as Egan (2007) and Petley (2011).
8. The album was reportedly a 'concept record', supposedly inspired by Evo's (the lead singer) continued fandom for Hammer's horror films and his own anticipation of the company's future developments. As he explained to the British fanzine *Samhain*: 'the album reflects the new Hammer as well as the old' ('Evo' cited in Evans 1990: 14). Appropriately, the record featured songs such as 'Baron Frankenstein' and 'The Phantom of the Opera', but is long out of print.

9. At the global box office, *Dracula* reportedly generated $216m and *Frankenstein* $112m (http://imdb.com/pro). On the decline in popularity of the slasher film, see Grove (2005: 187–8).

10. While I have spoken at length with some of Hammer's former employees, many of the reasons are unable to be revealed due to signed confidentiality agreements.

11. Many of Hammer's films were co-productions with American majors such as Warner Bros, who oversaw, for example, *The Curse of Frankenstein*, and Twentieth Century Fox, who was involved in the production of *The Nanny* (Seth Holt, 1965) among others.

12. Examples include the compilation *Music from Hammer Films* (1990).

13. For example, a Hammer playing cards set was issued, which featured stills from Hammer's back catalogue of gothic horror films.

14. Humphreys remains most famous for having painted the original British film posters for *A Nightmare on Elm Street* (Wes Craven, 1984) and *The Evil Dead*. His work can be found at http://grahamhumphreys.com.

15. Credits included the modestly successful DVD horror film, *The Locals* (Greg Page, 2003), and the critically acclaimed Western, *The Proposition* (John Hillcoat, 2005).

16. 'The Enterprise Investment Scheme (EIS) is designed to help smaller higher-risk trading companies to raise finance by offering a range of tax reliefs to investors who purchase new shares in those companies' (www.hmrc.gov.uk/eis, accessed 11 July 2014).

17. Stan Winston is best known for his special effects work on *Aliens* (James Cameron, 1986) and *Terminator 2: Judgement Day* (James Cameron, 1991).

18. Paul Andrew Williams' comedy horror, *The Cottage*, is one such film, and was subsequently funded by the UKFC, Isle of Man Film, Screen Yorkshire and Steel Man Pictures.

19. www.libertyglobal.com (accessed 24 September 2014).

20. *Lesbian Vampire Killers* had been the victim of several stop–starts during its development dating back to 2005. As Phil Claydon told *Fangoria*, Hammer's initial enthusiasm for the project subsided, resulting in the company offering 'only a basic option for three years' that would have potentially stalled the project again (Claydon cited in Jones 2010: 59).

21. In I. Q. Hunter's words, 'For many Hammerphiles' the company's 'tendencies towards camp and sexploitation' during this period constitute 'signs of exhaustion, inauthenticity and a slide into bad taste' (2013: 47). See also Chapter 4 of this book.

22. Hammer initially issued a limited collector's edition DVD (5000 copies) that was available direct from the company website. A vanilla release followed.

23. http://boxofficemojo.com/movies/?id=lettherightonein09.htm. Director Matt Reeves had recently made the alien-invasion film *Cloverfield* (Matt Reeves, 2008) – a much anticipated movie from the producer of the prime-time US TV show *Lost* (2004–10), which had taken $168,000,000 at the worldwide box office.

24. This is apparent even in light of the decline in DVD sales since 2006. Websites like boxofficemojo.com and imdb.com/pro attest in part to the emphasis and value placed on knowing a film's box-office gross, whereas video sales figures remain tricky to find.

25. www.hammerfilms.com/news/article/newsid/143/hammer-to-broadcast-first-production-for-over-twenty-years-in-joint-venture-with-myspace (12 December 2007, accessed 20 March 2014).

26. News Corp acquired Myspace in 2005 for a reported $580m. The property was sold on again in 2011 for a reported $35m – a drop in value that evidences the

subsequent market hold of competitors Facebook and Twitter (see Cellan-Jones 2011).

27. www.puregrassfilms.com/AboutUs.aspx (accessed 8 December 2011).

28. Incidentally, the film was also directed by Johannes Roberts, who would go on to direct one of the pivotal hoodie horror films, *F*.

29. One of the more extreme reviews came from the popular horror site dreadcentral. com, in which the reviewer called the film a 'one-note, shit-out, steaming, failure-pile of cinematic travesty' (Barton 2008).

30. It should be stated at this point that Myspace had a policy in place whereby spectators had to agree that they were aged eighteen or over before accessing the content. Nevertheless, Hammer's advertising was visible to all, regardless of age (moreover, such age restrictions are relatively easily outstepped in the digital age, which Hammer, presumably, would have been aware of).

31. Hammer produced a series of mugs that replicated classic poster images, such as *Dracula*, *Quatermass II* (Val Guest, 1957), *Legend of the 7 Golden Vampires* (Roy Ward Baker, 1974), as well as two *Let Me In* variants. These mugs, however, were not all that widely available, being limited to cult stores such as Forbidden Planet, and Hammer's own website.

32. Notable among these releases were Warner's three-disc *Hammer Horror Originals* box set, which included *The Curse of Frankenstein*, *Dracula* and *The Mummy* ('The first three horror films from the infamous Hammer Studios') and Studio Canal's twenty-one disc box set, *The HAMMER Collection*, a black cardboard cube that opened up to reveal four DVD booklets that, when placed on top of one another, formed the image of a Gothic crucifix.

33. Blu-ray discs and players were first made commercially available in 2006.

34. Lee played the role of Dracula in the following Hammer films: *Dracula*, *Dracula Prince of Darkness* (Terence Fisher, 1966), *Dracula Has Risen from the Grave* (Freddie Francis, 1968), *Taste the Blood of Dracula* (Peter Sasdy, 1970), *Scars of Dracula* (Roy Ward Baker, 1970), *Dracula AD 1972* and *The Satanic Rites of Dracula* (Alan Gibson, 1973). For an extended discussion of Lee, and his associations with the role, see Hutchings (2003b: 91–5).

35. Oakes, for example, claimed that the film is 'a homage to old Hammer in the *Wicker Man* vein' (Oakes cited in Wells 2010); the *Daily Record* stated that '*Wake Wood* will please horror fans with its . . . neat nods to the best of 70s British horror' (Anon. 2011); and the *i* characterised the film, as 'a throwback to exactly the kind of nonsensical hokum the studio was so fondly remembered for' (Phelan 2013).

36. For a discussion of the global popularity of *Sharknado* – that became a social media phenomenon in 2013 – see Block (2014).

7. A KINGDOM OF HORROR

Contemporary British Horror Cinema: Industry, Genre and Society has documented how, from 2000 to 2014, British horror witnessed its biggest boom period since the 1970s. The book has shown how British horror films during this period were in constant dialogue with other nations, whether in terms of film economics or textual reflexivity, and also how they managed to retain specific cultural mores. It has been revealed that, while British horror was not as globally visible, as profitable or as written about, as other examples of popular British cinema – such as the romantic comedy or heritage film – it nevertheless remained one of the most persistent and consistent, varied and heterogeneous, innovative and widely distributed, genre of films.

This chapter, as a means of closure, will reflect briefly on the key issues that have been addressed over the last six chapters, before considering some of the directions that the study of British horror cinema could – or, indeed, should – take in the future. It is hoped that this chapter will provide a springboard for further scholarship that will be as dynamic as the films themselves.

The book began by identifying some of the problematic ways that British horror has been discussed in the past: namely, under the auspices of David Pirie's (1973, 2008) influential 'heritage of horror' argument. With this in mind, Chapter 2 sought to examine the industrial – rather than the cultural – reasons from British horror's revival in the 2000s, examining how the films were funded, marketed and distributed. It was argued that horror was initially conceived as a widely marketable genre that could aid in the successful 're-launch' of a British film industry following the instating of the UKFC in 2000, and the subsequent buzz (and controversy) that surrounded it. Citing industry data and reports, film reviews and industry testimonies, it was maintained, that, while in the past it has 'more or less [been] impossible to think of British cinema without reference to its relationship with Hollywood' (Street 2009: 240), Hollywood and American finance was, on the whole, absent from the production of British horror films in the first years of the twenty-first century. The chapter also documented how tax breaks that were available in continental Europe led to a multitude of British horror co-productions that employed European monies, locations and crew, and how, through DVD channels and the Internet, many horror films were able to reach audiences without the backing of American finance (unlike in other areas of contemporary British cinema). It was shown how, with the general lack of interest in films that 'looked British' or had a 'British sensibility', Hollywood's distancing from British horror film production opened doors for European countries to produce films that would appeal to – above all else – local audiences, and, in turn, testify to several national film industries that were able to turn a profit without Hollywood pulling the strings.[1] Certainly, countries such as Spain, France, Germany and the UK itself remained the most fertile ground for success for British horror and associated co-productions. This success was achieved through the fruitful utilisation of European stars and locations, people and studios. Moreover, what with the realisation that British horror was most popular at home, there was now scope to produce more 'nationally specific' films and, as the success of films such as *28 Days Later*, *Shaun of the Dead* and *The Descent* attested, scope to exploit British actors lesser-known to an international mainstream audience, and still turn a profit.

One of the early concerns of this book was how British film production, in the first part of the decade, experimented with the horror genre as a means of targeting international audiences, through the casting of actors and the addressing of themes that had been popular with both sexes and a variety of age groups. It was acknowledged that, where some movies failed (such as the Colin Firth vehicle *Trauma*), others (such as *Shaun of the Dead* and *The Descent*) proved how it was in fact possible to generate big box-office receipts – by either hybridising with other genres that were seen to have an appeal to female audiences (*Shaun of the Dead* and the rom-com, for instance), or trumping traditional male-centric horror with well-rounded female characters (as with *The Descent*).

As well as having considered statistical and economic factors that led to the production of British horror, the book has also drawn attention to some of the primary creative impulses behind British horror cinema of this period, arguing how certain films sought to 'appear British' in a market that was otherwise super-saturated with European and American product. By analysing specific directors and some of their key films, Chapter 3 argued, how, through the nostalgic recollection of the 'video nasty era', several films offered satirical commentary on the censorious opinions on video violence that had characterised the past, through the use of visceral horror in *Creep* and *The Devil's Chair*, and the invoking of video technology in *The Last Horror Movie* and *Resurrecting the Street Walker*. It was revealed, with reference to some of the criticisms that contemporary British horror has faced from the press, how these case studies provocatively addressed the creative 'influence' of the video nasty on impressionable youngsters (the filmmakers themselves), in a way that captured the sensationalist rhetoric of the video nasty panic, and resulted in films that may have appeared indicative of trends in horror cinema abroad, but were also nationally distinctive.

This national distinctiveness, however, was not solely restricted to the invocation of the video nasty era, although the prevalence of filmmakers who openly aligned themselves with fan practices remained a driving force during the production of British horror after 2000. By intertextually targeting eras and themes that remain of specific interest to cult film fan communities, this book has positioned contemporary British horror as an outlet for new directors to develop a genre profile, and exploit their own fan allegiances with horror cinema. These factors were touched on in Chapter 3 in reference to the films of Neil Marshall, Adam Mason, Christopher Smith and Julian Richards, but were further considered in Chapter 4 in relation to horror-comedies such as *Shaun of the Dead*, *Lesbian Vampire Killers* and *Doghouse*. These horror-comedies were analysed to illustrate how the stereotypical 'fan boy' has been shaped by pop culture and theorised within academia, and how self-critiquing filmmakers often knowingly exacerbate such stereotypes in a playful, often self-deprecating, way. By seemingly 'pandering' to what some feminist critics would consider 'dangerous' about the perceived 'masculinity' of cult film discourse, filmmakers Jake West, Edgar Wright and Phil Claydon were shown to acknowledge the regressive nature of their stereotype, by enjoying the horror, mocking their stereotypical identity (and the masculine insecurities supposedly contained within it) and questioning the hyperbolic theoretical paradigms that have sought to explain their cult interests away.

One of the central thrusts of this book, therefore, has been the prominence of the fan filmmaker as a driving force in the production of contemporary British horror cinema. Yet, while intertextuality and irony have functioned to provoke, and poke-fun at, detractors of the genre, British horror films have also been recognised and remain partly defined by their more 'serious' socio-cultural preoccupations. As a means of illustrating this, Chapter 5 considered how recent British horror cinema engaged with the pressing (and predominantly right-wing) concerns regarding 'broken Britain' through the 'hoodie horror' cycle. Through the textual examination of *Eden Lake*, *Cherry Tree Lane*, *Heartless* and *F*, the chapter argued how such films worked to expound the media stereotyping that was imposed on the vulnerable British working class during this period. And drawing on the typical rhetoric of the contemporary British news media, it was shown how the children of the working class have been conveyed as 'monstrous' and as 'feral' within recent news reportage, and how, consequently, the British horror film appropriated these sensationalist images as a source of horror. Discourses surrounding the popular academic binary of 'realism' and 'genre' were explored to identify how these films created a dialogue between characteristics of British social realism and the horror film, and to question the accuracy and social function of sensationalist media stereotyping. This strand was continued by further examining the locations where each of these films was set: the countryside, the middle-class household, the city and the school.

Finally, the book returned to a primarily industry-focus in Chapter 6, addressing the re-launch of British horror's most iconic company, Hammer Films. Charting the several restarts that the company witnessed throughout the 1980s and 90s, the chapter showed that, for all Hammer retained a central position in cult film discourse and fan communities, the company name had little to no bearing on its international success in the wake of the theatrical release of its biggest hit *The Woman in Black*. This was slightly different in the home video market where, the chapter argued, Hammer was able to feature more prominently – and, indeed, more purposefully – in its marketing.

Contemporary British Horror Cinema has covered a lot of ground; but, as with any study dedicated to a specific period in cinema history, it has faced limitations. One of these limitations has been the process of studying contemporary cinema itself, which, mostly without the benefit of retrospect, has at times seemed all the more sprawling and incoherent. Indeed, the writing of this book was often complicated by the seemingly never-ending number of films that were being released on a week-by-week basis.[2] But what also proved tricky was keeping up to date with the rapid technological changes that continued to impact film itself, and, as a result, the definition of what cinema *actually means* in the twenty-first century (Klinger 2007; Cunningham and Iordanova 2012).

Such factors certainly brought, and continue to bring, into light questions of the usefulness of the 'cohesion' that grand historical narratives appear to offer us. As Peter Hutchings has argued in his conclusion to *The Horror Film*, 'retrospective views of horror history have often tidied up the genre in their attempts to categorise and make sense of it', yet, 'things are never that simple and generic patterns never that obvious' (2004a: 217). To this end, one of the benefits of studying contemporary cinema – horror or otherwise – presents us with an opportunity to capture the dynamism of the films and trends as they happen, and restricting the focus to such a short time period allows for detail to flourish that may have had to have been compromised in a study of a broader period. Therefore, while *Contemporary British Horror Cinema* has attested to the differences in British horror, it has also sought to identify those similarities between, not simply the horror films, but also the wider goings-on within the British film industry and those overseas, and how horror cinema specifically has navigated this period of industrial and technological change.

Inevitably, I haven't had space to consider everything in as much detail as I would have liked. Some things have simply had to be sidelined altogether. So, as a means of drawing things to as neat a close as possible, I will now address some of the areas that I've skirted over in these last six chapters. It is hoped that what follows will open other research avenues to further broaden our understanding of British horror cinema in the twenty-first century. I will also ponder, as a means of reflection, where the genre may be headed, the technology that will take it there, and, ultimately, how these factors may impact on the way that British horror is historicised in the future.

'I have seen the future . . . and it is a kingdom of horror'[3]

It now seems ironic that Richard Stanley heralded the death of British horror cinema in 2002, precisely due to the 'poverty row budgets and Z-grade casting' that many horror films produced before and after 2000 boast (2002: 193). After all, the majority of the films considered in this book could quite comfortably fall within Stanley's remit. But, as I have claimed here, such films' lack of gloss – or their 'fannishness', 'boyishness' or their prevailing lack of 'quality', or however one wants to phrase it – does not need to be perceived as something that makes them unworthy objects of study, nor should we recoil in horror at the thought of British horror continuing down this road in the future. In fact, it is inevitable that it will. As Stuart Heritage noted in a recent *Guardian* article that appeared in the wake of the theatrical success of *The Woman in Black*, a low-budget paracinema opus like the horror-comedy *Kill Keith* will always be 'far more representative of the British horror scene than [Hammer's film] will ever be'. The horror film's assumed lowliness, yet the ease with which the genre continues to be made, bought and sold, surely is reason enough to make it worthy of our attention. Of course, by dividing British horror up into 'the mainstream' and 'the marginal' in this way, there is a risk here of holding up two oppositional strands of inverted snobbery: the kinds that Jeffrey Sconce attests to when he claims that paracinema, and the 'caustic rhetoric' which its champions and detractors assert, 'suggests a pitched battle between a guerrilla band of cult film viewers and an elite cadre of would-be cinematic tastemakers' (1995: 372). Nevertheless, there is more truth to this binary than evaluative opinion, especially when we consider not simply British horror's recent past, but also as we look to its future.

As Julian Petley and Steve Chibnall (2002) once argued, it was the fan cultures that kept the spirit of British horror alive even when the production of films was at an all-time low in the 1990s, and one can surmise that, what with the increasing affordability of 'prosumer' filmmaking equipment (not to mention the closure of the UK Film Council in 2011), it is the amateur filmmaker who is mostly likely to hold the torch for British horror cinema long after the other producers have abandoned it. Already, there has been a push within the academy to consider the 'small-gauge storytelling' of filmmaking novices (see, for instance, Shand and Craven 2013), and it makes sense that future studies should more explicitly assess the horror genre's role in this phenomenon.[4] Indeed, films of the most obscure nature and lowest production values continue to be disseminated widely thanks to the growth in 'online distribution' (Iordanova and Cunningham 2012). As Ramon Labato has recently argued, the increasing centrality of user-driven content sharing sites such as YouTube and DailyMotion, as well as social networking sites such as Facebook and Twitter, 'have forever changed the way we communicate, replacing top-down corporate content delivery with a many-to-many model of dispersed circulation and sharing' (2012: 112). This has been found, for instance, through initiatives such as CreateSpace on Amazon.com, which, as I have discussed elsewhere, has provided an outlet for amateur/semi-pro filmmakers to distribute their films globally, while avoiding the outlay or slippery legal implications of obtaining a certificate from the (increasingly expensive) British Board of Film Classification (Walker 2014). Moreover, websites such as Openfilm.com, which alleges to bring 'the best elements of the film industry together', and from which amateur filmmakers specialising in horror and exploitation titles such as Jason Impey have benefited, offer a similar service. As its website (rather hyperbolically) states: 'With an innovative platform designed to change the process of discovering great independent film, Openfilm is dedicated to developing, marketing and distributing great works' (www. openfilm.com). Another fitting example of this practice is TheHorroShow. tv: a VoD rental service that caters exclusively for the low-budget horror film market.

Of course, the increasing ubiquity and availability of feature films on informal VoD platforms has not yet fully excised formal distribution companies.[5] And while it is fair to argue that the rising visibility of participatory culture forums challenge 'formal' distribution, it is highly debateable whether they will fully surpass it. As far as free 'open content' goes, the social network platform Facebook, which has proven so essential to raising profiles for lo-fi British horror films and their directors, has begun charging 'businesses' – which includes any organisation whether it be a band, Laundromat or film company – for the full exposure of their 'news feeds' to 'friends', following the development of the so-called 'Promoted Posts' programme. The programme, which 'lets businesses pay anywhere from a few dollars to a few thousand to ensure that hundreds of thousands of Facebookers see your post' (Kaplan

2012) is likely to make it even more difficult for lesser-/unknown directors and producers to generate awareness of their film(s). With that said, several companies that specialise in the distribution of ultra-low-budget/amateur/niche horror films – such as Troma, and more obscure factions such as World-Wide Multi-Media (WWMM) – continue to provide an outlet for such material via DVD and pay-to-play VoD with some success, including several British titles, which are featured alongside other similarly unusual 'cult B-movies' in the hope of targeting a hardcore genre audience. As with other DVD/Blu-ray labels such as Dimension Extreme (discussed in Chapter 2 of this book), such companies grant British horror films that may fail to get distribution through other formal channels 'acceptance' in their catalogues with other international obscurities. Notable British distributors who have aided in the distribution of British horror in a similar way are Metrodome, High Fliers, 101 Films and 4Dgitial Media: all of which have a pronounced presence in the online and DVD market, with British horror films such as *Hollow*, *Peter: Portrait of a Serial Killer*, *Outpost 11* and *The Captive*, respectively. Another good example is Mill Creek Entertainment, which specialises in the distribution of low-budget/low-quality/public-domain films. It advertises itself as 'The Best Source for Value DVD Entertainment', from which British horror films such as *Sick Bastard* and *The Summer of the Massacre* have received distribution in North American territories (www.millcreekent.com). Finally, another niche distributer, Chemical Burn Entertainment, claims to 'cross boundaries and destroy preconceived notions with its remarkable diversity of shocking and provocative films from the US, Asia and Europe' (www.chemicalburn.org), including contemporary British titles such as *Naked Trip* (Alex Baekshav, 2008), *Idol of Evil* (Kevin Mcdonagh, 2009), *Tales of the Dead* (Kemal Yildirim, 2010) and *Bane* (James Eaves, 2008).

Whereas amateur/semi-pro filmmakers – thanks mostly to their general willingness to be undeterred by their lack of mainstream popularity – are likely to lead the charge in terms of *quantity*, and arguably sustain 'a valuable sense of community' among fans through pastiche, parody and intertextuality (Chibnall and Petley 2002: 1), there continues to be stirrings beyond poverty row. That said, most productions remain of a lower-than-average budget (often way under £500,000), and released directly to DVD. Steve Jones (2012), writing of recent developments in American cinema, has suggested that the super-saturation of DVD and the horror genre within this has exacerbated the production of horror films for what he calls the 'DVD ghetto', that seek to 'embrace what [the American] grindhouse [films] represented in budgetary terms, using nostalgic homage to excuse their own budgetary restrictions'. Many contemporary British horror films fit this model, with the DVD sector continuing to provide an outlet for British filmmakers wanting to either homage *British* horror's past, or build on the trends initiated by

British horror in the present. For instance, the 'portmanteau film' initiated by the ground-breaking *Dead of Night* (Cavalcanti *et al.*) in 1945, and subsequently appropriated by Amicus Films in the 1970s with *Tales from the Crypt* (Freddie Francis, 1972) and *The Vault of Horror* (Roy Ward Baker, 1973), has flourished once more with the neat pairing of the DVD films *Bordello Death Tales* (James Eaves *et al.* 2009, released 2012) and *Battlefield Death Tales* (James Eaves *et al.* 2012), as well as *Little Deaths* and the US/New Zealand co-production *ABCs of Death* (Andrews *et al.* 2012), which not only echo a time when British horror was attempting to innovatively break from 'the Hammer hegemony' (Hutchings 2002b: 131), they also bring together many directors who have become 'known' for British horror in some cult circles, including: James Eaves (*Hellbreeder* (2004; co-directed by Johannes Roberts), *Bane*), Pat Higgins (*Trashhouse* (2005), *Hellbride* (2007), *KillerKiller* (2007)), Sean Hogan (*Lie Still* (2005), *The Devil's Business*), Andrew Parkinson (*Dead Creatures, Venus Drowning* (2006)), Simon Rumley (*The Living and the Dead* (2006), *Red, White and Blue* (2010)) and Jake West (*Evil Aliens, Doghouse*).

The rapid developments in prosumer production technologies and distribution/circulation methods also continue to contribute to the growing upsurge in *short* British horror films: a phenomenon that I haven't been able to consider here at all. Most of these films enjoy exposure online via sites such as YouTube and through a variety of film festivals, including Fright Fest and Abertoir, or at festivals that showcase shorts exclusively, such as Short Cuts to Hell and 2 Days Later. Notably, Shortcuts to Hell offers filmmakers a platform to showcase their shorts with the incentive being that the winner, with the support of the festival, gets to develop their film into a feature.[6] 2 Days Later, comparatively, is a local council-endorsed 'short horror film competition specifically designed to encourage filmmakers, enthusiasts and students to produce a 10 minute horror film in only 48 hours on a micro-budget' (www.2dayslater. co.uk). While numbers are inevitably inconclusive, one can be certain that, whatever the final total, the horror shorts being made today continue to outnumber those films of 'feature length'. According to competition organiser Mick Etherton, 2 Days Later has encouraged the production of more than 500 short horror films alone: more than 90 per cent of which are British (Etherton 2012).[7]

This brings us to another area of study that requires further research: the role of horror and fantasy film festivals in the promotion and circulation of British horror films. As is noted across the *Film Festival Yearbook* (2009–) series published by St Andrews Film Studies, film festivals are able to tell us a lot about – among other things – film economics, film culture and film audiences. Perhaps most significantly, as Rod Stoneman and Duncan Petrie have recently noted, such festivals continue to 'play a crucial role in delivering the delicatessen of cultural cinema to niche audiences that remain for it' (Petrie and Stoneman 2014: 193) even if, at times, it may feel like festivals are 'not bringing cinema closer to the people' but instead are 'shielding it from wider audiences' (Iordanova 2013: 1). Horror and fantasy film festivals are of particular interest here, because they will often specifically show films that are never intended for a 'wider audience'.

With that said, some horror festivals have a higher profile than others. Fright Fest, for instance, is sponsored by the UK television station Channel 4, and will often be ran in conjunction with a TV season of horror movies. Yet there are many other, lower-profile, independent horror festivals that showcase new British horror, such as Abertoir in Wales, that lack the corporate infrastructure of Fright Fest, operate on a more ad-hoc basis and sometimes have an educational slant (Abertoir receives higher subsidy from the local government because it is set on the grounds of Aberystwyth University and often features public lectures by resident scholars). Irrespective of how they operate, the centrality of such festivals to horror film culture makes them a fertile arena for the continued academic analysis of British filmmaking and the spaces of horror film reception.

Having identified these areas for further study, and irrespective of what directions the genre will now take, it is hoped that *Contemporary British Horror Cinema* has done justice to a lively era of film production within and beyond Britain and that it has offered some insight into one of the most productive genres in the broad arena of twenty-first-century 'British cinema'. The last six chapters have revealed that, beyond the evaluative judgements that have underpinned much scholarly criticism of British horror, the genre remained a central component to a global cinema in the face of critical dismissal or academic voidance, and that British horror was at the forefront of new filmmaking technology, intertextual revelry and sophisticated social comment. What was once 'long time dead' has now risen from the grave.

NOTES

1. Of course, to what extent Hollywood control can be completely avoided is debatable, and it remains true that Hollywood continues to be highly instrumental in contemporary European cinema (Wood 2007: 1–2). That said, as Mary P. Wood notes, 'underneath the high-profile successes of European cooperation[s] lie a vibrant and seething strata of popular cinema, most of which rarely make it outside national borders' (83).
2. I have tried to make explicit the conveyor-belt-like release patterns of contemporary British horror, but to keep up to date, consult M. J. Simpson's blog: http://british-horror-revival.blogspot.co.uk.
3. A. J. (Noel Clarke) in *Heartless*.
4. Shand and Craven's volume does, however, offer a fascinating chapter by Ciara Chambers (2013) on the Spence Brothers: an amateur duo responsible for making innovative Super8 amateur science-fiction films.
5. Openfilm, for one, works in conjunction with several distribution companies.

6. According to the supplementary materials on each British DVD release, this festival offers an approach similar to that adopted by filmmakers Steven Sheil, Gerard Johnson and Lawrence Gough before they went on to make *Mum & Dad*, *Tony* and *Salvage*, respectively.
7. For example, of the forty shorts screened at the 2 Days Later Halloween Screening in October 2012, thirty-six were from Britain or the Republic of Ireland, with the other entries originating from elsewhere in Europe. The full programme is available at: www.2dayslater.co.uk/dare/promo/prog2012.pdf (accessed 3 November 2012).

BIBLIOGRAPHY

Anon. (1990) 'Sam's snippets', *Samhain* 10, p. 4.

Anon. (2002) '*Long Time Dead*', *Total Film*, 18 January, www.totalfilm.com/reviews/cinema/long-time-dead (accessed 11 March 2010).

Anon. (2003a) 'Production round up', *Screen International* 1,417, p. 20.

Anon. (2003b) 'ITALY Three-say weekend May 16–18', *Screen International* 1,406, p. 20.

Anon. (2005a) 'One bite – and you're hooked', *Screen International* 1,512, pp. 8–9.

Anon. (2005b) 'Under that hoodie is a child like yours', *Daily Mail*, 15 May, www.dailymail.co.uk/debate/columnists/article-348738/Under-hoodie-child-like-yours.html (accessed 16 June 2009).

Anon. (2007) 'Hammer horror to strike net', *Daily Mirror*, 13 December, http://lexisnexis.com (accessed 25 September 2014).

Anon. (2008a) 'Revolver release policy in firing line', *Cinema Business* 50, p. 38.

Anon. (2008b) '*Eden Lake* threatens to spread terror from cinema to the streets', *The Guardian*, 15 September, www.guardian.co.uk/film/filmblog/2008/sep/15/1 (accessed 11 September 2009).

Anon. (2009a) 'Critics maul *Lesbian Vampire Killers*', *BBC News*, 20 March, http://news.bbc.co.uk/1/hi/entertainment/7954681.stm (accessed 7 February 2010).

Anon. (2009b) '*Lesbian Vampire Killers* "biggest movie flop of 2009"', *Pink News: Europe's Largest Gay News Service*, 29 December, www.pinknews.co.uk/2009/12/29/lesbian-vampire-killers-biggest-movie-flop-of-2009/ (accessed 12 December 2012).

Anon. (2010a) 'Hammer Films: Back from the dead', *SFX* [special horror edition], p. 16.

Anon. (2010b) 'Let me in to the festival', *Bristol Post*, 28 October, http//lexisnexis.com (accessed 28 November 2014)

Anon. (2010c) 'Let me in', *Lincolnshire Echo*, 28 October, p. 5, http://lexisnexis.com (accessed 28 November 2014).

Anon. (2011) 'Hammer horror is dead creepy', *Daily Record*, 25 March. http://lexis-nexis.com (accessed 30 June 2014).

Anon. (2012) 'Porn actor "who mailed body parts" to Canadian government filmed himself beheading victim ... before posting horrific footage online titled 1 Lunatic 1 Pickaxe', *Daily Mail*, 31 May, www.dailymail.co.uk/news/article-2152600/Luka-Rocco-Magnotta-Porn-actor-hacked-victim-mailed-body-parts-posted-gruesome-video-online.html#ixzz2091uULp6 (accessed 31 May 2012).

Adams, M. and Raisborough, J. (2011) 'The self-control ethos and the "chav": Unpacking cultural representations of the white working class', *Culture & Psychology* 17: 1, pp. 81–97.

Aftab, K. (2009) 'Don't lose your head', *The Independent*, 5 June, www.independent.co.uk/arts-entertainment/films/features/drag-me-to-hell--dont-lose-your-head-1697053.html (accessed 3 April 2010).

Aldgate, A. and Richards, J. (2009) *Best of British: Cinema and Society from 1930 to the Present*. London: I. B. Tauris.

Altman, R. (2004 [1984]) 'A semantic/syntactic approach to film genre', in Braudy, L. and Cohen, M. (eds) *Film Theory and Criticism* (6th Edition), Oxford and New York: Oxford University Press, pp. 680–90.

Andrews, Hannah (2014) *Television and British Cinema: Convergence and Divergence since 1990*. Basingstoke: Palgrave.

Angry Lesbians, The (n.d.), '*Lesbian Vampire Killers*: NO WAY!', *The Petition Site*, www.thepetitionsite.com/1/wwwangrylesbiansbiz (accessed 12 May 2011).

Associates, The (n.d.) *Salvage*, *Surviving Evil* and *Tony* business and release data, www.the-associates.co.uk/displaytitle.php?id=269 (accessed 3 November 2011).

Attwood, F. (2005) '"Tits and ass and porn and fighting": Male heterosexuality in magazines for men', *International Journal of Cultural Studies* 8: 1, pp. 87–104.

Austin, G. (2012) 'Biological dystopias: The body in contemporary French horror cinema', *L'Esprit createur* 52: 2, pp. 99–113.

Bacal, S. (2004) 'Back from the dead', *Screen International* 1,448, p. 16.

Badley, L. (2010) 'Bringing it all back home: Horror cinema and video culture', in Conrich, I. (ed.) *Horror Zone: The Cultural Experience of Contemporary Horror Cinema*, London: I. B. Tauris, pp. 45–63.

Baker, S. (2009) '*Shameless* and the question of England: Genre, class and nation', the *Journal of British Cinema and Television* 6: 3, pp. 452–67.

Bal, M. (2001) *Quoting Caravaggio: Contemporary Art, Prosperous History*. Chicago: University of Chicago Press.

Bankston, D. (2003) 'All the rage', *American Cinematographer* 84: 7, pp. 82–90.

Barker, Martin (ed.) (1984) *The Video Nasties: Freedom and Censorship and the Media*. London: Pluto Press.

Barker, M. and Petley, J. (eds) (2001) *Ill Effects: The Media/Violence Debate*. London: Routledge.

Barker, M., Arthurs, J. and Harindranath, R. (2001) *The Crash Controversy: Censorship Campaigns and Film Reception*. London: Wallflower Press.

Barlow, G. and Hill, A. (1985) (eds) *Video Violence and Children*. London: Hodder and Stoughton.

Barton (2008) 'When Evil Calls', *Deadcentral.com*, 16 January, www.dreadcentral.com/reviews/5980/when-evil-calls-dvd (accessed 28 November 2014).

Bawden, F. (2009a) 'Hoodie-winked', *The Guardian*, 9 March, p. 2.

Bawden, F. (2009b) 'Hoodie or altar boys?', *Women in Journalism*, http://womeninjournalism.co.uk/hoodies-or-altar-boys (accessed 4 December 2014).

Bernard, M. (2014) *Selling the Splat Pack: The DVD Revolution and the American Horror Film*. Edinburgh: Edinburgh University Press.

Bishop, K. (2009) 'Dead man still walking: Explaining the zombie renaissance', *Journal of Popular Film and Television* 37: 1, pp. 16–25.

Blake, L. (2008) *Wounds of Nations: Horror Cinema, Historical Trauma and National Identity*. Manchester: Manchester University Press.

Blake, L. (2012) 'New Labour, new horrors: Genetic mutation, generic hybridity and gender crisis in British horror of the new millennium', in Allmer, P., Brick, E. and Huxley, D. (eds) *European Nightmares: Horror Cinema in Europe since 1945*. London: Wallflower, pp. 77–87.

Block, A. (2014), '*Sharknado*'s branding bite', *The Hollywood Reporter* 420 (23), p. 18

Bloom, C. (2012) *Riot City: Protest and Rebellion in the Capital*. Basingstoke: Palgrave.

Bode, L. (2010) 'Transitional tastes: Teen girls and genre in the critical reception of *Twilight*', *Continuum: Journal of Media and Cultural Studies* 24: 5, pp. 707–20.

Box Office Mojo, *Scream* business data, http://boxofficemojo.com/movies/?id=scream.htm (accessed 8 March 2011).

Box Office Mojo, *The Blair Witch Project* business data, http://boxofficemojo.com/movies/?id=blairwitchproject.htm (accessed 8 March 2011).

Box Office Mojo, *The Quiet Ones* business data, www.boxofficemojo.com/movies/?id=quietones.htm (accessed 8 October 2014).

Branaghan, Sim (2006) *British Film Posters: An Illustrated History*. London: BFI.

British Film Institute (BFI) (2011) *Opening Our Eyes: How Film Contributes to the Culture of the UK*. London: British Film Institute.

British Film Institute (BFI) (2012) *11 Statistical Yearbook*. London: BFI.

Broadbent, P. (2006) 'Losing yob battle', *Herald Express* (Torquay), 9 March, p. 9.

Brookes, X. (2005) 'Dazed and confused', the *Guardian*, 19 May, www.guardian.co.uk/film/2005/may/19/cannes2005.cannesfilmfestival3 (accessed 4 June 2010).

Brophy, P. (2000 [1985]) 'Horrality – the textuality of contemporary horror films', in Gelder, K. (ed.) *The Horror Reader*, London: Routledge, pp. 276–93.

Brouwer, Julian (2008) 'Bloody awful', *Daily Mirror*, 2 March, http://lexisnexis.com (accessed 14 July 2014).

Brown, C. (2004) '*Trauma*', *Screen International* 1,439, p. 34.

Brunsdon, C. (2007) *London in Cinema: The Cinematic City since 1945*. London: British Film Institute.

Burt, G. (1993) *After the Hole*. London: Black Swan.

Büssing, S. (1987) *Aliens in the Home: The Child in Horror Fiction*. New York: Greenwood Press.

Cameron, D. (2007) 'To fix broken Britain we will start at school', *The Telegraph*, 2 September, www.telegraph.co.uk/comment/personal-view/3642395/To-fix-broken-Britain-we-shall-start-at-school.html (accessed 4 December 2014)

Carolyn, A. (2009) *It Lives Again!: Horror Movies in the New Millennium*. Tolworth: Telos.

Carroll, N. (1990), *The Philosophy of Horror, or Paradoxes of the Heart*. London: Routledge.

Carruthers, J. (2010) 'An open letter to *Gorezone* magazine', *Let's Get Dangerous!*, 13 January, http://letsgetdangerous.wordpress.com/2010/01/13/an-open-letter-to-gorezone-magazine/ (accessed 7 April 2011).

Carter, Oliver (2013) '"Slash Production": Objectifying the serial 'kiler' in Euro-Cult Cinema fan production', in MacDonald, A. (ed.) *Murders and Acquisitions: Representations of the Serial Killer in Popular Culture*, London and New York: Bloomsbury, pp. 123–44.

Caterer, J. (2011) *The People's Pictures: National Lottery Funding and British Cinema*. Newcastle upon Tyne: Cambridge Scholars Publishing.

Cellan-Jones, Rory (2011) 'MySpace sold to Specific Media by Murdoch's News Corp',

BBC News, 29 June. www.bbc.co.uk/news/business-13969338 (accessed 15 July 2014).

Chambers, C. (2013) 'The Spence Brothers: Amateur sci-fi and cine culture in Northern Ireland' in Shand, R. and Craven, I. (eds) *Small-Gauge Storytelling: Discovering the Amateur Fiction Film*. Edinburgh: Edinburgh University Press, pp. 373–99.

Chapman, J. (2007) '"This ship in England": History, politics and national identity in *Master and Commander: The Far Side of the World* (2003)', in Chapman, J., Glancy, M. and Harper, S. (eds) *The New Film History: Sources, Methods, Approaches*. London: Palgrave, pp. 55–68.

Chapman, J., Glancy, M. and Harper, S. (2007) 'Introduction', in Chapman, J., Glancy, M. and Harper, S. (eds) *The New Film History: Sources, Methods, Approaches*. London: Palgrave, pp. 1–10.

Chatman, S. (2004 [1972]) 'The structure of narrative transmission', in Rivkin, J. and Ryan, M. (eds) *Literary Theory: An Anthology* (2nd Edition), Oxford: Blackwell, pp. 97–124.

Cherry, B. (2002) 'Screaming for release: Femininity and horror film fandom in Britain', in Chibnall, S. and Petley, J. (eds) *British Horror Cinema*. London: Routledge, pp. 42–57.

Cherry, B. (2009) *Horror*. London: Routledge.

Cherry, B. (2010) 'Stalking the web: Celebration, chat and horror film marketing on the Internet', in Conrich, I. (ed.) *Horror Zone: The Cultural Experience of Contemporary Horror*. London: I. B. Tauris, pp. 67–85.

Cherry, B. (2011) 'A cosy catastrophe: Genre, national cinema and fan responses to *28 Days Later*' in Hochscherf, T. and Leggott, J. (eds) *British Science Fiction Film and Television: Critical Essays*. Jefferson: McFarland, pp. 156–66.

Chibnall, S. (1998) *Making Mischief: The Cult Films of Pete Walker*. Godalming: FAB Press.

Chibnall, S. (2009) 'Travels in lad land: The British gangster film cycle – 1998–2001', in Murphy, R. (ed.) *The British Cinema Book* (3rd Edition), London: British Film Institute, pp. 375–86.

Chibnall, S. and Petley, J. (2002) 'The return of the repressed? – British horror's heritage and future', in Chibnall, S. and Petley, J. (eds) *British Horror Cinema*. London: Routledge, pp. 1–9.

Clark, P. (2002) 'Death is the prize in the board game from hell', The *Evening Standard*, 17 January, p. 30.

Claydon, P. (2010) *Lesbian Vampire Killers* DVD Commentary.

Clayton, W. and Harman, S. (eds) (2014) *Screening Twilight: Critical Approaches to a Cinematic Phenomenon*. London: I. B. Tauris.

Click, M. (2009) '"Rabid", "obsessed", "frenzied": Understanding *Twilight* fangirls and the gendered politics of fandom", *FlowTV* 12, 18 December, www.flowtv.org/2009/12 (accessed 7 May 2011).

Clover, C. (1992) *Men, Women and Chainsaws: Gender in the Modern Horror Film*. Princeton: Princeton University Press.

Cockwell, S (2010) '*Beyond the Rave*', *Eat My Brains*, 30 September, www.eatmybrains.com/showreview.php?id=528 (accessed 3 September 2011).

Cole, M. (2011) 'Day the mob came crashing through my door: One middle-class mother's harrowing account' *Daily Mail*, 12 August, www.dailymail.co.uk/f e-mail/article-2025097/London-riots-Notting-Hill-mother-day-mob-came-crashing-in.html (accessed 16 April 2012).

Collins, D. (2008) 'Family valupounds: *The People* looks at controversial bid to tame young thugs', *The People*, 1 June, p. 5, www.lexisnexis.com/uk/legal/results/enh docview.do?docLinkInd=true&ersKey=2*3_T16189337577&format=GNBFULL&

startDocNo=1&resultsUrlKey=0_T16189337589&backKey=2*0_T16189337590
&csi=1452*51&docNo=1 (accessed 4 October 2011).

Conrich, I. (1998) 'The contemporary British horror film: Observations on market-ing, distribution and exhibition', in Fenton, H. (ed.) *Flesh and Blood – Book One*. Guildford: FAB Press, pp. 27–31.

Creed, B. (1993) *The Monstrous-Feminine: Film, Feminism, Psychoanalysis*. London: Routledge.

Cripps, C. (2008) 'Spooked by a child who is spirited away', *The Independent* (Extra), 13 August, p. 16.

Cunningham, S. and Silver, J. (ed.) (2012) 'On-line film distribution: Its history and global complexion', in Cunningham, S. and Iordanova, D. (eds) (2012) *Digital Disruption: Cinema Moves On-line*, St Andrews: St Andrews Film Studies, pp. 33–66.

Curran, J. and Porter, V. (eds) (1983) *British Cinema History*. London: Weidenfeld and Nicolson.

Dams, T. (2003) 'Inward and upwards', *Screen International* 1,425, p. 25.

David, A. (2011) Telephone interview with author, 4 February.

Dennis, J. (2008) '*Eden Lake* review', *Twitch Film*, 15 September, http://twitchfilm.net/reviews/2008/09/eden-lake-review.php (accessed 15 September 2010).

Dougan, A. (2002) 'Alex could be the new Ewan', *Evening Times* (Glasgow), 17 January, p. 32.

Driscoll, R. (2010) 'Here's looking at chew . . .', *Western Mail*, 5 November, p. 2, http://lexisnexis.com (accessed 13 May 2014).

Duffett, M. (2013) *Understanding Fandom: An Introduction to the Study of Media Fan Culture*. London and New York: Bloomsbury.

Dyer, D. (2010) *Straight Up: The Real Me in My Own Words*. London: Random House.

Dyer, R. (2009 [1993]) 'The role of stereotypes', in Bassett, C., Marris, P. and Thornham, S. (eds) *Media Studies: A Reader* (3rd Edition), Edinburgh: Edinburgh University Press, pp. 206–12.

Edelstein, D. (2006) 'Now playing at your local multiplex: Torture porn', *The New York Times*, http://nymag.com/movies/features/15622 (accessed 29 March 2011).

Edwards, G. (2005) 'Hoodie horror', *South Wales Echo*, 15 December, p. 21.

Egan, K. (2007) *Trash or Treasure? – Censorship and the Changing Meanings of the Video Nasties*. Manchester: Manchester University Press.

Eric (2009) 'Steven Sheil talks *Mum & Dad*', *Bloody Good Horror*, www.bloodygoodhorror.com/bgh/interviews/05/06/2009/steven-sheil-talks-mum-dad (accessed 3 September 2011).

Etherton, M. (2012) E-mail interview with author, 28 November.

Evans, Graham (1990), 'The Vampire Lovers', *Samhain* 22, pp. 14–15.

Ezra, E. and Rowden, T. (2006b) 'What is transnational cinema?', in Ezra, E. and Rowden, T. (eds) *Transnational Cinema: The Film Reader*. London: Routledge, pp. 1–12.

Fahy, T. (ed.) (2010) *The Philosophy of Horror*. Lexington: The University Press of Kentucky.

Falk, B. (2012) 'Danny Dyer saves the world', *The Huffington Post*, 1 March, www.huffingtonpost.co.uk/ben-falk/danny-dyer-saves-the-worl_b_1304188.html (accessed 5 April 2012).

Fielding, H. (1996) *Bridget Jones's Diary*. London: Picador.

Finn, J (2014) E-mail interview with author, 14 October.

Fisher, A. (2011) *Radical Frontiers in the Spaghetti Western: Politics, Violence and Popular Italian Cinema*. London: I. B. Tauris.

Fitzherbert, H. (2010) 'Vamp it up with reborn Hammer', *Sunday Express*, 7 November, p. 62, http://lexisnexis.com (accessed 8 April 2014).

Forshaw, B. (2013) *British Gothic Cinema*. Basingstoke: Palgrave Macmillan.

Fouz-Hernández, S. (2005) *Mysterious Skin: Male Bodies in Contemporary Cinema*. London: I. B. Tauris.

Fradley, M., Godfrey, S. and Williams, M. (2013) *Shane Meadows: Critical Essays*. Edinburgh: Edinburgh University Press.

Freeland, C. (1995) 'Realist horror', in C. Freeland and T. Wartenberg (eds) *Philosophy and Film*, London: Routledge, pp. 126–42.

Garner, R. (2009) '"Hoodies, louts, scum": How media demonises teenagers; Research finds negative stories in the press make teenage boys frightened of each other', *The Independent*, 13 March, p. 13.

Gauntlett, D. (2008) *Media, Gender and Identity: An Introduction* (2nd Edition). London: Routledge.

Gentlemen, A. (2010) 'Is Britain broken?', *The Guardian*, 31 March, www.guardian. co.uk/society/2010/mar/31/is-britain-broken (accessed 31 March 2010).

Genz, S. and Brabon, B. A. (2009) *Postfeminism: Cultural Texts and Theories*. Edinburgh: Edinburgh University Press.

George, S., Kay, J., Macnab, G., Schilling, M., Blaney, M. and Rodier, M. (2005) 'Disc world', *Screen International* 1,507, pp. 14–15.

Gifford, D. (1975) *A Pictorial History of Horror Movies*. London: Hamlyn.

Gilbey, R. (2002) 'Reasons to be cheerful', *Sight and Sound* 12: 10, pp. 14–17.

Gilbey, R. (2011) 'Gilbey on film: Horror at the box office', *New Statesman*, 17 May, www.newstatesman.com/blogs/cultural-capital/2011/05/zombie-undead-bobbi-film-box (accessed 17 May 2011).

Godfrey, S. and Walker, J. (2015) 'From pinter to *Pimp*: Danny Dyer, class, cultism and the critics', *Journal of British Cinema and Television* 12: 1, pp. 101–20.

Golding, W. (1997 [1954]) *Lord of the Flies*. London: Faber and Faber.

Graham, J. (2009) 'Hoodies strike fear in British cinema', *The Guardian*, 5 November, www.guardian.co.uk/film/2009/nov/05/british-hoodie-films (accessed 20 May 2011).

Grant, B. K. (ed.) (1984) *Planks of Reason: Essays on the Horror Film*. Lanham: Scarecrow Press.

Grant, B. K. and Sharrett, C. (eds) (2004) *Planks of Reason: Essays on the Horror Film* (2nd Edition). Lanham: Scarecrow Press.

Grass, B. (2011) Skype interview with author, 15 October.

Grove, D. (2005) *Making Friday the 13th: The Legend of Camp Blood*. Surrey: FAB Press.

Hall, S. (2000) 'Cultural identity and cinematic representation', in Stam, R. and Miller, T. (eds) *Film and Theory: An Anthology*. Oxford: Blackwell, pp. 704–14.

Hallam, J. with Marshment, M. (2000) *Realism and Popular Cinema*. Manchester: Manchester University Press.

Hallenbeck, B. G. (2010) *The Hammer Vampire*. Bristol: Hemlock Books.

Hallenbeck, B. G. (2011) *Hammer Fantasy and Sci-Fi*. Bristol: Hemlock Books.

Hammond, W. (2009) '*Lesbian Vampire Killers*', *Sight and Sound* 19: 5, p. 68.

Hantke, S. (2010a) 'The military horror film: Speculations on a hybrid genre', *Journal of Popular Culture* 45: 4, pp. 701–19.

Hantke, S. (2010b) 'They don't make 'em like them used to: On the rhetoric of crisis and the current state of American horror cinema', in Hantke, S. (ed.) *American Horror Film: The Genre at the Turn of the Millennium*, Jackson: University of Mississippi Press, pp. vii–xxxii.

Harper, S. and Porter, V. (eds) (2007) *British Cinema in the 1950s: The Decline of Deference*. Oxford: Oxford University Press.

Harper, S. and Smith, J. (2012) *British Film Culture in the 1970s: The Boundaries of Pleasure*. Edinburgh: Edinburgh University Press.

Harries, D. (2002) 'Film parody and the resuscitation of genre', in Neale, S. (ed.) *Genre and Contemporary Hollywood*. London: BFI, pp. 281–93.

Hawkins, J. (2000) *Cutting Edge: Art-Horror and the Horrific Avant-garde*. Minneapolis: University of Minnesota Press.

Hawkins, J. (2003) 'Midnight sex-horror movies and the down-town avant-garde', in Jancovich, M, Lázaro Reboll, A., Stringer, J. and Willis, A. (eds) *Defining Cult Movies: The Cultural Politics of Oppositional Taste*, Manchester: Manchester University Press, pp. 223–34.

Hayton, N. (2011) 'Unconscious adaptation: *Hardy Candy* as *Little Red Riding Hood*', *Adaptation* 4: 1, pp. 38–54.

Hayward, K. and Yar, M. (2006) 'The "chav" phenomenon: Consumption, media and the construction of a new underclass', *Crime, Media, Culture* 2: 9, pp. 9–28.

Hearn, M. (2009) *Hammer Glamour*. London: Titan Books.

Hearn, M. and Barnes, A (1997) *The Hammer Story*. London: Titan Books.

Hebdige, D. (1983) 'Rape of our children's minds', *Daily Mail*, 30 June, p. 6.

Heller-Nicholas, A. (2014), *Found Footage Horror Films: Fear and the Appearance of Reality*. Jefferson: McFarland.

Henderson, S. (2009) 'From screen to shelf: Perspectives on independent distribution', *Journal of British Cinema and Television* 6: 3, pp. 468–80.

Heritage, S. (2012) '*Kill Keith*: Cheggers' horror is a film to die for', *The Guardian*, 22 March, www.guardian.co.uk/film/filmblog/2012/mar/22/kill-keith-british-horror (accessed 2 July 2012).

Higson, A. (1989) 'The concept of national cinema', *Screen* 30: 4, pp. 36–46.

Higson, A. (2011) *Film England: Culturally English Filmmaking since the 1990s*. London: I. B. Tauris.

Hill, A. (2001) '"Looks like it hurts": Women's responses to shocking entertainment', in Barker, M. and Petley, J. (eds) *Ill Effects: The Media/Violence Debate*, London: Routledge, pp. 135–49.

Hill, D. (1958) 'The face of horror', *Sight and Sound* 28: 1, pp. 6–11.

Hill, J. (1983) 'Working-class realism and sexual reaction: Some theses on the "British New Wave"', in Curran, James and Porter, Vincent (eds) *British Cinema History*, London: Weidenfeld and Nicolson, pp. 368–70.

Hill, J. (1999) *British Cinema in the 1980s: Issues and Themes*. Oxford: Oxford University Press.

Hill, J. (2000a), 'From the "New Wave" to "Brit-grit": Continuity and difference in working-class realism', in Ashby, Justine and Higson, Andrew (eds) *British Cinema: Past and Present*, Routledge: London, pp. 249-60.

Hill, J. (2000b) 'A working-class hero is something to be? Changing representations of class and masculinity in British cinema', in Babington, B., Davies, A. and Powrie, P. (eds) *The Trouble with Men: Masculinities in European and Hollywood Cinema*, London: Wallflower, pp. 100–9.

Hill, J. (2012) '"This is for the *Batman*s as well as the *Vera Drake*s": Economics, culture and UK government film production policy in the 2000s', *Journal of British Cinema and Television* 9: 3, pp. 333–56.

Hills, M. (2002) *Fan Cultures*. London: Routledge.

Hills, M. (2005) *The Pleasures of Horror*. London: Continuum.

Hills, M. (2014) 'Hammer 2.0: Legacy, modernization, and Hammer Horror as heritage brand', in Nowell, R. (ed.) *Merchants of Menace: The Business of Horror Cinema*, London and New York: Bloomsbury, pp. 229–49.

Hjort, M. (2003) 'The globalization of Dogma: The dynamics of metaculture and counter-publicity', in Hjort, M and MacKenzie, S. (eds) *Purity and Provocation: Dogma 95*, London: BFI, pp. 133–57.

Hjort, M. and MacKenzie, S. (2003) 'Introduction', in Hjort, M and MacKenzie, S. (eds) *Purity and Provocation: Dogma 95*, London: Palgrave, pp. 1–28.

Hockenhull, S. (2010) 'Sublime landscape in contemporary British horror: *The Last Great Wilderness* and *Eden Lake*', *Horror Studies* 1: 2, pp. 207–24.

Hollows, J. (2003) 'The masculinity of cult', in Jancovich, M, Lázaro Reboll, A., Stringer, J. and Willis, A. (eds) *Defining Cult Movies: The Cultural Politics of Oppositional Taste*, Manchester: Manchester University Press, pp. 35–53.

Holmes, R. (2012) Face-to-face interview with author, Leicester, 5 April.

Hood, S. (1983) 'John Grierson and the Documentary Film Movement', Curran, J. and Porter, V. (eds) *British Cinema History*, London: Weidenfeld and Nicolson, pp. 99–112.

Horeck, T. and Kendall, T. (eds) (2011) *The New Extremism in Cinema: From France to Europe*. Edinburgh: Edinburgh University Press.

Horvath, M., Hegarty, P., Tyler, S. and Mansfield, S. (2012) '"Lights on at the end of the party": Are lads' mags mainstreaming dangerous sexism?', *British Journal of Psychology* 103: 4, pp. 454–71.

Hunt, L. (1998) *British Low Culture: From Safari Suits to Sexploitation*. London: Routledge.

Hunt, L. (2002) 'Necromancy in the UK: Witchcraft and the occult in British horror', in Chibnall, S. and Petley, J. (eds) *British Horror Cinema*, London: Routledge, pp. 82–98.

Hunt, N. (2002) 'Case study: *The Last Great Wilderness*', *Screen International* 1,367, p. 14.

Hunt, N. (2003) 'The importance of trivia: Ownership, exclusion and authority in science fiction fandom', in Jancovich, M, Lázaro Reboll, A., Stringer, J. and Willis, A. (eds) *Defining Cult Movies: The Cultural Politics of Oppositional Taste*, Manchester: Manchester University Press, pp. 185–201.

Hunter, A. (2002) 'Brit talent shines at Edinburgh', *Screen International* 1,369, pp. 1–2.

Hunter, A. (2009) '*Lesbian Vampire Killers*', *Daily Express*, 20 March, www.express.co.uk/posts/view/90179/Lesbian-Vampire-Killers (accessed 5 April 2009).

Hunter, A. (2010) '*Cherry Tree Lane*', *Screen Daily*, 18 June, www.screendaily.com/reviews/latest-reviews/-cherry-tree-lane/5015137.article (accessed 18 June 2010).

Hunter, I. Q. (2011) '*A Clockwork Orange*, exploitation and the art film', in Hochscherf, T. and Leggott, J. (eds) *British Science Fiction Film and Television: Critical Essays*, Jefferson: McFarland, pp. 96–103.

Hunter, I. Q. (2012) 'From window cleaner to potato man: Confessions of a working-class stereotype' in Hunter, I. Q. and Porter, L. (eds) *British Comedy Cinema*, London: Routledge, pp. 154–70.

Hunter, I. Q. (2013) *British Trash Cinema*, London: British Film Institute.

Hutchings, P. (1993) *Hammer and Beyond: The British Horror Film*. Manchester: Manchester University Press.

Hutchings, P. (2001) *Terence Fisher*. Manchester: Manchester University Press.

Hutchings, P. (2002a) 'The Amicus house of horror', in Chibnall, S. and Petley, J. (eds) *British Horror Cinema*, London: Routledge, pp. 131–44.

Hutchings, P. (2002b) *Terence Fisher*. Manchester: Manchester University Press.

Hutchings, P. (2003a) 'The Argento Effect', in Jancovich, M, Lázaro Reboll, A., Stringer, J. and Willis, A. (eds) *Defining Cult Movies: The Cultural Politics of Oppositional Taste*. Manchester: Manchester University Press, pp. 127–41.

Hutchings, P. (2003b) *Dracula*. London: I. B. Tauris.

Hutchings, P. (2004a) *The Horror Film*. Harlow: Pearson Longman.

Hutchings, P. (2004b) 'Uncanny landscapes in British film and television', *Visual Culture in Britain* 5: 2, pp. 27–40.

Hutchings, P. (2008) *Historical Dictionary of Horror Cinema*. Lanham: Scarecrow Press.

Hutchings, P. (2009a) 'Horror London', *Journal of British Cinema and Television* 6: 2, pp. 190–206.

Hutchings, P. (2009b) '*A New Heritage of Horror: The English Gothic Cinema* by David Pirie', *Journal of British Cinema and Television* 6: 1, pp. 147–9.

Internet Movie Database Professional (n.d.a) *Doghouse* business data, http://pro.imdb.com/title/tt1023500/business (accessed 12 December 2012).

Internet Movie Database Professional (n.d.b) *Eden Lake* business data, http://pro.imdb.com/title/tt1020530/business (accessed 19 July 2012).

Internet Movie Database Professional (n.d.c) *Honest* business data, http://pro.imdb.com/title/tt0192126/business (accessed 19 July 2012).

Internet Movie Database Professional (n.d.d) *Lesbian Vampire Killers* business data, http://pro.imdb.com/title/tt1020885/business (accessed 12 December 2012).

Internet Movie Database Professional (n.d.e) *Manor Hunt Ball* production page, http://pro.imdb.com/title/tt1733218 (accessed 10 December 2012).

Internet Movie Database Professional (n.d.f) *My Little Eye* business data, http://pro.imdb.com/title/tt0280969/business (accessed 8 March 2011).

Internet Movie Database Professional (n.d.g) *Rancid Aluminum* business data, http://pro.imdb.com/title/tt0179443/business (accessed 19 July 2012).

Internet Movie Database Professional (n.d.h) *Scary Movie 3* business data, http://pro.imdb.com/title/tt0306047/business (accessed 13 July 2012).

Internet Movie Database Professional (n.d.i) *Scream 3* business data, http://pro.imdb.com/title/tt0134084/business (accessed 8 March 2011).

Internet Movie Database Professional (n.d.j) *The Amityville Horror* business data, http://pro.imdb.com/title/tt0384806/business (accessed 19 July 2012).

Internet Movie Database Professional (n.d.k) *The Descent* business data, http://pro.imdb.com/title/tt0435625/business (accessed 8 March 2011).

Internet Movie Database Professional (n.d.l) *The Exorcist* business data, http://pro.imdb.com/title/tt0070047/business (accessed 8 March 2011).

Internet Movie Database Professional (n.d.m) *The Texas Chainsaw Massacre* business data, http://pro.imdb.com/title/tt0324216/business (accessed 19 July 2012).

Internet Movie Database Professional (n.d.n) *The Wolfman* business data, http://pro.imdb.com/title/tt0780653/business (accessed 19 July 2012).

Internet Movie Database Professional (n.d.o) *The Woman in Black* business data, http://pro.imdb.com/title/tt1596365/business (accessed 19 December 2012).

Iordanova, D. (2013) 'Introduction', in *The Film Festival Reader*, St Andrews: St Andrews Film Studies, pp. 1–15.

Iordanova, D. and Cunningham, S. (2012) (eds) *Digital Disruption: Cinema Moves On-line*. St Andrews: St Andrews Film Studies.

Iordanova, Dina and Cheung, Ruby (eds) (2011) *Film Festival Yearbook 3: Film Festivals and East Asia*. St Andrews: St Andrews Film Studies.

Iordanova, Dina and Torchin, Leshu (eds) (2012) *Film Festival Yearbook 4: Film Festivals and Activism*. St Andrews: St Andrews Film Studies.

Iordanova, Dina and Van de Peer, Stefanie (eds) (2014) *Film Festival Yearbook 6: Film Festivals and the Middle East*. St Andrews: St Andrews Film Studies.

Iordanova, Dina with Rhyne, R. (eds) (2009) *Film Festival Yearbook 1: The Festival Circuit*. St Andrews: St Andrews Film Studies with College Gate Press.

Iordanova, Dina with Cheung, Ruby (eds) (2010) *Film Festival Yearbook 2: Film Festivals and Imagined Communities*. St Andrews: St Andrews Film Studies.

J. G. (2011) 'London burns', *The Economist*, 9 August, www.economist.com/blogs/blighty/2011/08/riots-london-0 (accessed 3 December 2014).

Jancovich, M. (2000) '"A real shocker": Authenticity, genre and the struggle for cultural distinctions', *Cultural Studies* 14: 1, pp. 22–35.

Jancovich, M. (2008 [2002]) 'Cult fictions: Cult movies, subcultural capital and the production of cultural distinctions', in Mathijis, E. and Mendik, X. (eds) *The Cult Film Reader*, Maidenhead: McGraw-Hill (Open University Press), pp. 149–62.

Jancovich, M, Lázaro Reboll, A., Stringer, J. and Willis, A. (2003) 'Introduction', in Jancovich, M, Lázaro Reboll, A., Stringer, J. and Willis, A. (eds) *Defining Cult Movies: The Cultural Politics of Oppositional Taste*, Manchester: Manchester University Press, pp. 1–13.

Jefferies, Mark (2007) 'Hammer mouse of horrors: Film to be released online', *Daily Record*, 13 December, http://lexisnexis.com (accessed 14 July 2014).

Jenkins, H. (1992) *Textual Poachers: Television Fans and Participatory Cultures*. London: Taylor and Francis.

Johnson, Derek (2012), 'Cinematic destiny: Marvel Studios and the trade stories of industrial convergence', *Cinema Journal* 52: 1, pp. 1–24.

Johnson, Tom (1997) *Censored Screams: The British Ban on Hollywood Horror in the Thirties*. London: McFarland and Company.

Jolin, D. (2005) '*The Last Horror Movie*', *Empire* 192, p. 35.

Jones, A. (1994) 'If I had a Hammer', *Shivers* 10, pp. 19–21.

Jones, A. (2001) 'Going to the dogs', *Shivers* 92, pp. 14–17.

Jones, A. (2009) '*Eden Lake*: Paradise bloodied', *Fangoria* 279, pp. 32–5.

Jones, A. (2010) '*Lesbian Vampire Killers*: Laughs at stake', *Fangoria* 289, pp. 58–61.

Jones, K. (2007) 'Americans are interested in the British', *Screen International* 1,606, p. 12.

Jones, O. (2011) *Chavs: The Demonization of the Working-Class*. London: Verso.

Jones, S. (2012) 'Post-torture porn: DVD as neo-grindhouse ghetto', www.drstevejones.co.uk/post%20torture%20porn.html (accessed 13 November 2012).

Jones, S. (2013) *Torture Porn: Popular Horror in the Era of* Saw. London: Palgrave.

Kaplan, J.A. (2012) 'Facebook to charge users to "promote" posts to friends", Fox News, 4 October, www.foxnews.com/tech/2012/10/04/facebook-to-charge-users-to-promote-posts-to-friends (accessed 5 October 2012).

Kay, J. (2006a) 'Vested interest', *Screen International* 1,559, p. 20.

Kay, J. (2006b) 'Katz, Moldo resurrect UK genre label Amicus', *Screen International*, 30 January, http://lexisnexis.com (accessed 14 July 2014).

Kay, J. (2008) '*Cloverfield*'s Matt Reeves to direct *Let the Right One In* remake', *Screen International*, 25 September, http://lexisnexis.com (accessed 6 November 2014).

Kemp, S. (2012) '*The Woman in Black* is the most successful British horror film in 20 years', *The Hollywood Reporter*, 28 February, www.hollywoodreporter.com/news/daniel-radcliffe-woman-in-black-box-office-295641 (accessed 28 November 2012).

Kendrick, J. (2004) 'A nasty situation: Social panics, transnationalism and the video nasty', in Hantke, S. (ed.) *Horror Film: Creating and Marketing Fear*, Jackson: University Press of Mississippi, pp. 153–72.

Kennedy, M. (2012) 'BFI sets out five year plan for British film industry funding', *The Guardian*, 14 May, www.guardian.co.uk/film/2012/may/14/bfi-273m-funding-british-film (accessed 27 October 2012).

Kerekes, D. and Slater, D. (1993) *Killing for Culture: An Illustrated History of Death Film from Mondo to Snuff*. London: Creation Books.

Kerekes, D. and Slater, D. (2000) *See No Evil – Banned Films and Video Controversy*. Manchester: Headpress.

Kermode, M. (2001) 'I was a teenage horror fan: or, "How I learned to stop worrying and love Linda Blair"', in Barker, M and Petley, J. (eds) *Ill-Effects: The Media/ Violence Debate*, London: Routledge, pp. 126–34.

Kermode, M. (2002) 'The British censors and horror cinema', in Chibnall, S. and Petley, J. (eds), *British Horror Cinema*, London: Routledge, pp. 10–22.

Kermode, M. (2005) '*The Last Horror Movie*', *Sight & Sound* 15: 2, pp. 56–7.

Kerner, A. (2015) *Torture Porn in the Wake of 9/11: Horror, Exploitation, and the Cinema of Sensation*. New Brunswick, NJ: Rutgers University Press.

Kimber, Shaun (2011) *Henry: Portrait of a Serial Killer*. London: Palgrave.

Kinsey, W. (2002) *Hammer Films: The Bray Studio Years*. London: Reynolds and Hearn.

Kinsey, W. (2007) *Hammer Films: The Elstree Studios Years*. London: Tomahawk Press.

Kinsey, W. (2010) *Hammer Films: The Unsung Heroes: The Team behind the Legend*. New York: Midpoint Trade Books.

Kirby, J. (2006) 'The hoodie needs a daddy, not a hug', *The Sunday Times*, 16 July, p. 16.

Klinger, B. (1994) *Melodrama and Meaning: History, Culture and the Films of Douglas Sirk*. Hoboken: John Wiley & Sons.

Klinger, B. (2007) *Beyond the Multiplex: Cinema, New Technologies and the Home*. Berkley: University of California Press.

Labato, R. (2012) *Shadow Economies of Cinema: Mapping Informal Film Distribution*. London: BFI.

Landy, M. (1991) *British Genres: Cinema and Society, 1930–1960*. Princeton: Princeton University Press.

Leake, M. (1999a) 'The *Lighthouse* saga part 2: Getting the money', *Reel Scene* 7: 5, pp. 8–11.

Leake, M. (1999b) 'The *Lighthouse* saga part 3', *Reel Scene* 7: 6, pp. 8–11.

Lee, Marc (2008) 'A new lease of life for the undead', *The Daily Telegraph*, 24 March, http://lexisnexis.com (accessed 14 July 2014).

Leggott, J. (2004) 'Like father?: Failing parents and angelic children in contemporary British social realist cinema', in Babington, Bruce, Davies, Ann and Powrie, Phil (eds), *The Trouble With Men: Masculinities in European and Hollywood Cinema*, London: Wallflower Press, pp. 163–73.

Leggott, J. (2008) *Contemporary British Cinema: From Heritage to Horror*, London: Wallflower.

Littlejohn, R. (2011) 'So where are the parents? They are out looting too', *Daily Mail*, 12 August, p. 17.

Lovell, A. (1996) 'Landscapes and stories in 1960s British Realism', in Higson, A. (ed.) *Dissolving Views: Key Writings on British Cinema*, London: Cassell, pp. 157–77.

Lowe, Tom (2008), 'Horror "rave" to hit Myspace', *Press Association Mediapoint*, 18 March. http://lexisnexis.com (accessed 14 July 2014).

Lowenstein, A. (2005) *Shocking Representation: Historical Trauma, National Cinema and the Modern Horror Film*. New York: Columbia University Press.

Lury, K. (2000) 'Here and then: Space, place and nostalgia in British Youth Cinema', in Murphy, R. (ed.) *British Cinema of the 90s*, London: Routledge, pp. 100–8.

Lyons, J. (2007) '"We're seeing a wave of new young talent"', *Screen International* 1,606, p. 13.

McDonagh, M. D. (2012) '*The Devil's Business* Review', *The Hollywood News*, 10 September, www.thehollywoodnews.com/2012/07/01/the-devils-business-review (accessed 19 July 2012).

McDonald, P. (2007) *Video and DVD Industries*. London: BFI.

McKay, S. (2007) *A Thing of Unspeakable Horror: The History of Hammer Films*. London: Aurum.

McLean, G. (2005) 'In the hood', *The Guardian*, 13 May, www.guardian.co.uk/poli tics/2005/may/13/fashion.fashionandstyle (accessed 19 May 2010).

McRobbie, A. (2009) *The Aftermath of Feminism: Gender, Culture and Social Change.* London: SAGE Publications.

Macmillan, S. (2002) 'Case study: *Deathwatch*', *Screen International* 1,381, p. 14.

Macnab, G. (2002) 'That shrinking feeling', *Sight and Sound* 12: 10, pp. 18–20.

Macnab, G. (2004a) 'The wages of fear', *Screen International* 1,438, p 6.

Macnab, G. (2004b) 'Production: The UK', *Screen International* 1,467, p. 20.

Macnab, G. (2005a) '*The Descent*', *Screen International* 1,507, p. 17.

Macnab, G. (2005b) 'Scare tactics', *Screen International* 1,565, pp. 11–12.

Macnab, G. (2005c) 'Random Harvest teams with Hammer, Winston on horror', *Screen International*, 14 January, http://lexisnexus.com (accessed 11 June 2014).

Macnab, G. (2006a) '*The Descent*', *Screen International* 1,530, p. 26.

Macnab, G. (2006b) '*Severance*', *Screen International* 1,559, p. 19.

Macnab, G. (2008a) 'Wish you were here', *Screen International* 1,645, pp. 6–7.

Macnab, G. (2008b) 'Hammer resurrection as production of *The Wake Wood* begins', *Screen International*, 22 September, http://lexisnexis.com (accessed 6 November 2014).

Macnab, G. (2009) 'Fresh blood', *Screen Daily*, 23 January, http://lexisnexis.com (accessed 23 May 2013).

Macnab, G. (2010) 'Still haunted by the ghosts of the past', *The Independent*, 15 November, www.independent.co.uk/arts-entertainment/films/features/still-haunted-by-the-ghosts-of-the-past-2134039.html (accessed 23 January 2013).

Magot, M. and Schelsinger, P. (2009) '"For this relief much thanks": Taxation, film policy and the UK government', *Screen* 50: 3, pp. 299–317.

Maher, K. (2002) 'Be scared. Be very scared', *The Guardian*, 4 August, www.the guardian.com/film/2002/aug/04/edinburghfilmfestival2002.culturaltrips (accessed 28 November 2014).

Maher, Kevin (2008) 'The kids are all frights', *The Times*, 26 June, pp. 13–14.

Manzoor, S. (2009) 'My £45 hit film: Marc Price on his zombie movie *Colin*', *The Guardian*, 30 July, www.guardian.co.uk/film/2009/jul/30/marc-price-zombie-film-colin (accessed 11 November 2012).

Marlow-Mann, Alex (ed) (2013) *Film Festival Yearbook 5: Archival Film Festivals.* St Andrews: St Andrews Film Studies.

Marriott, J. (2002) 'They just don't make 'em like they used to', *The Scotsman*, 17 January, p. 8.

Marsh, K. A. (2004) 'Contextualizing Bridget Jones', *College Literature* 31: 1, pp. 52–72.

Marshall, N. (2003) *Dog Soldiers* DVD Commentary.

Marshall, N. and Winckler, A. (2009) 'UK stars of tomorrow: Neil Marshall and Alex Winckler', *Screen International* 1,694, pp. 24–5.

Martin-Jones, D. (2005) 'Sexual healing: Representations of the English in post-devolutionary Scotland', *Screen* 45: 2, pp. 227–33.

Martin-Jones, D. (2011) *Scotland: Global Cinema – Genres, Modes and Identities.* Edinburgh: Edinburgh University Press.

Mason, A. (2010), E-mail interview with author, 23 August.

Mathijs, E. and Sexton, J. (2011) *Cult Cinema*. London: Wiley Blackwell.

Meikle, D. (1996) *A History of Horrors: The Rise and Fall of the House of Hammer.* Lanham and London: Scarecrow Press.

Meikle, D. (2009) *A History of Horrors – The Rise and Fall of the House of Hammer* (2nd Edition). Plymouth: Scarecrow Press.

Mendik, X. and Mathijs, E. (2008) 'Editorial introduction: What is cult film?', in Mendik, X. and Mathijs, E. (eds) *The Cult Film Reader.* New York: Open University Press, pp. 1–11.

Midgley, C. (2006) 'They have hoodies, too', *The Times*, 10 November, www.lexisn exis.com/uk/legal/results/enhdocview.do?docLinkInd=true&ersKey=23_T15893129 580&format=GNBFULL&startDocNo=121&resultsUrlKey=0_T1589313 8250&backKey=20_T15893138251&csi=10939&docNo=131 (accessed 10 March 2011).

Milmo, D. and Gibson, O. (2005) 'Treasury's culture test aims to boost UK filmmaking', *The Guardian*, 30 July, www.theguardian.com/politics/2005/jul/30/uk.filmnews (accessed 25 July 2014).

Minns, A. (2000) 'Entertainment gurus resurrect Hammer horror label', *Screen International*, 7 February, http://lexisnexis.com (accessed 10 January 2014).

Minns, A. (2001) 'Parker and the vicious cycle', *Screen International* 1,380, p. 13.

Minns, A. (2001a) 'Gathering of evil in the UK', *Screen International* 1,335, p. 26.

Minns, A. (2002) 'Buena Vista rides with UK's Four Horsemen', *Screen Daily*, www.screendaily.com/buena-vista-rides-with-uks-four-horsemen/408753.article (accessed 7 January 2010).

Minns, A. (2004a) 'Distributing support', *Screen International* 1,451, p. 8.

Minns, A. (2004b) 'Dead funny', *Screen International* 1,444, p. 7.

Mitchell, R. (2002) 'Marketing drives *28 Days*', *Screen International* 1,380, p. 6.

Mitchell, R. (2005a) 'Film fans sink teeth into horror rebirth', *Screen International* 1,499, p. 24.

Mitchell, R. (2005b) 'Where did all the rom-coms go?', *Screen International* 1,524, pp. 24–25.

Mitchell, W. (2005) 'The UK', *Screen International* 1,512, p. 17.

Mitchell, W. (2007a) 'Hammer Film relaunched with European investors including Cyrte', *Screen International*, 10 May, www.lexisnexis.com (accessed 6 November 2014).

Mitchell, W. (2007b) 'Hammer's first new film to air episodes on MySpace', *Screen International*, 13 December, www.lexisnexis.com (accessed 6 November 2014).

Mitchell, W. (2008) '"We're total Anglophones right now"', *Screen International* 1,642, pp. 14–17.

Monk, C. (2000a) 'Men in the 90s', in Murphy, R. (ed.) *British Cinema of the 90s*, London: BFI, pp. 156–66.

Monk, C. (2000b) 'Underbelly UK: The 1990s underclass film, masculinity and the ideologies of "new" Britain', in Ashby, Justine and Higson, Andrew (eds), *British Cinema, Past and Present*, London and New York: Routledge, pp. 274–87.

Mortimer, Lynne (2010) 'New wave of Hammer horrors set to be a hit', *East Anglian Daily Times*, 27 October, http//lexisnexis.com (accessed 25 September 2014).

Muir, K. (2010) 'Hammer returns with chilling vampire tale', *The Times*, 15 October, p. 21, http://lexisnexis.com (accessed 3 April 2013).

Mulvey, L. (1975) 'Visual pleasure and narrative cinema', *Screen* 16: 3, pp. 6–18.

Murphy, B. M. (2013) *The Rural Gothic in American Popular Culture: Backwoods Horror and Terror in the Wilderness*, Basingstoke: Palgrave.

Murphy, R. (1998) 'Popular British cinema', *Journal of Popular British Cinema* 1, pp. 6–12.

Murphy, R. (ed.) (1999a) *British Cinema of the 90s*. London: Routledge

Murphy, R. (1999b) 'A path through the moral maze', in Murphy, R. (ed.) *British Cinema of the 90s*, London: Routledge, pp. 1–16.

Murphy, R. (2002) 'Another false dawn? The Film Consortium and the franchise scheme', *Journal of Popular British Cinema* 5, pp. 31–6.

Murphy, R. (ed.) (2009) *The British Cinema Book* (3rd Edition). London: BFI.

Murray, C. (1990) *The Emerging British Underclass*. London: Institute of Economic Affairs.

Murray, J. (2012) 'Blurring borders: Scottish cinema in the twenty-first century', *Journal of British Cinema and Television* 9: 3, pp. 400–18.

Murry, J., Roberrs, D. and Drake, M. (2008) 'Should hooded youths be banned from our streets and shops?', *Sunday Express*, 30 March, www.express.co.uk/posts/view/39640/Should-hooded-youths-be-banned-from-our-streets-and-shops (accessed 13 March 2010).

Newman, K. (1988) *Nightmare Movies*. London: Bloomsbury.

Newman, K. (2009) 'Horror will eat itself', *Sight and Sound* 19, p. 5.

Newman, K. (2011) *Nightmare Movies: Horror on Screen since the 1960s* (3rd Edition). London: Bloomsbury.

Norman, N. (2010) 'Back from the dead', *Daily Express*, 22 October, p. 38, http://lexisnexis.com (accessed 28 November 2014).

Nowell, R. (2010) *Blood Money: A History of the First Teen Slasher Cycle*. London and New York: Continuum.

Parker, Robin (2007) 'When evil calls', *Broadcast*, 16 August, http://lexisnexis.com (accessed 2 July 2014).

Pearson, Geoffrey (2006) 'Disturbing continuities: "Peaky blinders" to "hoodies"', *CJM* 65, pp. 6–7.

Pegg, S. (2011) *Nerd Do Well*. London: Arrow Books.

Peirse, A. (2009) 'Destroying the male body in British Horror Cinema', in Fouz-Hernández, S. (ed.) *Mysterious Skin: Male Bodies in Contemporary Cinema*, London: I. B. Tauris, pp. 159–73.

Peirse, A. (2013) *After Dracula: The 1930s Horror Film*. London: I. B. Tauris.

Peirse, A. and Martin, D. (eds) (2013) *Korean Horror Cinema*. Edinburgh: Edinburgh University Press.

Percival, S. (2009) *MySpace Marketing: Creating a Social Network to Boom your Business*. Indianapolis: QUE.

Perkins, S. (2012) 'Film in the UK, 2001–10: A statistical overview', *Journal of British Cinema and Television* 9: 3, pp. 310–32.

Perks, M. (2002) 'A descent into the underworld: *Death Line*', in Chibnall, S. and Petley, J. (eds) *British Horror Cinema*, London: Routledge, pp. 145–55.

Petley, J. (1996 [1986]) 'The lost continent', in Barr, C. (ed.) *All Our Yesterdays: 90 Years of British Cinema* (3rd Edition), London: BFI, pp. 98–119.

Petley, J. (2000) '"Snuffed out": Nightmares in a trading standards officer's orain', in Mendik, X. and Harper, G. (eds) *Unruly Pleasures: The Cult Film and Its Critics*, Surrey: FAB Press, pp. 205–19.

Petley, J. (2002a) '"A crude sort of entertainment for a crude sort of audience": The British critics and horror cinema', in Chibnall, Steve and Petley, Julian (eds) *British Horror Cinema*, London: Routledge, pp. 23–41.

Petley, J. (2002b) 'From Brit-flicks to shit-flicks: The cost of public subsidy', *Journal of Popular British Cinema* 5, pp. 37–52.

Petley, J. (2011) *Film and Video Censorship in Modern Britain*. Edinburgh: Edinburgh University Press.

Petley, J. and Chibnall, S. (2002) 'The return of the repressed? British horror's heritage and future', in Chibnall, Steve and Petley, Julian (eds) *British Horror Cinema*, London: Routledge, pp. 1–9.

Petrie, D. (2002) 'British low-budget production and digital technology', *Journal of Popular British Cinema* 5, pp. 64–76.

Petrie, D. and Stoneman, R. (2014) *Educating Filmmakers: Past, Present and Future*. Bristol: Intellect.

Phelan, Laurence (2013) 'Film choice: *Wake Wood*', *i*, 21 December, http://lexisnexis.com (accessed 30 June 2014).

Pinedo, I. (2004) 'Postmodern elements of the contemporary horror film', in Prince, S. (ed.) *The Horror Film*, Piscataway: Rutgers University Press, pp. 85–117.

Pirie, D. (1973) *A Heritage of Horror: The English Gothic Cinema 1946–1972*. London: Gordon Fraser.

Pirie, D. (2008) *A New Heritage of Horror: The English Gothic Cinema* (2nd Edition). London: I. B. Tauris.

Ponsford, D. (2009) 'Magazines ABCs: Lads' mags take circulation hit', *Press Gazette*, 12 February, www.pressgazette.co.uk/node/43071 (accessed 11 May 2010).

Powell, A. (2005) *Deleuze and Horror Film*. Edinburgh: Edinburgh University Press.

Powlson, N. (2009) 'Why Dyer is back in the doghouse', *Derby Evening Telegraph*, 12 June, p. 21.

Prawer, S. S. (1980) *Caligari's Children: The Film as Tale of Terror*. New York: Da Capo Press.

Pre-Cert Video Forum, *Love Camp 7* data, www.pre-cert.co.uk, www.pre-cert.co.uk/search.php?q=Love+Camp+7&t=Title&c=UK (accessed 9 July 2012).

Pre-Cert Video Forum, *Night Train Murders* data, www.pre-cert.co.uk, www.pre-cert.co.uk/search.php?q=night+train&t=Title&c=UK (accessed 9 July 2012).

Pyatt, J. (2007) 'He is nothing but a monster', *The Sun*, 4 October, www.thesun.co.uk/sol/homepage/news/5964/He-is-nothing-but-a-monster.html (accessed: 4 June 2010).

Quinn, T. (2007) '"I'm a huge fan of British film"', *Screen International* 1,606, p. 12.

Radner, H. (2011) *Neo-Feminist Cinema: Girly Films, Chick Flicks and Consumer Culture*. London: Routledge.

Ramaswamy, C. (2010) '"People are going to be offended by this film"', *The Scotsman*, 31 August, p. 38.

Read, J. (2003) 'The cult of masculinity', in Jancovich, M, Lázaro Reboll, A., Stringer, J. and Willis, A. (eds), *Defining Cult Movies: The Cultural Politics of Oppositional Taste*, Manchester: Manchester University Press, pp. 54–70.

Reed, B. (2012) 'Interview: *Inbred* director Alex Chandon', *This Is Fake DIY*, 20 September, www.thisisfakediy.co.uk/articles/film/interview-inbred-director-alex-chandon (accessed 3 December 2012).

Rehling, N. (2011) '"It's all about belonging": Masculinity, collectivity, and community in British hooligan films', *Journal of Popular Film and Television* 39: 4, pp. 162–73.

Richards, J. (2000) 'Rethinking British cinema', in Ashby, J. and Higson, A. (eds) *British Cinema Past and Present*, London: Routledge, pp. 21–34.

Richards, J. (2005) *The Last Horror Movie* DVD Commentary. Tartan Films.

Richardson, J. and O'Neill, R. (2011) '"Stamp on the camp": The social construction of gypsies and travellers in media and political debate', in Richardson, J. and Ryder, A. (eds) *Gypsies and Travellers: Empowerment and Inclusion in British Society*. Bristol: The Policy Press, pp. 169–88.

Rigby, J. (2000) *English Gothic: A Century of Horror Cinema*. London: Reynolds and Hearn.

Rigby, J. (2002) *English Gothic: A Century of Horror Cinema* (2nd Edition). London: Reynolds and Hearn.

Rigby, J. (2004) *English Gothic: A Century of Horror Cinema* (3rd Edition). London: Reynolds and Hearn.

Rigby, J. (2006) *English Gothic: A Century of Horror Cinema* (4th Edition). London: Reynolds and Hearn.

Rigby, J. (2013) Personal email correspondence.

Rigby, J. (2015) *English Gothic: Classic Horror Cinema*. London: Signum Books.

Roberts, J. (2010a) Face-to-face interview with author, *Bloodlines: British Horror Past and Present*, Leicester, 5 March.

Roberts, J. (2010b) Face-to-face interview with author, Cambridge, 17 September.

Robey, T. (2009) 'Lesbian Vampire Killers, review', The Telegraph, 19 March, www.telegraph.co.uk/journalists/tim-robey/5016281/Lesbian-Vampire-Killers-review.html (accessed 5 April 2009).

Rogers, S. (2011) 'England riots: Which shops were looted?', The Guardian. www.guardian.co.uk/uk/datablog/2011/dec/06/england-riots-shops-raided (accessed 14 May 2012).

Rose, J. (2009) Beyond Hammer: British Horror Cinema since 1970. Leighton Buzzard: Auteur.

Rosser, M. (2013) 'Hammer to reboot The Abominable Snowman', Screen International, 21 November, www.lexisnexis.com (accessed 22 November 2013).

Ryall, T. (1998) 'British cinema and genre', Journal of Popular British Cinema 1: 1, pp. 18–24.

Ryall, T. (2002) 'New Labour and the cinema: Culture, politics and economics', Journal of Popular British Cinema 5, pp. 5–20.

Sanjek, D. (1990) 'Fans' notes: The horror film fanzine', Literature Film Quarterly 18: 3, pp. 150–60.

Sanjek, D. (1994) 'Twilight of the monsters: The English horror film 1968–1975', in Dixon, W. W. (ed.) Re-Viewing British Cinema: 1900–1992., Albany: State University of New York Press, pp. 195–209.

Saunders, R. (2012) 'Undead spaces: Fear, globalisation, and the popular geopolitics of zombiism', Geopolitics 17: 1, pp. 80–104.

Sawyer, A. (1999) '"A stiff upper lip and a trembling lower one": John Wyndham on screen', in Hunter, I. Q. (ed.) British Science Fiction Cinema, London: Routledge, pp. 74–87.

Sconce, J. (1995) '"Trashing" the academy: Taste, excess and an emerging politics of cinematic style', Screen 36: 4, pp. 371–93.

Seguin, D. (2005) 'Hey! Big spender', Screen International 1,528, pp. 24–9.

Seguin, D. (2007) 'Specialty forces', Screen International 1,598, pp. 14–15.

Shackleton, L. and Mitchell, R. (2002) 'Triumphant debut for Deathwatch', Screen International 1,381, p. 51.

Shail, R. (ed.) (2008) Seventies British Cinema. London: BFI.

Shand, R. and Craven, I. (eds) (2013) Small-gauge Storytelling: Discovering the Amateur Fiction Film. Edinburgh: Edinburgh University Press.

Sharrett, C. (2009) 'The problem of Saw: "Torture porn" and the conservatism of contemporary horror films', Cineaste (winter), pp. 32–7.

Sheil, S. (2010a) Skype interview with author, 10 November.

Sheil, S. (2010b) E-mail interview with author, 9 March.

Shin, C. (2008) 'Art of branding: Tartan "Asia Extreme" films', Jump Cut: A Review of Contemporary Media 50, www.ejumpcut.org/archive/jc50.2008/TartanDist/index.html (accessed 30 April 2010).

Simmons, D. (2011) 'Hammer horror and science fiction', in Hochscherf, T. and Leggott, J. (eds) British Science Fiction Film and Television: Critical Essays, Jefferson: McFarland, pp. 50–9.

Simpson, M. J. (2012) Urban Terrors: New British Horror Cinema, 1998–2008. Bristol: Hemlock Books.

Simpson, R. J. E. (2014) Telephone interview with author, 4 July.

Sitarskiego, P. (ed.) (2001) Kino Europy. Cracow: Rabid Publishing House.

Smith, C. C. (2011) 'Day the mob came crashing through my door', Daily Mail, 12 August, p. 9.

Smith, Christopher (2005), DVD Commentary track for Creep. Pathé Distribution.

Smith, L. S. (2002), 'Filmography of British horror films of the sound era,' in

Chibnall, S. and Petley, J. (eds) *British Horror Cinema*, London: Routledge, pp. 196–237.

Sneak, The (2008), 'The Sneak: *Eden Lake*', *The Sun*, 11 September, www.thesun. co.uk/sol/homepage/showbiz/film/movie_reviews/article1676823.ece (accessed 20 July 2011).

Sothcott, J. (2011) E-mail interviews with author, 11–14 November.

Spicer, A. (2001) *Typical Men: The Representation of Masculinity in Popular British Cinema*. London: I. B. Tauris.

Stanley, R. (2002) 'Dying light: An obituary for the great British horror film', in Chibnall, S. and Petley, J. (eds) *British Horror Cinema*, London: Routledge, pp. 183–95.

Stratton, A. (2011) 'David Cameron on riots: Broken society is top of my political agenda', *The Guardian*, 15 August, www.guardian.co.uk/uk/2011/aug/15/david-cameron-riots-broken-society (accessed 15 August 2011).

Street, S. (2002) *Transatlantic Crossings: British Feature Films in the USA*. London and New York: Continuum.

Street, S. (2009) *British National Cinema* (2nd Edition). London: Routledge.

Street, S. (2012) 'Digital Britain and the spectre/spectacle of new technologies', *Journal of British Cinema and Television* 9: 3, pp. 377–99.

Telotte, J. P. (2008 [2001]) 'The Blair Witch Project: Film and the Internet', in Mathijs, E. and Mendik, X. (eds) *The Cult Film Reader*, New York: Open University Press, pp. 263–73.

Tilly, C. (2008) 'Hoodie horror disappoints', *IGN*, 12 September, http://uk.movies.ign. com/articles/909/909659p1.html (accessed 15 September 2010).

Tookey, C. (2008a) '*Mum & Dad*: This gorefest is just torture for the taxpayer', *Daily Mail*, 25 December, www.dailymail.co.uk/tvshowbiz/reviews/article-1101734/Mum--Dad-This-gore-fest-just-torture-taxpayer.html (accessed 30 June 2011).

Tookey, C. (2008b), '*Eden Lake*: A great movie (if you can stomach it)', *Daily Mail*, 11 September, www.dailymail.co.uk/tvshowbiz/article-1054787/Eden-Lake-A-great-movie-stomach-it.html (accessed 30 June 2011).

Tookey, C. (2009) 'Consistently abominable: *Lesbian Vampire Killers*', *Daily Mail*, 20 March, www.dailymail.co.uk/tvshowbiz/reviews/article-1163268/Consistently-abominable-Lesbian-Vampire-Killers.html (accessed 5 April 2009).

Tookey, C. (2011) 'Hoodies you want to hug: A teen gang fights aliens in the best monster movie since *Shaun of the Dead*', *Daily Mail*, 13 May, www.dailymail.co.uk/ tvshowbiz/reviews/article-1386562/Attack-The-Block-review-The-best-monster-movie-Shaun-Of-The-Dead.html (accessed 28 November 2012).

Treneman, A. (2005) 'All he's asking is for a little respect', *The Times*, 13 May, p. 25.

Tudor, A. (2002) 'From paranoia to postmodernism? The horror movie in late modern society', in Neale, S. (ed.) *Genre and Contemporary Hollywood*, London: BFI, pp. 104–16.

Tudor, A. (2003) 'Genre', in Grant, B. K. (ed.) *Film Genre Reader III*, Austin: University of Texas Press, pp. 1–11.

Turney, J. (2009) *The Culture of Knitting*. London: BERG.

Twitchell, J. (1985) *Dreadful Pleasures: An Anatomy of Modern Horror*. Oxford: Oxford University Press.

Tyler, I. (2008) '"Chav Mum, Chav Scum"': Class disgust in contemporary Britain', *Feminist Media Studies* 8: 1, pp. 17–34.

Tyler, I. (2013) *Revolting Subjects: Social Abjection and Resistance in Neoliberal Britain*. London: Zed Books.

UK Film Council (UKFC) (2000) *Towards a Sustainable UK Film Industry*, www. ukfilmcouncil.org.uk/media/pdf/p/r/TASFI.pdf (accessed 7 January 2011).

UK Film Council (UKFC) (2003) *UK Film Council Statistical Year Book 2002*, London: UK Film Council.

UK Film Council (UKFC) (2004) *UK Film Council Statistical Year Book: Annual Review* 2003–2004, www.ukfilmcouncil.org.uk/media/pdf/l/r/Final_Yearbook_0304. pdf (accessed 7 January 2011).

UK Film Council (UKFC) (2005) *UK Film Council Statistical Year Book 2004–2005*, www.bfi.org.uk/sites/bfi.org.uk/files/downloads/uk-film-council-statistical-year-book-annual-review-2004-2005.pdf (accessed 27 December 2012).

UK Film Council (UKFC) (2006) *UK Film Council Statistical Year Book 2005–2006*, www.ukfilmcouncil.org.uk/media/pdf/l/r/Statistical_Yearbook_05-06.pdf (accessed 7 January 2011).

UK Film Council (UKFC) (2007) *UK Film Council Statistical Year Book 2006–2007*, www.bfi.org.uk/sites/bfi.org.uk/files/downloads/uk-film-council-statistical-year-book-2006-2007.pdf (accessed 27 December 2012).

UK Film Council (UKFC) (2008) *UK Film Council Statistical Year Book 2008*, www. bfi.org.uk/sites/bfi.org.uk/files/downloads/uk-film-council-statistical-yearbook-2008. pdf (accessed 27 December 2012).

UK Film Council (UKFC) (2009) *UK Film Council Statistical Year Book 2009*, www. bfi.org.uk/sites/bfi.org.uk/files/downloads/uk-film-council-statistical-yearbook-2009. pdf (accessed 27 December 2012).

UK Film Council (UKFC) (2010) *UK Film Council Statistical Year Book 2010*, www. bfi.org.uk/sites/bfi.org.uk/files/downloads/uk-film-council-statistical-yearbook-2010. pdf (accessed 27 December 2012).

Vidal, B. (2012) *Heritage Film: Nation, Genre and Representation*. London: Wallflower Press.

Virtue, G. (2011) 'Hoodies are goodies in Joe Cornish's *Attack the Block*', *The Herald Scotland*, 8 May, www.heraldscotland.com/arts-ents/film-tv-features/hoodies-are-goodies-in-joe-cornish-s-attack-the-bloc-1.1099324 (accessed 4 December 2014).

Vitali, V. and Willemen, P. (eds) (2006) *Theorizing National Cinema*. London: BFI Publishing.

Walker, J (2011) 'F for "frightening"?: Johannes Roberts takes on hoodie horrors', *Diabolique* 3, pp. 24–32.

Walker, J. (2012) 'A wilderness of horrors? British horror cinema in the new millennium', *Journal of British Cinema and Television* 9: 3, pp. 436–56.

Walker, J. (2013) *The Contemporary British Horror Film: 2000–2010*. Unpublished PhD thesis, De Montfort University.

Walker, J. (2014) 'Low budgets, no budgets and digital video nasties: Recent British horror and informal distribution', in Nowell, R. (ed.) *Merchants of Menace: The Business of Horror Cinema*, London and New York: Bloomsbury, pp. 215–28.

Ware, J. (2009) 'Yes family breakdown IS behind broken Britain', *Daily Mail*, 11 July, www.dailymail.co.uk/debate/article-1198962/Yes-family-breakdown-IS-broken-Britain-Top-judge-says-national-tragedy-attacks-BBC-suppressing-debate. html (accessed 4 December 2014).

Warren, B. (2000) *The Evil Dead Companion*. London: Titan Books.

Waters, D. (2006) 'On the trail of *Lesbian Vampire Killers*', BBC News, 22 May, http://news.bbc.co.uk/1/hi/entertainment/5006368.stm (accessed 3 December 2010).

Watkins, J. (2012) *The Woman in Black* DVD Special Features. Hammer Films.

Weitz, K., Hinsliff, G., and Bright, M. (2005) 'The youth debate: When the hoodies met the housewife', *The Observer*, 15 May, p. 14.

Wells, Dominic (2010), 'Resurrected from the dead', *The Times*, 30 October, http://lexisnexis.com (accessed 16 July 2014).

Whelehan, I. (2000) *Overloaded: Popular Culture and the Future of Feminism*. London: The Women's Press.

Williams, A. (ed.) (2001) *Film and Nationalism*. New Brunswick, NJ: Rutgers University Press.

Williams, G. C. (2007) 'Birthing an undead family: Reification of the mother's role in the Gothic landscape of *28 Days Later*', *Gothic Studies* 9: 2, pp. 33–44.

Williams, L. (1984) 'When the woman looks', in Doane, M. A., Mellencamp, P. and Williams, L. (eds) *Re-Vision: Essays in Feminist Film*, Los Angeles: American Film Institute, pp. 83–99.

Williams, L. (1991) 'Film bodies: Gender, genre, and excess', *Film Quarterly* 44: 4, pp. 2–13.

Williams, Linda Ruth (2005) *The Erotic Thriller in Contemporary Cinema*. Edinburgh: Edinburgh University Press.

Williams, P. A. (2000) *Cherry Tree Lane* Director's Commentary, UK DVD. Momentum Pictures.

Willis, A. (2003) 'Spanish horror and the flight from "art" cinema, 1967–73', in Jancovich, M, Lázaro Reboll, A., Stringer, J. and Willis, A. (eds) *Defining Cult Movies: The Cultural Politics of Oppositional Taste*, Manchester: Manchester University Press, pp. 71–83.

Wood, M. P. (2007) *Contemporary European Cinema*. London: Hodder Arnold.

Wood, R. (1985 [1979]) 'Introduction to the American horror film', in Nichols, B. (ed.) *Movies and Methods*, Berkley: University of California Press, pp. 195–219.

Wordsworth, W. (1979) *The Prelude 1850*. New York and London: Norton.

Worland, R. (2007) *The Horror Film: An Introduction*. Oxford: Blackwell Publishing.

Wright, E. (2005) *Shaun of the Dead* DVD Commentary. Working Title.

Wu, Harmony H. (2003) 'Trading in horror, cult and matricide: Peter Jackson's phenomenal bad taste and New Zealand fantasies of inter/national cinematic success', in Jancovich, M, Lázaro Reboll, A., Stringer, J. and Willis, A. (eds) *Defining Cult Movies: The Cultural Politics of Oppositional Taste*, Manchester: Manchester University Press, pp. 84–108.

Young, S. (2005) 'Snapping up school girls: Legitimation crisis in recent Canadian horror', in Schneider, S.J. and Williams, T. (eds) *Horror International*, Detroit: Wayne State University Press, pp. 235–57.

Specialist web resources/databases

2 Days Later Film Festival, www.2dayslater.co.uk

British Horror Films, www.britishhorrorfilms.co.uk.

British Horror Revival, http://british-horror-revival.blogspot.co.uk.

Chemical Burn Entertainment, www.chemicalburn.org

Film Index International, http://fii.chadwyck.co.uk/home

LexisLibrary, www.lexisnexis.com/uk

Maxim Media, www.emaximmedia.com

Mill Creek Entertainment, www.millcreekent.com

Openfilm, www.openfilm.com

Pass The Marmalade: Darrell Buxton's British Horror Film Pages, www.buxton.freeserve.co.uk

Pre-Cert Video database, www.pre-cert.co.uk

UK Film Council's (UKFC's) Awards Database, http://industry.bfi.org.uk/awards (accessed 19 July 2012).

FILMS AND TELEVISION PROGRAMMES

British horror films that appeared post-2000 appear in bold.

13th Sign, The, UK, 2000, dirs Jonty Acton and Adam Mason.
28 Days Later, UK, 2002, dir. Danny Boyle.
28 Weeks Later, UK/Spain, 2007, dir. Juan Carlos Fresnadillo.
ABCs of Death, US/New Zealand, 2012, dirs Kaare Andrews *et al.*
Abominable Snowman, The, UK, 1957, dir. Val Guest.
Adulthood, UK, 2008, dir. Noel Clarke.
Alien: Resurrection, US, 1997, dir. Jean-Pierre Jeunet.
Aliens, US, 1986, dir. James Cameron.
American Beauty, US, 1999, dir. Sam Mendes.
American Haunting, An, UK/Canada/Romania/US, 2005, dir. Courtney Solomon.
American Pie, US, 1999, dir. Paul Weitz.
American Werewolf in London, An, UK/US, 1981, dir. John Landis.
Amityville Horror, The, US, 2005, dir. Andrew Douglas.
Anatomie (Anatomy), Germany, 2000, dir. Stefan Ruzowitsky.
Antichrist, Denmark/Germany/France/Sweden/Italy/Poland, 2009, dir. Lars von Trier.
Army of Darkness, US, 1992, dir. Sam Raimi.
Attack the Block, UK, 2011, dir. Joe Cornish.
Awakening, The, UK, 2011, dir. Nick Murphy.
Bad Karma, UK, 1991, dir. Alex Chandon.
Ban the Sadist Videos, UK, 2005, dir. David Gregory.
Bane, UK, 2008, dir. James Eaves.
Basic Instinct, US, 1992, dir. Paul Verhoeven.
Battle Royale, Japan, 2000, dir. Kinji Fukasaku.
Battlefield Death Tales, UK, 2012, dirs James Eaves *et al.*
Beacon 77 (The 7th Dimension), UK, 2009, dir. Brad Watson.
Behemoth, US/Canada, 2011, dir. W. D. Hogan.

Beyond, The, Italy, 1980, dir. Lucio Fulci.
Beyond the Rave, UK, 2008, dir. Matthias Hoene.
Big Fat Gypsy Gangster, UK, 2011, dir. Ricky Grover.
Black Death, UK/Germany, 2010, dir. Christopher Smith.
Blade, US, 1998, dir. Stephen Norrington.
Blair Witch Project, The, US, 1999, dirs Daniel Myrick and Eduardo Sánchez.
Blood Feast, US, 1963, dir. Herschell Gordon Lewis.
Blood Feast 2: All U Can Eat, US, 2002, dir. Herschell Gordon Lewis.
Blood on Satan's Claw, The, UK, 1971, dir. Piers Haggard.
Bordello Death Tales, UK, 2012, dirs James Eaves, Pat Higgins and Alan Ronald.
Borderlands, The, UK, 2013, dir. Elliot Goldner.
Botched, Germany/Ireland/UK/USA, 2007, dir. Kit Ryan.
Boy Eats Girl, Ireland/UK, 2005, dir. Stephen Bradley.
Bram Stoker's Dracula, US, 1992, dir. Francis Ford Coppola.
Breeders, UK, 1998, dir. Paul Matthews.
Bridget Jones: The Edge of Reason, UK/France/Germany/Ireland/US, 2004, dir. Beeban Kidron.
Bridget Jones's Diary, UK/France/US/Ireland, 2001, dir. Sharon Maguire.
Broken, UK, 2006, dir. Adam Mason and Simon Boyes.
Brookside [TX], UK, 1982–2003, dirs various.
Bunker, The, UK, 2001, dir. Rob Green.
Business, The, UK/Spain, 2005, dir. Nick Love.
Byzantium, UK/US/Ireland, 2012, dir. Neil Jordan.
Cabin Fever, US, 2002, dir. Eli Roth.
California Axe Massacre (Axe), US, 1974, dir. Fredrick R. Friedel.
Calvaire, Belgium, 2004, dir. Fabrice Du Welz.
Cannibal Apocalypse, Italy/Spain, 1980, dir. Antonio Margheriti.
Cannibal Ferox, Italy, 1981, dir. Umberto Lenzi.
Cannibal Holocaust, Italy, 1980, dir. Ruggero Deodato.
Captive, The (Armistice), UK, 2013, dir. Luke Massey.
Casino Royale, UK/Czech Republic/US/Germany/Bahamas, 2006, dir. Martin Campbell.
Chatroom, UK, 2010, dir. Hideo Nakata.
Cherry Falls, US, 2000, dir. Geoffrey Wright.
Cherry Tree Lane, UK, 2010, dir. Paul Andrew Williams.
Child's Play 3, US, 1991, dir. Jack Bender.
Children of the Corn, US, 1984, dir. Fritz Kiersch.
Children, The, UK, 2008, dir. Tom Shankland.
Citadel, Ireland/UK, 2012, dir. Ciaran Foy.
Clinic, The (The Addicted), UK, 2014, dir. Sean J. Vincent.
Clive Barker's Book of Blood, UK, 2009, dir. John Harrison.
Clockwork Orange, A, UK/US, 1971, dir. Stanley Kubrick.
Cloverfield, US, 2008, dir. Matt Reeves.
Cockneys versus Zombies, UK, 2012, dir. Matthias Hoene.
Cold and Dark, UK, 2005, dir. Andrew Goth.
Colin, UK, 2009, dir. Marc Price.
Comedown, UK, 2012, dir. Menhaj Huda.
Community, UK, 2012, dir. Jason Ford.
Company of Wolves, The, UK, 1984, dir. Neil Jordan.
Cottage, The, UK, 2008, dir. Paul Andrew Williams.
Cradle of Fear, UK, 2001, dir. Alex Chandon.
Crash, Canada/UK, 1996, dir. David Cronenberg.
Credo, UK, 2008, dir. Toni Harman.

Creep, UK/Germany, 2004, dir. Christopher Smith.
Curse of Frankenstein, The, UK, 1957, dir. Terence Fisher.
Cut & Paste, UK, 2009, dir. Jason Impey.
Cycle, UK, 2005, dir. Robbie Moffat.
Daisy Chain, The, Ireland/UK, 2008, dir. Aisling Walsh.
Dark, The, Germany/UK, 2005, dir. John Fawcett.
Dark Knight, The, US/UK, 2008, dir. Christopher Nolan.
Darklands, UK, 1996, dir. Julian Richards.
Dawn of the Dead, US, 1978, dir. George A. Romero.
Dawn of the Dead, US, 2004, dir. Zack Snyder.
Day of Violence, A, UK, 2010, dir. Darren Ward.
Dead Cert, UK, 2010, dir. Steve Lawson.
Dead Creatures, UK, 2001, dir. Andrew Parkinson.
Dead Even (Method), UK/Romania/Switzerland/US, 2004, dir. Duncan Roy.
Dead of Night, UK, 1945, dirs Cavalcanti *et al.*
Dead Outside, The, UK, 2008, dir. Kerry Anne Mullaney.
Dead Wood, UK, 2007, dirs David Bryant, Sebastian Smith and Richard Stiles.
Death Line, UK, 1973, dir. Gary Sherman.
Deathwatch, UK, 2002, dir. Michael J. Bassett.
Deliverance, US, 1972, dir. John Boorman.
Demons Never Die, UK, 2011, dir. Arjun Rose.
Deranged, UK, 2009, dir. Jason Impey.
Deranged, UK/Spain, 2012, dir. Neil Jones.
Descent, The, UK, 2005, dir. Neil Marshall.
Descent: Part 2, The, UK, 2009, dir. Jon Harris.
Deviation, UK, 2012, dir. J. K. Amalou.
Devil's Bridge, UK, 2010, dir. Chris Crow.
Devil's Business, The, UK, 2011, dir. Sean Hogan.
Devil's Chair, The, UK/US, 2007, dir. Adam Mason.
Devil's Playground, UK, 2010, dir. Mark McQueen.
Devil's Rejects, The, 2005, US/Germany, dir. Rob Zombie.
Dodgeball, US/Germany, 2004, dir. Rawson Marshall Thunder.
Dog Soldiers, UK/Luxembourg/US, 2002, dir. Neil Marshall.
Doghouse, UK, 2009, dir. Jake West.
Don't Look Now, UK/Italy, 1972, dir. Nicolas Roeg.
Donkey Punch, UK, 2008, dir. Oliver Blackburn.
Dracula, UK, 1958, dir. Terence Fisher.
Dracula AD 1972, UK, 1972, dir. Alan Gibson.
Dracula Has Risen from the Grave, UK, 1968, dir. Freddie Francis.
Dracula Prince of Darkness, UK, 1966, dir. Terence Fisher.
Dread, UK/US, 2009, dir. Anthony DiBlasi.
Dream Demon, UK, 1988, dir. Harley Cokeliss.
Dust Devil, UK/South Africa, 1991, dir. Richard Stanley.
Eden Lake, UK, 2008, dir. James Watkins.
Evil Aliens, UK, 2005, dir. Jake West.
Evil Dead, The, US, 1981, dir. Sam Raimi.
Evil Dead II, US, 1987, dir. Sam Raimi.
Exam, UK, 2009, dir. Stuart Hazeldine.
Exhibit A, UK, 2007, dir. Dom Rotheroe.
Exorcist, The, US, 1973, dir. William Friedkin.
F, UK, 2010, dir. Johannes Roberts.
Faces of Death, US, 1978, dir. John Alan Schwartz.

Faculty, The, US, 1998, dir. Robert Rodriguez.
Fallow Field, The, UK, 2013, dir. Leigh Dovey.
Fat Slags, UK, 2004, dir. Ed Bye.
Fatal Attraction, US, 1987, dir. Adrian Lyne.
Ferryman, The, New Zealand/UK, 2007, dir. Chris Graham.
Festen, Denmark/Sweden, 1998, dir. Thomas Vinterberg.
Field in England, A, UK, 2013, dir. Ben Wheatley.
Final Destination, US/Canada, 2000, dir. James Wong.
Flesh and Blood: The Hammer Heritage of Horror, UK, 1994, dir. Ted Newsom.
Fly, The, US, 1986, dir. David Cronenberg.
Football Factory, The, UK, 2005, dir. Nick Love.
Forest of the Damned, UK, 2005, dir. Johannes Roberts.
Freeze Frame, UK/Ireland, 2004, dir. John Simpson.
Friday the 13th, US, 1980, dir. Sean S. Cunningham.
Frightmare, UK, 1974, dir. Pete Walker.
Frontier(s), France/Switzerland, dir. Xavier Gens.
Full Monty, The, UK, 1997, Peter Cattaneo.
Funny Man, UK, 1994, dir. Simon Sprackling.
Gathering, The, UK, 2003, dir. Brian Gilbert.
Gavin and Stacey [TX], UK, 2007-.
Ghostbusters, US, 1984, dir. Ivan Reitman.
Gnaw, UK, 2008, dir. Gregory Mandry.
Graveyard Shift: A Zomedy of Terrors, UK, 2010, dirs Sapphira Sen-Gupta and Denise Channing.
Great Ecstasy of Robert Carmichael, The, UK, 2005, dir. Thomas Clay.
Grudge, The, US/Japan, 2004, dir. Takashi Shimizu.
Halloween, US, 1978, dir. John Carpenter.
Halloween H20, US, 1998, dir. Steve Miner.
Hammer House of Horror [TX], 1980, UK, dirs various.
Hammer House of Mystery and Suspense [TX], UK, 1984, dirs various.
Hardware, UK/US, 1990, dir. Richard Stanley.
Harry Brown, UK, 2009, dir. Daniel Barber.
Harry Potter and the Philosopher's Stone, US/UK, 2001, dir. Chris Columbus.
Haute Tension (Switchblade Romance), France/Romania, 2003, dir. Alexandre Aja.
Heartless, UK, 2009, dir. Philip Ridley.
Hellboy II: The Golden Army, US/Germany, 2008, dir. Guillermo del Toro.
Hellbreeder, UK, 2004, dirs James Eaves and Johannes Roberts.
Hellbride, UK, 2007, dir. Pat Higgins.
Hellraiser, UK, 1987, dir. Clive Barker.
Henry: Portrait of a Serial Killer, 1986, dir. John McNaughton.
Hills Have Eyes, The, US, 1977, dir. Wes Craven.
Hills Have Eyes, The, US, 2006, dir. Alexandre Aja.
Hole, The, UK, 2001, dir. Nick Hamm.
Hollow, UK, 2011, dir. Michael Axelgaard.
Honest, UK, 2000, dir. David A. Stewart.
Hostel, US, 2005, dir. Eli Roth.
Hot Fuzz, UK/France, 2007, dir. Edgar Wright.
House of Whipcord, UK, 1974, dir. Pete Walker.
Human Traffic, UK/Ireland, 1999, dir. Justin Kerrigan.
Hush, UK, 2008, dir. Mark Tonderai.
I Bought a Vampire Motorcycle, UK, 1990, dir. Dirk Campbell.
I Know What You Did Last Summer, US, 1997, dir. Jim Gillespie.

I Spit on Your Grave, US, 1978, dir. Meir Zarchi.
I Spit on Your Grave, US, 2010, dir. Steven R. Monroe.
Ichi the Killer, Japan, 2001, dir. Takashi Miike.
Idol of Evil, UK, 2009, dir. Kevin Mcdonagh.
Ils, France/Romania, 2005, dirs Xavier Palud and David Moreau.
Inbred, UK, 2011, dir. Alex Chandon.
Inferno, Italy, 1980, dir. Dario Argento.
Infestation, UK, 2005, dir. Ed Evers-Swindell.
Innocent Lies, UK/France, 1995, dir. Patrick DeWolf.
Isolation, UK/Ireland, 2005, dir. Billy O'Brien.
It's Alive, US, 2008, dir. Josef Rusnak.
Kannibal, UK, 2001, dir. Richard Driscoll.
Kidulthood, UK, 2006, dir. Menhaj Huda.
Kill Keith, UK, 2011, dir. Andrew Thompson.
Kill List, UK, 2011, dir. Ben Wheatley.
Killer Bitch, UK, 2010, dir. Liam Galvin.
KillerKiller, UK, 2007, dir. Pat Higgins.
King Kong, New Zealand/US/Germany, 2005, dir. Peter Jackson.
La Haine, France, 1995, dir. Mathieu Kassovitz.
Lady Vanishes, The, UK, 1938, dir. Alfred Hitchcock.
Land of the Dead, US, 2005, dir. George A. Romero.
Last Great Wilderness, The, UK/Denmark, 2002, dir. David Mackenzie.
Last Horror Movie, The, UK, 2003, dir. Julian Richards.
Last House on the Left, The, US, 1972, dir. Wes Craven.
Last House on the Left, The, US, 2009, dir. Dan Iliadis.
Last Seven, The, UK, 2010, dir. Imran Naqvi.
Låt den rätte komma in (Let the Right One In), Sweden, 2008, dir. Thomas Alfredson.
Legend of the 7 Golden Vampires, UK/Hong Kong, 1974, dir. Roy Ward Baker.
Lesbian Vampire Killers, UK, 2009, dir. Phil Claydon.
Let Me In, US/UK, 2010, dir. Matt Reeves.
Let the Right One In, Sweden, 2008, dir. Tomas Alfredson.
Lethal Dose: 50 (LD50), UK, 2003, dir. Simon De Selva.
Lie Still, UK, 2005, dir. Sean Hogan.
Lighthouse, UK, 2000, dir. Simon Hunter.
Little Britain [TX], UK, 2003–6, dirs various.
Little Deaths, UK, 2012, dirs Andrew Parkinson *et al.*
Living and the Dead, The, UK, 2006, dir. Simon Rumley.
Locals, The, New Zealand, 2003, dir. Greg Page.
Lock, Stock and Two Smoking Barrels, UK, 1998, dir. Guy Ritchie.
Lola rennt (Run Lola Run), Germany, 1998, dir. Tom Tykwer.
Long Time Dead, UK, 2002, dir. Marcus Adams.
Lost [TX], US, 2004–10, dirs various.
Lost, The, UK, 2006, dir. Neil Jones.
Love Camp 7, US, 1968, dir. R. L. Frost.
Lovely Bones, The, US/UK/New Zealand, 2009, dir. Peter Jackson.
Lullaby of Clubland, UK, 2002, dir. Mikey Myers.
Lust for a Vampire, UK, 1971, dir. Jimmy Sangster.
Made in Britain, UK, 1982, dir. Alan Clarke.
Mamma Mia!, US/UK/Germany, 2008, dir. Phyllida Lloyd.
Man Bites Dog, Belgium, 1992, dirs Rémy Belvaux, André Bonzel and Benoît Poelvoorde.
Mandela: Long Walk to Freedom, UK/South Africa, 2013, dir. Justin Chadwick.

Mansfield Park, UK, 1999, dir. Patricia Rozema.
Mary Poppins, US, 1964, dir. Robert Stevenson.
Mary Shelley's Frankenstein, US/Japan, 1994, dir. Kenneth Branagh.
Matrix: Revolutions, The, Australia/US, 2003, dirs The Wachowski Brothers.
Method, UK/Romania/Switzerland/US, 2004, dir. Duncan Roy.
Monsters, UK, 2010, dir. Gareth Edwards.
Morvern Callar, UK, 2002, dir. Lynne Ramsay.
Mum & Dad, UK, 2008, dir. Steven Sheil.
Mummy, The, UK, 1959, dir. Terence Fisher.
Mummy: Tomb of the Dragon Emperor, The, US/China/Germany, 2008, dir. Rob Cohen.
My Big Fat Gypsy Wedding [TX], UK, 2011–, dirs various.
My Little Eye, UK, 2002, dir. Marc Evans.
Naked Trip, UK, 2008, dir Alex Baekshav.
Nanny, The, UK, 1965, dir. Seth Holt.
Natural Born Killers, US, 1994, dir. Oliver Stone.
Never Play with the Dead, UK, 2001, dir. Ray Kilby.
Night Junkies, UK, 2007, dir. Lawrence Pearce.
Night of the Living Dead, US, 1968, dir. George A. Romero.
Night of the Living Dead: Resurrections, UK, 2012, dir. James Plumb.
Night Train Murders, Italy, 1975, dir. Aldo Lado.
Nightmare on Elm Street, A, US, 1984, dir. Wes Craven.
Nil by Mouth, UK/France, 1997, dir. Gary Oldman.
Octane, UK/Luxembourg, 2003, dir. Marcus Adams.
Omen, The, UK/US, 1976, dir. Richard Donner.
Open Space, 'Suitable for Viewing in the Home?' [TX], BBC, 1985, dirs various.
Other Half, The, UK, 2006, dir. Marlowe Fawcett.
Others, The, US/Spain/France/Italy, 2001, dir. Alejandro Amenábar.
Ouija Board, UK, 2009, dir. Matt 'M. J.' Stone.
Outcast, UK, 2010, dir. Colm McCarthy.
Outpost, UK, 2008, dir. Steve Barker.
Panic Button, UK, 2011, dir. Chris Crow.
Paranormal Activity, US, 2007, dir. Oren Peli.
Patrol Men, UK, 2010, dirs David Campion and Ben Simpson.
Peeping Tom, UK, 1960, dir. Michael Powell.
Pervirella, UK, 1997, dir. Alex Chandon.
Phantasm, US, 1979, dir. Don Coscarelli.
Phantasmagoria, UK, 2005, dir. Jake West.
PIG, US, 2010, dir. Adam Mason.
Pride and Prejudice [TX], UK, 1995, dir. Simon Langton.
Proposition, The, Australia/UK, 2005, dir. John Hillcoat.
Psycho, US, 1960, dir. Alfred Hitchcock.
Psychosis, UK, 2010, dir. Reg Traviss.
Puffball, UK/Ireland/Canada, 2007, dir. Nicolas Roeg.
Pumpkinhead, US, 1988, dir. Stan Winston.
Quatermass II, UK, 1957, dir. Val Guest.
Quatermass Xperiment, The, UK, 1955, dir. Val Guest.
Quiet Ones, The, US/UK, 2014, dir. John Pogue.
Rancid Aluminium, UK, 2000, dir. Ed Thomas.
Rasputin the Mad Monk, UK, 1966, dir. Don Sharp.
Ratcatcher, UK, 1999, dir. Lynne Ramsay.
Rawhead Rex, UK/Ireland, 1986, dir. George Pavlou.

Razor Blade Smile, UK, 1998, dir. Jake West.
Red Canopy, UK, 2006, dir. Ian Weeks.
Red Mist (*Freakdog*), UK, 2008, dir. Paddy Breathnach.
Red, White and Blue, UK/US, 2010, dir. Simon Rumley.
Reeds, The, UK, 2010, dir. Nick Cohen.
Reign of Fire, UK/Ireland/US, 2002, dir. Rob Bowman.
Reptile, The, UK, 1966, dir. John Gilling.
Resident, The, UK/US, 2010, dir. Antti Jokinen.
Resident Evil, UK/Germany/France, 2002, dir. Paul W. S. Anderson.
Resurrecting the Street Walker, UK, 2009, dir. Özgür Uyanık.
Reverb, UK, 2008, dir. Eitan Arrusi.
Reverend, The, UK, 2011, dir. Neil Jones.
Ring, The, USA/Japan, 2002, dir. Gore Verbinski.
Ringu, Japan, 1998, dir. Hideo Nakata.
Salvage, UK, 2009, dir. Lawrence Gough.
Sand Serpents, Canada, 2009, dir. Jeff Renfroe.
Sanitarium, UK, 2001, dirs Johannes Roberts and James Eaves.
Satanic Rites of Dracula, The, UK, 1973, dir. Alan Gibson.
Saw, US/Australia, 2004, dir. James Wan.
Saw II, US/Canada, 2005, dir. Darren Lynn Bousman.
Scars of Dracula, UK, 1970, dir. Roy Ward Baker.
Scary Movie 3, US, 2003, dir. David Zucker.
Scream, US, 1996, dir. Wes Craven.
Scream 2, US, 1997, dir. Wes Craven.
Scream 3, US, 2000, dir. Wes Craven.
Scream 4, US, 2011, dir. Wes Craven.
Scum, UK, 1977/79, dir. Alan Clarke.
Seed of Chucky, Romania/US/UK, 2004, dir. Don Mancini.
Sentinels of Darkness, UK, 2002, dir. Manos Kalaitzakis.
Severance, UK/Germany, 2006, dir. Christopher Smith.
Sex Lives of the Potato Men, UK, 2004, dir. Andy Humphries.
Sexy Beast, UK/Spain, 2000, dir. Jonathan Glazer.
Shameless [TX], UK, 2004–13, dirs various.
Sharknado, US, 2013, dir. Anthony C. Ferrante.
Shaun of the Dead, UK, 2004, dir. Edgar Wright.
Shining, The, US/UK, 1980, dir. Stanley Kubrick.
Shrooms, Ireland/UK, 2007, dir. Paddy Breathnach.
Sick House, The, UK, 2008, dir. Curtis Radclyffe.
Sick Bastard, UK, 2007, dir. Jason Impey.
Sixth Sense, The, US, 1999, dir. M. Night Shyamalan.
Skyfall, UK/US, 2012, dir. Sam Mendes.
Snuff, US/South America, 1976, dirs Michael Findlay and Roberta Findlay.
Snuff Movie, UK/US/Romania, 2005, dir. Bernard Rose.
Somers Town, UK, 2008, dir. Shane Meadows.
Son of Rambow, France/UK/Germany, 2007, dir. Garth Jennings.
Sopranos, The [TX], US, 1999–2007.
Soulmate, UK, 2013, dir. Axelle Carolyn.
Spaced [TX], UK, 1999–2001, dir. Edgar Wright.
Spiderhole, UK, 2010, dir. Daniel Simpson.
Spirit Trap, UK, 2005, dir. David Smith.
Splintered, UK, 2010, dir. Simeon Halligan.
Stag Night of the Dead, UK, 2009, dir. Neil 'Napoleon' Jones.

Stalled, UK, 2013, dir. Christian James.
Star Wars Episode I: The Phantom Menace, US, 1999, dir. George Lucas.
Stitches, UK/Ireland, 2012, dir. Conor McMahon.
Stolen Face, UK, 1952, dir. Terence Fisher.
Storage 24, UK, 2012, dir. Johannes Roberts.
Straw Dogs, US/UK, 1971, dir. Sam Peckinpah.
Strigoi, UK/Romania, 2009, dir. Faye Jackson.
Stuck, Canada/UK/US/Germany, 2007, dir. Stuart Gordon.
Summer of the Massacre, The, UK, 2006, dir. Bryn Curt James Hammond.
Summer Scars, UK, 2007, dir. Julian Richards.
Sunshine, UK/US, 2007, dir. Danny Boyle.
Surviving Evil, UK/South Africa, 2009, dir. Terence Daw.
Suspiria, Italy, 1977, dir. Dario Argento.
Tales from the Crypt, UK, 1972, dir. Freddie Francis.
Tales of the Dead, UK, 2010, dir. Kemal Yildirim.
Taste of Fear, UK, 1961, dir. Seth Holt.
Taste the Blood of Dracula, UK, 1970, dir. Peter Sasdy.
Ted Bundy, UK/US, 2002, dir. Matthew Bright.
Tenebre, Italy, 1982, dir. Dario Argento.
Terminator 2: Judgement Day, US, 1991, dir. James Cameron.
Texas Chain Saw Massacre, The, US, 1974, dir. Tobe Hooper.
Texas Chainsaw Massacre, The, US, 2003, dir. Marcus Nispel.
Texas Chainsaw Massacre Part 2, The, US, 1986, dir. Tobe Hooper.
The Lady Vanishes, UK, 1938, dir. Alfred Hitchcock.
The Lady Vanishes, UK, 1979, dir. Anthony Page.
Thing, The, US, 1982, dir. John Carpenter.
This is England, UK, 2006, dir. Shane Meadows.
This is Not a Love Song, UK, 2001, dir. Billie Eltringham.
Tony (Tony: London Serial Killer), UK, 2009, dir. Gerard Johnson.
Torment, The (The Possession of David O'Reilly), UK, 2010, dirs Andrew Cull and Steve Isles.
Tormented, UK, 2009, dir. Jon Wright.
Tortured AKA Sex Slave, UK, 2011, dir. Jason Impey.
Trainspotting, UK, 1996, dir. Danny Boyle.
Trashhouse, UK, 2005, dir. Pat Higgins.
Trauma, UK, 2004, dir. Marc Evans.
Travellers , UK, 2011, dir. Kris McManus.
True Blood [TX], US, 2008–, dirs various.
Truth or Die, UK, 2012, dir. Robert Heath.
Twilight Zone, The [TX], US, 1959–64, dirs various.
Twin Town, UK, 1997, dir. Kevin Allen.
Twins of Evil, UK, 1971, dir. Tudor Gates.
Under the Skin, UK/US/Switzerland, 2013, dir. Jonathan Glazer.
Underworld, UK/Germany/Hungary/US, 2003, dir. Len Wiseman.
Urban Ghost Story, UK, 1998, dir. Geneviève Jollife.
Urban Legend, US/France, 1998, dir. Jamie Blanks.
Vampire Circus, UK, 1972, dir. Robert Young.
Vampire Diary, UK, 2006, dirs Mark James and Phil O'Shea.
Vampire Lovers, The, UK, 1970, dir. Roy Ward Baker.
Vanguard, The, UK, 2008, dir. Matthew Hope.
Vault of Horror, The, UK, 1973, dir. Roy Ward Baker.
Venus Drowning, UK, 2006, dir. Andrew Parkinson.

Video Nasties: Moral Panics, Censorship and Videotape, UK, 2011, dir. Jake West.
Village of the Damned, UK, 1960, dir. Wolf Rilla.
Vipers, US/Canada, 2008, dir. Bill Corcoran.
w Delta z, UK/Ireland, 2007, dir. Tom Shankland.
Wake Wood, UK/Ireland, 2009, dir. David Keating.
War of the Worlds, US, 2005, dir. Steven Spielberg.
What Lies Beneath, US, 2000, dir. Robert Zemeckis.
When Evil Calls, UK, 2006, dir. Johannes Roberts.
White Settlers, UK, 2014, dir. Simeon Halligan.
Wicker Man, The, UK, 1973, dir. Robin Hardy.
Wicker Tree, The, UK, 2010, dir. Robin Hardy.
Wild Country, UK, 2005, dir. Craig Strachan.
Wilderness, UK, 2006, dir. Michael J. Bassett.
Wind Chill, US/UK, 2007, dir. Gregory Jacobs.
Wolfman, The, US/UK, 2010, dir. Joe Johnston.
Woman in Black, The, UK, 2012, dir. James Watkins.
Woman in Black, The, Angels of Death, UK, 2015, dir. Tom Harper.
World of Hammer, The, UK, 1990, dir. Robert Sidaway.
Wuthering Heights, UK, 2012, dir. Andrea Arnold.
X2, Canada/USA, 2003, dir. Bryan Singer.
Zombie Creeping Flesh, Italy/Spain, 1980, dir. Bruno Mattei.
Zombie Diaries, The, UK, 2006, dirs Michael Bartlett and Kevin Gates.
Zombie Ferox, UK, 2002, dir. Jonathon Ash.
Zombie Flesh-Eaters, Italy, 1979, dir. Lucio Fulci.
Zombie Undead, UK, 2010, dir. Rhys Davies.
Zombie Women of Satan, UK, 2009, dir. Steve O'Brien.
Zombies of the Night, UK, 2008, dir. Stuart Brennan.

INDEX